THE COMPLETE PLAIN WORDS

Sir Ernest Gowers, who was an Hon. D.Litt. of Manchester University, an Hon. Fellow of Clare College, Cambridge, an Hon. A.R.I.B.A., and a Past President of the English Association, was born in 1880. He was educated at Rugby School and Clare College, Cambridge, where he was a scholar and took a 'First' in Classics. He entered the Inland Revenue Department in 1903, and it was as chairman of that Board that he left the civil service twenty-seven years later on his appointment as chairman of the Coal Mines Reorganization Commission (later the Coal Commission). In the meantime he had served in several departments and had been at one time principal private secretary to Lloyd George as Chancellor of the Exchequer. During the Second World War he was London Regional Commissioner for Civil Defence, and afterwards chairman of numerous committees and commissions on a wide variety of subjects, including the admission of women into the Foreign Service, the conditions of work in shops and offices, the preservation of historic houses, foot-and-mouth disease, and capital punishment. Sir Ernest Gowers died in 1966.

Sir Bruce Fraser was born in 1910 and educated at Bedford School and Trinity College, Cambridge, where he took a 'Double First' in Classics and English. He entered the Scottish Office in 1933 and the Treasury in 1936. He became Permanent Secretary of the Ministry of Health in 1960–64 and from 1966 till his retirement in 1971 he was Comptroller and Auditor General.

THE
COMPLETE PLAIN
WORDS

SIR ERNEST GOWERS

REVISED BY SIR BRUCE FRASER

'As if plain words, useful and intelligible instructions, were not as good for an esquire, or one that is in commission from the King, as for him that holds the plough.' JOHN EACHARD, *The Grounds and Occasions of the Contempt of the Clergy and Religion enquired into*, 1670.

PENGUIN BOOKS

Penguin Books Ltd, Harmondsworth, Middlesex, England
Viking Penguin Inc., 40 West 23rd Street, New York, New York 10010, U.S.A.
Penguin Books Australia Ltd, Ringwood, Victoria, Australia
Penguin Books Canada Limited, 2801 John Street, Markham, Ontario, Canada L3R 1B4
Penguin Books (N.Z.) Ltd, 182–190 Wairau Road, Auckland 10, New Zealand

—

Plain Words first published 1948
The ABC of Plain Words first published 1951
First published together as *The Complete Plain Words* by
H.M. Stationery Office, 1954
Published in Pelican Books 1962
Reprinted 1963, 1964, 1966, 1967, 1968, 1969, 1970, 1971, 1972
Second edition published by H.M. Stationery Office 1973
Published in Pelican Books 1973
Reprinted 1974, 1975 (twice), 1976, 1977
Reprinted with revisions 1977
Reprinted 1978, 1979, 1980, 1982, 1983, 1984, 1985, 1986

—

Made and printed in Great Britain by
Hazell Watson & Viney Limited,
Member of the BPCC Group,
Aylesbury, Bucks
Set in Linotype Times

CONTENTS

6

PREFACE

Plain Words first appeared in 1948. The Treasury invited Sir Ernest Gowers, a distinguished civil servant, to write it as a contribution to what they were doing to improve official English. It made an immediate impact, which was by no means limited either to officialdom or to this country. It was followed in 1951 by *The ABC of Plain Words* and in 1954 by *The Complete Plain Words*, in which Gowers brought together in one volume, with additions and alterations, what he had written in the previous two.

The Complete Plain Words has been repeatedly reprinted, and Gowers made a number of amendments in succeeding impressions. Had he lived he would himself have produced a new edition: unhappily he had no time to do so after completing his monumental revision of Fowler's *Modern English Usage* (1965). The task has instead been entrusted to me.

Gowers' work is undoubtedly a classic. Not only is it elegantly and wittily written: it affords to the reader profit as well as pleasure, for it concentrates on what matters to the ordinary practitioner, not on what interests only grammarians and scholars. It is eminently sensible. Indeed there can be few writers on the use of English whose judgments and preferences command such ready agreement from sensible people, whether amateur or professional.

Its influence in the public service has been deep and lasting. I sought an up-to-date assessment from heads of Government Departments, and the replies had an impressive similarity. The work is recommended reading in most parts of the service, and it is widely read, or at least widely referred to, by both senior and junior staff. Its influence is felt even by those who have never read it, for its precepts, and many of its illustrations, are used in many booklets for staff and in many training and refresher courses.

7

It is no light task to revise a classic, and I owe it to the reader to explain what I have done.

In his Preface to *The Complete Plain Words* Gowers wrote:

> I am not a grammarian, and *The Complete Plain Words*, like its predecessors, makes no claim to be a grammar of the English language, though for reasons I have explained in the text I felt bound, reluctantly and diffidently, to give one chapter (9) to some points of grammar and one (10) to punctuation. Apart from these two chapters, this book is wholly concerned with what is described in one of the quotations that head the first chapter as the choice and arrangement of words in such a way as to get an idea as exactly as possible out of one mind into another. Even so I must not be credited with too high an ambition: the scope of the book is circumscribed by its being intended primarily for those who use words as tools of their trade, in administration or business.

This general description holds good for the revised edition. My task was not to produce a new book – this is not 'Fraser' but 'Gowers revised by Fraser' – and I have tried to keep as much as possible of the flavour and spirit of the original. Nevertheless there is no doubt that revision is now necessary if Gowers is to be as useful in the future as he has been in the past (just as there is no doubt that this revised edition will before very long need revision in its turn).

First, though most of his precepts are still sound and still need stressing, many of his illustrations were collected when war-time rationing and controls were still with us; and their subject-matter gives them a dated air.* I have substituted contemporary illustrations wherever I could, lest the precepts might look out of date too.

Second, developments in the language and in accepted usage since Gowers first wrote have, I think, made a few passages

---

* War-time shortages seem to have been a particularly prolific source of contorted language, as in Gowers' example *The fats position will then be relieved*, meaning *Fats will then be more plentiful*. But peace-time shortages seem to have the same quality: a 1970 White Paper told us that 'Last winter there was a *tight situation in the supply* of solid smoke-less fuels'. The five italicised words mean no more than *shortage* or *scarcity*.

either questionable or unnecessary. For instance, Gowers said in 1951 that *worth-while* as an adjective ('a worth-while job') had not yet reached more than colloquial status: I think it now has. Again, Gowers devoted much space to castigating absurd uses of *bottleneck*, *target* and *literally*: these particular villains, though not dead, seem now to be moribund, and I have saved some space accordingly.

But these same developments seem to call for additions as well as excisions; I have made additions throughout the text and I have written four completely new chapters.

Third, the nature of education has changed greatly since the late 1940s and it seems to me that here and there Gowers assumes in his readers a more literary education than most readers now have. I have reluctantly cut out a number of literary allusions which, though apt and charming, may (to quote one of my correspondents) 'look highbrow and irrelevant in the swinging and illiterate seventies'. I have, I hope, left enough to rebut a charge of indiscriminate vandalism.

Fourth, Gowers was much concerned to urge a less stilted style of writing in letters from Government Departments to members of the public. One hesitates to say that the battle has been won, for no doubt there is still much room for improvement. But the general standard is certainly far higher now than it was when he wrote. Out-dated pomposities in the formal framework of such letters ('I am directed to inform you' and so on) have almost disappeared. 'Thank you for your letter' is now much commoner than 'Receipt of your letter is acknowledged'. All Departments pay much more attention than they did to staff training, and the great virtues which Gowers preached of clarity, simplicity and friendliness are daily preached in staff training programmes throughout the service. I have therefore felt justified in shortening and remodelling what Gowers wrote on this subject (mostly in Chapter 3).

Finally, I found a few passages which I could not persuade myself to agree with. What should an honest and respectful reviser do when honesty and respect conflict? I sought guidance from what Gowers himself did when revising Fowler. Sometimes he reproduced Fowler's view and added his own, and sometimes he simply substituted Gowers for Fowler without indicating that he had done so. I have felt justified, here and there, in following this example, though I do not claim to be nearly as close to Gowers in stature as Gowers was to Fowler. But these displays of arrogance are few, for Gowers was a much less quirky preceptor than Fowler and much more difficult to disagree with.

This tempts me into moralising about the duty of anyone who writes about the use of English for the general practitioner. He must, as I see it, have the courage of his convictions, but must not express them too dogmatically on points which fairly admit of a different opinion. He must avoid pedantry, and must also recognise that what seems obviously right to one man seems pedantic to another. He must offer resistance to undesirable innovations, but must not assume that every innovation is sure to be undesirable. He must respect the genius of the language, which includes a wonderful capacity for change. All this requires personal judgment, and every man's judgment is fallible. Gowers' judgment was less fallible than most and I can only hope that I have not deviated too far from the course he followed among the shoals and rocks of dogmatism, pedantry and ultra-conservatism. I would rather, on the whole, be blamed (as he was) for being too liberal than for being too restrictive.

I take this view partly because I endorse Gowers' general principle that the official writer (to whom this book is mainly though not wholly addressed) should keep within the limits of currently accepted usage and should not, save very rarely, place himself in the van of change. This seems to me sound, because his readers are not reading him by choice and they may resent it if they think he is writing either above or below their heads. It follows that he should take a fairly liberal view of what currently accepted usage actually is; for his writing should appear up to date rather than old-fashioned. But if he wants to go further, if he wants to experiment with the unorthodox, to blaze a trail to new heights of eloquent and evocative prose, let him try it in his spare time on some work of his own. If people will pay to read it, good luck to him. But he should not go on 'demo's' in official time.

Gowers' frequent use of the first person presented me with a difficulty. It would clearly be wrong to flatten the tone of his book by depersonalising his views. So where Gowers wrote 'I think', I have left it like that. But then comes the problem – am I going to add any 'I thinks' of my own? If I do not, I shall not be keeping to the flavour and spirit of the original. But if I do, the reader may be cross at not knowing whether he is reading genuine Gowers or only Fraser. Perhaps I should use 'I' for Gowers and 'i' for Fraser?

I decided that my best course was to adopt a personal tone, as Gowers did, but not to place my views surreptitiously under his protection. Here, then, are the clues necessary to distinguish Fraser from Gowers. I have re-written much of Chapter 1 (the Prologue); its first half is largely Gowers, its second largely Fraser. Chapters 2, 11, 12 and 13 are wholly Fraser. Chapter 14 (the Epilogue) is Gowers, untouched but for some trifling amendments. Chapters 3 to 10 form the core of the book, the part that matters most. In these chapters I have conscientiously followed Gowers, whose mind I can fairly claim by now to know pretty well; and except where the contrary is clearly indicated by footnote or otherwise the reader may take it that 'I' means either 'Gowers agreed with by Fraser' or 'Fraser, confident that Gowers would agree with him'. A few of the footnotes in these chapters express views that need to be identified as mine rather than his, and to these I have added my initials.

I asked all heads of major Government Departments to help me in collecting material for this edition. The response was overwhelming. I received contributions from all over the public service at home and overseas, providing far more quotations, both of bad writing and of good, than I could possibly use, as well as many apt comments and penetrating suggestions. The quotations came both from officials' writings and from others, and they confirmed my own impression that 'officialese', in the sense of a species of bad writing peculiarly characteristic of public officials, is not nearly as serious an offender as it was.

11

One sees plenty of bad official writing, but nowadays its faults are not usually of a kind peculiar to officials: they are to be found in even greater profusion elsewhere, and the official is to be blamed more often for following a bad example than for setting one.*

In general, I have not given the source of my quotations. Sometimes I have concealed it by omitting identifying words. Sometimes too I have altered the original by correcting irrelevant mistakes, whether of spelling, punctuation or syntax. Take, for example, this remarkable specimen of student prose:

> Anyhow, is it not the case that opponents of student representation argue that the proceeds of a meeting of governors is confidential?

If I had wanted to use this simply as an illustration of the intrusiveness of the word 'case' (*is it not the case that* instead of *do not* or *surely* or just nothing at all) I might have altered *proceeds* to *proceedings* and *is* to *are.*†

But I have played fair: I have quoted accurately whatever is relevant to my context and nothing presented as a quotation is in fact invented.

I express my deep sense of obligation to all who helped me. It would be invidious to particularise, but I hope that those who find that I have simply purloined their comments and criticisms

---

*The following comment by a Permanent Secretary is fairly typical:

Our impression is that the worst offenders against the Queen's English nowadays are academics, businessmen and journalists. We ourselves have no cause for complacency, but we have gained some ground in the battle for plain words and we believe that much of the credit must go to Gowers. What troubles us now is not the pompous circumlocution which was once the mark of official writing, but the threat of 'expert' writing which characteristically tends towards abstraction and jargon. The battle must be continued on a different front.

† I will not conceal the source of this one. It is from a formal memorandum submitted by the Students' Representative Council of Aberdeen College of Education to the House of Commons Select Committee on Education and Science 1969–70. The whole memorandum is so startlingly illiterate as to make one very gloomy, not only about its authors but also about those who taught them and about those whom they are destined to teach.

without acknowledgement, and paraded them as my own, will take this as a mark of my special gratitude. Some of the comments I received seemed to me so apt and pithy that I have used them as chapter headings.

Finally, I am very grateful to the staff of Her Majesty's Stationery Office, who have taken immense pains in the production of this work and whose skill and forbearance have greatly eased my task.

BRUCE D. FRASER

Note to 1977 reprint

Since this revised edition was first published in April 1973 I have received a great many letters about it, nearly all gratifying, and I here express my thanks to all who have written, whether I have replied to them individually or not.

Even in so short a time, changes have become apparent in the use of words. *Basically*, for instance, leapt into riotous life as soon as the copy was with the printers; and *arguably* has joined it as a vogue word. I came across only a single instance of a *low profile* while I was preparing the revised edition, and I decided that it was either a freak or a mistake. I was wrong; it was a seedling, which has now sprouted copiously in all directions.

Among fairly new usages which I noted without condemning them (as some of my correspondents think I should have done), the use of *hopefully* in the sense *it is to be hoped that* has gained a lot more ground; so has the use of the subjunctive in such a sentence as *I suggest that he go* (rather than *should go*).

Among usages which I did condemn, I think I can detect a decline in the use of *data* and *media* as singular nouns – though one of my correspondents reports that computer-land not only still treats *data* as singular but has produced *datae* as its plural. I wish I could report a much steeper decline in horrible or nonsensical uses of *in terms of*, *marginal*, *situation* and *overall*. But I fear that so far these words are not even in a marginal improvement situation in terms of their misuse overall.

But developments in the language are not yet, I think, so extensive as to call for a major revision. I have taken the opportunity to make a few changes, some of them suggested by correspondents, but none are very important. It seems to me wise to wait a few more years before attempting anything more ambitious. I am not sure whether it would be equally wise to say that, hopefully, further reprints will afford the opportunity.

B.D.F.

1

PROLOGUE

> Do but take care to express yourself in a plain, easy Manner,
> in well-chosen, significant and decent Terms, and to give a
> harmonious and pleasing Turn to your Periods; study to ex-
> plain your Thoughts, and set them in the truest Light, labouring
> as much as possible, not to leave them dark nor intricate, but
> clear and intelligible.
>
> CERVANTES, *Preface to Don Quixote*

> The final cause of speech is to get an idea as exactly as possible
> out of one mind into another. Its formal cause therefore is
> such choice and disposition of words as will achieve this end
> most economically.
>
> G. M. YOUNG

THE main purpose of this book is to help officials in their use of
written English as a tool of their trade. I suspect that this project may be received by many of them without any marked
enthusiasm or gratitude. 'Even now,' they may say, 'it is all we
can do to keep our heads above water by turning out at top
speed letters in which we say what we mean after our own
fashion. Not one in a thousand of the people we write to knows
the difference between good English and bad. What is the use of
all this highbrow stuff? It will only prevent us from getting on
with the job.'

But what is this job that must be got on with? Writing is an
instrument for conveying ideas from one mind to another; the
writer's job is to make his reader apprehend his meaning readily
and precisely. Do these letters always say just what the writer
means? Nay, does the writer himself always know just what he
means? Even when he knows what he means, and says it in a
way that is clear to him, is it always equally clear to his reader?
If not, he has not been getting on with the job. 'The difficulty',
said Robert Louis Stevenson, 'is not to write, but to write what
you mean, not to affect your reader, but to affect him precisely

14

as you wish.' Let us take one or two examples to illustrate particular faults, and, applying this test to them, ask ourselves whether the reader is likely to grasp at once the meaning of

Prices are basis prices per ton for the representative-basis-pricing specification and size and quantity,

or of

Where particulars of a partnership are disclosed to the Executive Council the remuneration of the individual partner for superannuation purposes will be deemed to be such proportion of the total remuneration of such practitioners as the proportion of his share in partnership profits bears to the total proportion of the shares of such practitioner in those profits.

or of

The treatment of this loan interest from the date of the first payment has been correct – i.e. tax charged at full standard rate on Mr X and treated in your hands as liability fully satisfied before receipt.

All these were written for plain men, not for experts. What will the plain man make of them? The recipient of the last may painfully and dubiously reach the right conclusion – that no more money is wanted from him. But the recipient of the first example will be unable to unlock the secret of the jargon without a key, and what the second will make of the explanation given to him is anyone's guess. Yet the writers may be presumed to have known exactly what they meant; the obscurity was not in their thoughts but in their way of expressing themselves. The fault of writing like this is not that it is unscholarly but that it is inefficient. It wastes time: the reader's time because he has to puzzle over what should be plain, and the writer's time because he may have to write again to explain his meaning. A job that needed to be done only once has had to be done twice because it was bungled the first time.

Professional writers realise that they cannot hope to affect their readers precisely as they wish without care and practice in the proper use of words. The need for the official to take pains is even greater, for if what the professional writer has written is

15

wearisome and obscure the reader can toss the book aside and read no more, but only at his peril can he so treat what the official has tried to tell him. By proper use I do not mean grammatically proper. It is true that there are rules of grammar and syntax, just as in music there are rules of harmony and counterpoint. But one can no more write good English than one can compose good music merely by keeping the rules. On the whole they are aids to writing intelligibly, for they are in the main no more than the distillation of successful experiments made by writers of English through the centuries in how best to handle words so as to make a writer's meaning plain. Some, it is true, are arbitrary. One or two actually increase the difficulty of clear expression, but these too should nevertheless be respected, because lapses from what for the time being is regarded as correct irritate the educated reader, and distract his attention, and so make him the less likely to be affected precisely as you wish. But I shall not have much to say about text-book rules because they are mostly well known and well observed in official writing.

The golden rule is not a rule of grammar or syntax. It concerns less the arrangement of words than the choice of them. 'After all,' said Lord Macaulay, 'the first law of writing, that law to which all other laws are subordinate, is this: that the words employed should be such as to convey to the reader the meaning of the writer.' The golden rule is to pick those words and to use them and them only. Arrangement is of course important, but if the right words are used they generally have a happy knack of arranging themselves.

This golden rule applies to all prose, whatever its purpose, and indeed to poetry too. Illustrations could be found throughout the gamut of purposes for which the written word is used. At the one end of it we can turn to Shakespeare, and from the innumerable examples that offer themselves choose the lines

> Kissing with golden face the meadows green,
> Gilding pale streams with heavenly alchymy

which, as a description of what the rising sun does to meadows and rivers on a 'glorious morning', must be as effective a use of thirteen words as could be found in all English literature. At the other end we can turn (for the golden rule can be illustrated from official writing in its observance as well as in its breach) to the unknown member of the staff of the General Post Office who by composing the notice that used to be displayed in every post office

Postmasters are neither bound to give change nor authorised to demand it

used twelve words hardly less efficiently to warn customers of what must have been a singularly intractable dilemma. At first sight there seems little in common between the two. Their purposes are different; one is descriptive and emotional, the other instructional and objective. But each serves its purpose perfectly, and it is the same quality in both that makes them do so. Every word is exactly right; no other word would do as well; each is pulling its weight; none could be dispensed with. As was said of Milton's prose in the quotation that heads Chapter 6, 'Fewer would not have served the turn, and more would have been superfluous'.

Moreover you need to choose the right words in order that you may make your meaning clear not only to your reader but also to yourself. The first requisite for any writer is to know just what meaning he wants to convey, and it is only by clothing his thoughts in words that he can think at all. 'What a man cannot state he does not perfectly know, and conversely the inability to put his thoughts into words sets a boundary to his thought. . . . English is not merely the medium of our thought; it is the very stuff and process of it.'* And the less one makes a habit of thinking, the less one is able to think: the power of thinking atrophies unless it is used. The following was written about politicians, but it is true of all of us:

A scrupulous writer in every sentence that he writes will ask himself . . . What am I trying to say? What words will express it? . . . And he probably asks himself . . . . Could I put it more shortly? But

* *Report of the Departmental Committee on the Teaching of English in England* (H.M. Stationery Office, 1921).

you are not obliged to go to all this trouble. You can shirk it by
simply throwing open your mind and letting the ready-made phrases
come crowding in. They will construct your sentences for you – even
think your thoughts for you to a certain extent – and at need they
will perform the important service of partially concealing your
meaning even from yourself.*

'Go to all this trouble' is not an overstatement. Few common
things are more difficult than to find the right word, and many
people are too lazy to try. This form of indolence sometimes
betrays itself by a copious use of inverted commas. 'I know this
is not quite the right word', the inverted commas seem to say,
'but I can't be bothered to think of a better'; or, 'please note that
I am using this word facetiously'; or, 'don't think I don't know
that this is a cliché'. If the word is the right one, do not be
ashamed of it: if it is the wrong one, do not use it. The same
implied apology is often made in conversation by interposing
'you know' or by ending every sentence with phrases such as 'or
something' or 'sort of thing'. Officials cannot do that, but in
them the same phenomenon is reflected in an unwillingness to
venture outside a small vocabulary of shapeless bundles of
uncertain content – words like *position, situation, arise, involve,
in connexion with, in terms of, issue, consideration* and *factor* –
a disposition, for instance, to 'admit with regret the position
which has arisen in connexion with' rather than to make the
effort to tell the reader specifically what is admitted with regret.
Clear thinking is hard work, but loose thinking is bound to
produce loose writing. And clear thinking takes time, but time
that has to be given to a job to avoid making a mess of it cannot be time wasted and may in the end be time saved.

It is wise therefore not to begin to write, or to dictate, until
you are quite certain what you want to say. That sounds elementary, but the elementary things are often the most likely
to be neglected. Some, it is true, can never be sure of clarifying
their thoughts except by trying to put them on paper. If you are
one of these, never be content with your first draft; always revise

it; and you will find that practice, though it may not make perfect, will greatly improve your efficiency.

'But', you may object, 'my work is very urgent. There's no time for this pernickety perfectionism.' Well, maybe. We can make allowances for what is produced under great stress for internal communication. But not all your work is desperately urgent and not all is for departmental reading only; and when it comes to external communication I am sure that you should fear more the danger of putting out slipshod work by omitting to revise it than that of delaying public business by excessive polishing. Very few can write what they mean and affect their readers precisely as they wish without revising their first attempt; and there *is* a happy mean between being content with the first thing that comes into your head and the craving for perfection that makes a Flaubert spend hours or even days on getting a single sentence to his satisfaction. The article you are paid to produce need not be polished but it must be workmanlike.

A few readers of earlier editions of this book have objected that to write as it recommends is to write flat, flavourless, unexciting stuff. I do not think this criticism is well conceived. First, even if it were true there would be gain, not loss, in eliminating what is muddled, obscure or pretentious. But second, and more important, it is not true.

Much official writing, such as routine letters to other authorities or to members of the public, explanatory circulars, and so on, needs merely to be clear, workmanlike and inoffensive. It had much better be flat and clear than eloquent and obscure, or even eloquent and clear; for the reader is looking only for plain, honest bread and butter and he does not want it spread with jam, or even caviar, any more than he wants it spread with glue or engine-grease. True, there is also much official writing, including certain White Papers and committee reports and certain sorts of correspondence, where plain bread and butter is not quite good enough. The writer has to get an argument across, to carry conviction to readers who have so far thought differently, or not at all, on the matter in hand; and he

The Complete Plain Words

will be more persuasive if he writes vividly and forcefully as well as correctly. But there is nothing whatever in this book which forbids vivid and forceful expression. On the contrary, its original author himself showed, in many passages lovingly preserved in this edition, how vigorously and persuasively he could write in perfect compliance with his own precepts.

Moreover the faults that he castigated make a man's writing less persuasive, not more. Some writers, by no means only in the public service, seem to think that if they can drag in plenty of long or unfamiliar or technical or modish words, arranged in long and involved sentences, their readers will regard them as clever fellows and be stunned into acquiescence. Not so: most readers will be more likely to think 'This man is a pompous ass. I'm not going to agree with *him* if I can help it.'

Here are two passages advocating certain sensible financial procedures. The first is addressed to farmers, the second to hospital planners. There is no doubt which is the more persuasive.

There are several very good reasons why the farmer, busy man as he is, should keep proper records of his business. It is the only way in which he can find out how much profit he has made, and how one year's profit compares with another. It helps him to manage his farm efficiently, and shows him how the various operations compare in outlay and in receipts.

[There is] a need for flexible resource allocation procedures to allow updating of investment decisions (capital and revenue) so that at any given point in time of the planning design process an optimum investment decision can be made rather than one which may have been valid at the inception of planning but has become progressively non-optimal.

The first of these passages is not memorable literature; but, for its purpose, it is as nearly perfect as it can be. And it did not need any great literary talent to produce it. We can all write like this if we try, just as we can all avoid writing like the second passage if we try. Indeed, any normal and sensible person finds it easier to write like the first than like the second.

20

Prologue

This book is no more intended as an aid to fine writing than as a text-book on grammar. Fine writing is not certain if its precepts are followed: shoddy writing is certain if they are not. A man who is incapable of writing a routine letter simply and clearly is unlikely (unless perhaps he is a literary genius) to be able to write acceptably for any higher purpose. Indeed, it will probably be found that the more loftily he tries to write, the more (as the author of the second passage might have put it) will his writing tend to become progressively non-optimal.

'Style', in the full literary sense, is a different matter altogether. A civil servant, writing rather disrespectfully about Gowers' original work (but in language that wholly complies with its precepts), concludes by saying:

In any case the prescriptions of any author can only tend towards one pattern of clarity and elegance. A good draftsman does not have just 'style' but his own style. I would therefore deprecate in principle any attempt to set up a single drafting model, however distinguished its author.

He is not, I am sure, denying that for stock letters and routine correspondence a single drafting model is both desirable and convenient. He has more elaborate writing in mind. And I agree with him. We all have our own preferences and pet aversions, our favourite phrases and turns of expression. We may think of them as constituting our 'style', and others may see them more as mannerisms. But for present purposes this does not matter. All that this book seeks to do is to point out certain elementary merits and certain common defects. If we do no more than pay attention to these we shall at least write fairly efficiently, and we all can and should acquire the habit of doing so. The merits that belong to literary 'style' – grace, wit, eloquence, force, astringency, grandeur and so on – cannot be taught in a book, and most of us must be content to do without them. But even the most gifted stylists build on sound foundations; they know that the loveliest of their architectural masterpieces, no less than our humble three-room cottages, would be spoilt by rising damp or smelly drains. I regard

21

Insufficient information has been received at the time of going out to print to facilitate a comprehensive revision, but this will be effected in the earliest subsequent edition possible

as rising damp, and

Design could be more calculatedly goal-directed

as a smelly drain. Both specimens come, appropriately enough, from a splendid collection sent to me by what used to be the Ministry of Public Building and Works.

Let us therefore agree, before we go any further, that a reasonably good standard of writing is a mark not of preciosity but of good sense, not of prissiness but of efficiency; that such a standard can be attained by anyone with a little effort; that the effort is well worth while (or, if I *must* put it this way to convince the sort of man whose soul I seek, that significant results in terms of cost-effectiveness may be anticipated to stem from the resource-input); that it requires neither hair-splitting nor self-consciousness but merely a willingness to acquire good habits; and, finally, that a writer with good habits may be allowed to make an occasional slip, just as a good doctor or lawyer may occasionally give the wrong advice or a good cashier the wrong change, without incurring eternal damnation.

If we cannot agree on these propositions we had better part company at this point.

2

A PRELIMINARY DIGRESSION

So as to avoid any misunderstanding about the scope of this book, it will be as well to begin with a digression explaining why certain uses of language are outside it.

LEGAL ENGLISH

Acts of Parliament, statutory rules and other legal instruments have a special purpose, to which their language has to be specially adapted. The legal draftsman, whether he is a public official or not, has to ensure to the best of his ability that what he says will be found to mean precisely what he intended, even after it has been subjected to detailed and possibly hostile scrutiny by acute legal minds. For this purpose he has to be constantly aware, not only of the natural meaning which his words convey to the ordinary reader, but also of the special meaning which they have acquired by legal convention and by previous decisions of the Courts.

Legal drafting must therefore be unambiguous, precise, comprehensive and largely conventional. If it is readily intelligible, so much the better; but it is far more important that it should yield its meaning accurately than that it should yield it on first reading, and the legal draftsman cannot afford to give much attention, if any, to euphony or literary elegance. What matters most to him is that no one will succeed in persuading a court of law that his words bear a meaning he did not intend, and, if possible, that no one will think it worth while to try.

All this means that his drafting is not to be judged by normal standards of good writing, and that he is not really included among those for whom this book is primarily intended – 'those who use words as tools of their trade, in administration or business'.

By normal standards of good writing legal drafting is usually both cumbrous and uncouth. No doubt it is sometimes un-

necessarily so;* it would be surprising indeed if it were not.
But it often needs a skilled lawyer to say whether a particular
passage could have been put more prettily without losing its
accuracy; the layman should be slow to criticise – or to imitate.

EXPERT TO EXPERT

When an expert is writing only for his fellow experts his aim
of 'affecting his reader precisely as he wishes' may be achieved
to perfection by the use of language which the rest of us find
obscure or even quite unintelligible. Any issue of any learned
journal will yield copious examples. I am not concerned with
this kind of writing. I could cite passages which, as it seems
to me, could have been put more clearly, with fewer technical
or unfamiliar words. But the layman is not really entitled to
criticise scientific or technical writing on this score; what is
unclear to him may be perfectly clear to the intended reader.

This is not to say that such writing always *is* clear, even to the
intended reader. Its obscurities are sometimes due, not to the
exigences of the subject matter, but to muddled thinking or
mere pretentiousness; and for obscurities of this kind, as for
any other misuses of language, the writer is not to be forgiven
merely because he is writing for fellow experts.

But writing on scientific or technical subjects is, of course,
entirely within the scope of this book if it is addressed to the
non-expert reader, and I have more to say about this in Chapter
11.

DEPARTMENTAL SHORTHAND

This is really a variant of what I have called 'expert to expert'.
It occurs not only in Government Departments but in most
large organisations where there has to be written communication on the business in hand between different parts of the
organisation. Familiar words take on unfamiliar special meanings; procedures and categories acquire pet names; new words

*For a striking example, see p. 220.

and new terms of art are invented to meet particular needs; the language becomes allusive and, to the uninitiated, hopelessly obscure.

Take the following (imaginary) examples:

These are all time-expired clause 4 optants and delay in referral would distort the quarterly submission-ratio.

If the claimant is ineligible for transitional supplement only because he has no dormant assets, the initiating officer should consider extra-statutory disregard.

All Wilberforce concessions should be separately recorded on Q A B 4's and the relevant claims in the non-grant-aidable list should be de-asterisked.

These passages are, in the strict sense of the word, jargon. But they are entirely justifiable, ugly though they are, because they are doing efficiently what they set out to do. Both writer and reader know precisely what a *time-expired clause 4 optant* is, what special meanings attach to *referral*, *submission-ratio*, *dormant* and *disregard*, what is the difference between a *Wilberforce concession* and (say) a Shaftesbury one, and so on. The purist may blench at *non-grant-aidable list* and *de-asterisked*, and I would not recommend either for general use. But the purist does not know, as the official does, that in this particular context a lot turns on whether a claim is categorised as asterisked, unasterisked or de-asterisked; he must not even recommend *de-starred* instead, because for all he knows *starred*, *unstarred* and *de-starred* are already in use for some quite different and equally precise purpose. And I cannot blame busy officials for using *non-grant-aidable list* as shorthand for *list of claims that do not satisfy the conditions for grant*.

To put these passages in a form intelligible to the uninitiated would probably take at least five times the space and render them, if anything, less clear to the initiated – to whom alone they are addressed. They are therefore a laudable way of 'getting an idea as exactly as possible out of one mind into another', and I shall have nothing to say by way of objection to 'departmental shorthand'.

The danger for the official, or for anyone else who habitually uses private language of this kind for internal communication, is that he may slip into using it for external communication too. Clearly this is inefficient as well as unmannerly, for the reader will be puzzled as well as annoyed. To call a man a time-expired clause 4 optant in a departmental minute may earn official approval: to call him one in reply to his letter may earn an unofficial punch on the nose.

THE SPOKEN WORD

The spoken word (whether conversation or oratory or the coy mixture of the two which is now familiar to us on television) is a very different thing from the written word. What is effective or allowable or desirable in the one may be quite the reverse in the other, and the extempore speaker cannot correct himself by revision as the writer can and should. It is therefore not fair to take a report of a speech or of an oral statement and criticise it as if it were a piece of considered writing.

What has been prepared in writing and is then read out (such as a paper to a learned society, or a formal statement or lecture) is, however, fair game. So are speeches, as soon as the author has revised them for publication. Many reported speeches, for instance in Parliament, are partly prepared and partly extempore, and it is not always easy to tell from reading them which parts are which. To be on the safe side, I have not looked for illustrations from speeches in *Hansard* – only from prepared statements and prepared answers to Parliamentary Questions. The few incidental quotations from speeches are identified as such.

3

THE ELEMENTS

If any man were to ask me what I would suppose to be a perfect style of language, I would answer, that in which a man speaking to five hundred people, of all common and various capacities, idiots or lunatics excepted, should be understood by them all, and in the same sense which the speaker intended to be understood.

DEFOE

There is one golden rule to bear in mind always: that we should try to put ourselves in the position of our correspondent, to imagine his feelings as he writes his letters, and to gauge his reaction as he receives ours. If we put ourselves in the other man's shoes we shall speedily detect how unconvincing our letters can seem, or how much we may be taking for granted.

INLAND REVENUE STAFF INSTRUCTION

HAVING thus cleared the decks we can return to the various other purposes for which official writing has to be used. The relative importance of these, in quantity at any rate, has been changed by the immense volume of modern social legislation and the innumerable ways in which public authorities, and the laws which they administer, now impinge on the life of the community. Official writing used to consist mostly of departmental minutes and instructions, inter-departmental correspondence, and despatches to Governors and Ambassadors. These things still have their places. But in volume they have been left far behind by the vast output now necessary for explaining the law to the public and telling them what their rights and obligations are.

Explaining the law can be a difficult and delicate task. An official interpreting the law is often looked on with suspicion. It is for the legislature to make the laws, for the executive to administer them, and for the judiciary to interpret them. The official must avoid all appearance of encroaching on the province of the Courts. For this reason it used to be a rule in the service that when laws were brought to the notice of those affected by them the actual words of the statute must be used; in no other way could the official be sure of escaping all imputation of putting his own interpretation on the law. But this rule, which was perhaps never quite so important as it was made out to be, has long since yielded to the pressure of events.

A new technique has been developed for those pamphlets and leaflets that are necessary to explain the law to the man in the street in such matters as PAYE and National Insurance. Its guiding principles are to use the simplest language and avoid technical terms, to employ the second person freely, not to try to give all the details of the law relevant to the subject, but to be content with stating the essentials, to explain, if these are stated in the writer's words and not the words of the Act, that they are an approximation only, to tell the reader where he can find fuller information and further advice, and always to make sure that he knows what are his rights of appeal. Immense pains are taken nowadays in the preparation of such pamphlets and leaflets. The reader's difficulties are often anticipated by questions and answers.

But there is another part of this subject: the answering of letters from individual correspondents about their own cases. These answers cannot be written, like the pamphlets and leaflets, by people who are experts both in the subject matter and in English composition. Often, it is true, an existing leaflet provides the answer to the correspondent's query, and the reply can merely say 'You will see from the enclosed leaflet that . . .' Or the same query may be posed so often that a stock form of reply has been devised to save the individual official the trouble of composing a reply himself. But these easy expedients are often not available. The official is then on his own. Writing a letter on behalf of the Government needs in some respects a special technique, but the principles of it are the same as those of all good writing, whatever its purpose. We have here in its most elementary form – though not on that account its least difficult – the problem of writing what one means and affecting one's reader precisely as one wishes. If therefore we begin our study of the problems of official English by examining the technique of this part of it, that will serve as a good introduction to the rest of the book, for it will bring out most of the points that we shall have to study more closely later. It is in this field of an official's duties more than in any other that good English can be defined simply as English which is readily understood by the reader. To be clear is to be efficient; to be obscure is to be inefficient. Your style of letter-writing is to be judged not by literary conventions or grammatical niceties but by whether it carries out efficiently the job you are paid to do.

But 'efficiency' must be broadly interpreted. It connotes a proper attitude of mind towards your correspondent. He may not care about being addressed in literary English, but he will care very much about being treated with sympathy and under-standing. It is not easy nowadays to remember anything so contrary to all appearances as that officials are the servants of the public; and the official must try not to foster the illusion that it is the other way round. So your style must not only be simple but also friendly, sympathetic and natural, appropriate to one who is a servant, not a master.

In the original *Plain Words* these generalities were translated into a number of practical rules, which are here repeated in shortened form.

(1) Be sure that you know what your correspondent is asking before you begin to answer him. Study his letter carefully. If he is obscure, spare no trouble in trying to get at his meaning. If you conclude that he means something different from what he says (as he well may) address yourself to his meaning not to his words, and do not be clever at his expense. Get into his skin, and adapt the atmosphere of your letter to suit that of his. If he is troubled, be sympathetic. If he is rude, be specially courteous. If he is muddle-headed, be specially lucid. If he is pig-headed, be patient. If he is helpful, be appreciative. If he convicts you of a mistake, acknowledge it freely and even with gratitude. But never let a flavour of the patronising creep in.

(2) Begin by answering his question. Do not start by telling

him the relevant law and practice, and gradually lead up to a statement of its application to his case. Give him his answer briefly and clearly at the outset, and only then, if explanation is needed, begin your explanation. Thus he will know the worst, or the best, at once, and can skip the explanation if he likes.

(3) So far as possible, confine yourself to the facts of the case you are writing about and avoid any general statement about the law.

(4) Avoid a formal framework if you can. Formal official letters are sometimes necessary to notify matters of policy or important decisions made by or on behalf of the Minister. Such letters must be written in a precise and dignified manner but must not be pompous. (An official letter to a big firm or a local authority may have to be read aloud at a board or council meeting. It is salutary to consider how it will sound there.)

But ordinary letters to the public should be cast in as informal and friendly a way as possible. The use of the impersonal passive, with its formal unsympathetic phrases such as 'it is felt', 'it is regretted', 'it is appreciated', is a sure sign that the wrong note has been struck. It gives the reader the impression that he is dealing with robots rather than human beings. How feeble is the sentence 'It is thought you will now have received the form of agreement' compared with 'I expect you will have received the form of agreement by now'.

(5) Be careful to say nothing that might give your correspondent the impression, however mistakenly, that you think it right that he should be put to trouble in order to save you from it. Do not use paper stamped 'Date as postmark'. Do not ask him to give you over again information he has already given you unless there is some good reason for doing so, and, if there is, explain the reason.

(6) Use no more words than are necessary to do the job. Superfluous words waste your time and official paper, tire your reader and obscure your meaning. There is no need, for instance, to begin each paragraph with phrases like *I am further to point out*, *I would also add*, *You will moreover observe*. Go straight to what you have to say, without precautionary words,

and then say it in as few words as are needed to make your meaning clear.

(7) Keep your sentences short. This will help both you to think clearly and your correspondent to take your meaning. If you find you have slipped into long ones, split them up.

(8) Be compact; do not put a strain on your reader's memory by widely separating parts of a sentence that are closely related to one another. Why, for instance, is this sentence difficult to grasp on first reading?

A deduction of tax may be claimed in respect of any person whom the individual maintains at his own expense, and who is (i) a relative of his, or of his wife, and incapacitated by old age or infirmity from maintaining himself or herself, or (ii) his or his wife's widowed mother, whether incapacitated or not, or (iii) his daughter who is resident with him and upon whose services he is compelled to depend by reason of old age or infirmity.

The structure of the sentence is too diffuse; the reader has to keep in mind the opening words all the way through. It ends by telling him that a deduction of tax may be claimed 'in respect of any person whom the individual maintains at his own expense and who is his daughter', but 'his daughter' is separated from 'who is' by no fewer than 32 words. This sentence, taken from a leaflet of Income Tax instructions, was later rewritten as follows:

If you maintain a relative of yourself or your wife who is unable to work because of old age or infirmity, you can claim an allowance of. . . . You can claim this allowance if you maintain your widowed mother, or your wife's widowed mother, whether she is unable to work or not. If you maintain a daughter who lives with you because you or your wife are old or infirm, you can claim an allowance of. . . .

Why is the new version so much easier to grasp than the old? Partly it is because a sentence of eighty-one words has been split into three, each making a statement complete in itself. But it is also because a device has been employed that is a most use-

ful one when an official writer has to say, as he so often has, that
such-and-such a class of people who have such-and-such attributes, and perhaps such-and-such other attributes, have such-
and-such rights or obligations. The device is to use conditional
clauses in the second person instead of relative clauses in the
third – to say: *if* you belong to such-and-such a class of people,
and *if* you have such-and-such attributes, you have such-and-
such a right or obligation. The advantage of this is that it avoids
the wide separation of the main verb from the main subject; the
subject *you* comes immediately next to the verb it governs.

(9) Do not say more than is necessary. The feeling that
prompts you to tell your correspondent everything when explaining is commendable, but you will often help him more by
resisting it, and confining yourself to the facts that will enable
him to understand what has happened.

I regret however that the Survey Officer who is responsible for the
preliminary investigation as to the technical possibility of installing
a telephone at the address quoted by any applicant has reported that
owing to a shortage of a spare pair of wires to the underground
cable (a pair of wires leading from the point near your house right
back to the local exchange and thus a pair of wires essential for the
provision of telephone service for you) is lacking and that therefore
it is a technical impossibility to install a telephone for you at. . . .

This explanation is obscure partly because the sentence is
too long, partly because the long parenthesis has thrown the
grammar out of gear, and partly because the writer, with the
best intentions, says far more than is necessary even for a thoroughly polite and convincing explanation. It might have run
thus:

I am sorry to have to tell you that we have found that there is no
spare pair of wires on the cable that would have to be used to con-
nect your house with the exchange. I fear therefore that it is impossible to install a telephone for you.

(10) Explain technical terms in simple words. You will soon
become so familiar with the technical terms of the law you are

administering that you will feel that you have known them all your life, and may forget that to others they are unintelligible.

(11) Do not use what have been called the 'dry meaningless formulae' of commercialese. Against some of these a warning is not needed: officials do not write *your esteemed favour to hand* or address their correspondents as *your good self*. But if they are not careful they may find themselves using *same* as a pronoun (on which see pp. 196–7), or *enclosed please find* instead of *I enclose*. *Per* should not be permitted to get too free with the English language. Such convenient abbreviations as *m.p.h.* and *r.p.m.* are no doubt with us for good. But generally it is well to confine *per* to its own language – e.g. *per cent*, *per capita*, *per stirpes*, *per contra*, and not to prefer *per day* to *a day*, or *per passenger train* to *by passenger train*, or *as per my letter* to *as I said in my letter*.

Even for phrases in which *per* is linked to a Latin word there are often English equivalents which serve as well, if not better. A letter can as well be signed *AB for CD* as *CD per pro AB*. £100 *a year* is more natural than £100 *per annum*. *Per se* does not ordinarily mean anything more than *by itself* or *in itself*.

Another Latin word better left alone is *re*. This is the ablative case of the Latin word *res*. It means *in the matter of*. It is used by lawyers for the title of lawsuits, such as '*In re* John Doe deceased'. It has passed into commercialese as an equivalent of the English preposition *about*. It has no business there, or anywhere else outside a lawyer's office. It is not needed either to introduce a heading ('*re* your application for a grant'), which can stand without its support, or in the body of a letter, where an honest *about* will serve your purpose better. Avoid that ugly and unnecessary symbol *and/or* when writing letters; it is fit only for forms and lists and specifications and things of that sort. It can always be dispensed with. Instead of writing (say) 'soldiers and/or sailors' we can write 'soldiers or sailors or both'. Finally, there is no reason for preferring the Latin abbreviations *inst.*, *ult.* and *prox.* to the name of the month, which is also capable of abbreviation and has the advantage over them of conveying an immediate and certain meaning.

Here is an example of the baleful influence of commercialese:

Payment of the above account, which is now overdue at the date hereof, appears to have been overlooked, and I shall be glad to have your remittance by return of post, and oblige.

> Yours faithfully,

The superfluous *at the date hereof* must have been prompted by a feeling that *now* by itself was not formal enough and needed dressing up. The word *oblige* is grammatically in mid-air. It has no subject, and is firmly cut off by a full stop from what might have been supposed to be its object, the writer's signature.

The fault of commercialese is that its mechanical use has a bad effect on both writer and reader – the writer because it deadens his appreciation of the meaning of words, the reader because he feels that the writer's approach to him lacks sincerity.

(12) Use words with precise meanings rather than vague ones. Since, as we have seen, you will not be doing your job properly unless you make your meaning readily understood, this is an elementary duty. Yet it is still too often disregarded. Every entrant into the service comes equipped with a vocabulary of common words of precise meaning adequate for all ordinary purposes. But when he begins to write as an official he has a queer trick of forgetting them and relying mainly on a smaller vocabulary of less common words with a less precise meaning. It is a curious fact that in the official's armoury of words the weapons readiest to hand are weapons not of precision but of rough and ready aim; indeed, they are of a sort that were constructed as weapons of precision but have been bored out by him into blunderbusses.* They have been put in the front rank of the armoury; he reaches out for a word and uses one of these without troubling to search in the ranks behind for one that is more likely to hit the target in the middle. For instance, the blunderbuss *integrate* is now kept in front of *join*,

*The *OED* defines this word as 'A short gun with a large bore, firing many balls or slugs, and capable of doing execution within a limited range without exact aim'.

combine, amalgamate, co-ordinate and other words, and the
hand stretching out for one of these gets no farther. *Develop*
blocks the way to *happen, occur, take place* and *come. Alternative* (a converted weapon of precision) stands before many
simple words such as *different, other, new, fresh, revised. Realistic* is in front of others, such as *sensible, reasonable, practicable,
workable* and *feasible. Involve* throws a whole section of the
armoury into disuse, though not so big a one as that threatened
by *overall*; and rack upon rack of simple prepositions are left
untouched because before them are kept the blunderbusses of
vague phrases such as *in relation to, in regard to, in connexion
with* and *in the case of*.

It may be said that it is generally easy enough to guess what is
meant. But you have no business to leave your reader guessing
at your meaning, even though the guess may be easy. That is
not doing your job properly. If you make a habit of not troubling to choose the right weapon of precision you may be sure
that sooner or later you will set your reader a problem that is
past guessing.

(13) If two words convey your meaning equally well, choose
the common one rather than the less common. Do not prefer
regarding, respecting or *concerning* to *about*, or say *advert* for
refer, or *state, inform, acquaint* or *advise* when you might use
the word *say* or *tell. Furthermore* is a prosy word used too often.
It may be difficult to avoid it in cumulative argument (moreover . . . in addition . . . too . . . also . . . again . . . furthermore),
but prefer one of the simpler words if they have not all been
used up. Do not say *hereto, herein, hereof, herewith, hereunder*,
or similar compounds with *there*, unless, like *therefore*, they
have become part of everyday language. Most of them put a
flavour of legalism into any document in which they are used.
Use a preposition and pronoun instead. For instance:

With reference to the second paragraph thereof. (With reference
to its second paragraph.)
I have received your letter and thank you for the information contained therein. (. . . contained in it.)
I am to ask you to explain the circumstances in which the gift was

made and to forward any correspondence relative thereto. (. . . any correspondence about it.)

To take a few more examples of unnecessary choice of stilted expressions, do not say *predecease* for *die before*, *ablution facilities* for *wash basins*, *it is apprehended that* for *I suppose*, *capable of locomotion* for *able to walk*, *will you be good enough to advise me* for *please tell me*, *I have endeavoured to obtain the required information* for *I have tried to find out what you wanted to know*, *it will be observed from a perusal of* for *you will see by reading*. The reason why it is wrong for you to use these starchy words is not that they are bad English; most of them are perfectly good English in their proper places. The reason is twofold. First, some of the more unusual of them may actually be outside your correspondent's vocabulary and convey no meaning at all to him. Secondly, their use runs counter to your duty to show that officials are human. These words give the reader the impression that officials are not made of common clay but are, in their own estimation at least, beings superior and aloof. They create the wrong atmosphere; the frost once formed by a phrase or two of this sort is not easily melted. If you turn back to the example given under rule (8) you will see how careful the writer of the revised version has been about this. The word *individual* (a technical term of income tax law to distinguish between a personal taxpayer and a corporate one) was unnecessary and has disappeared. *Deduction of tax* is translated into *allowance*, *incapacitated* into *unable to work*, *is resident with* into *lives with*, and *by reason of old age or infirmity* into *because you are old or infirm*.

These rules can be briefly summarised as 'Be short, be simple, be human'. Since they were formulated they have been used by all Government Departments in their own way. They are the foundation of a short booklet, *The Written Word*, issued for general service use by the Civil Service Department; also of more specialised booklets produced by other Departments for their own particular purposes, in which the lessons are rubbed home by practical examples drawn from the Department's daily work. For instance, local offices of the Department of

Health and Social Security are enjoined not to write about 'making arrangements for you to be granted an interview' but rather to say something like:

I should be glad if you would call at this office as soon as convenient to you to discuss your claim for dependant's allowance. We are open from 10 a.m. to 4 p.m. If you are too ill to call and will let me know, I will arrange for someone to visit you.

And managers of Employment Exchanges are advised not to write like this:

It is regretted that no suitable vacancy has been found for you up to date, and though every endeavour is being made to do so, you will appreciate the difficulty in view of your qualifications.

but like this:

I am sorry that I have been unable, so far, to find a suitable vacancy for you, but I will continue to do all I can. The difficulty is that most of the vacancies require particular technical qualifications that you do not possess.

There is no point in quoting extensively from these admirable productions. Sometimes, no doubt, they are not complied with, but they have certainly done a great deal to raise the standard of letters sent by Government Departments to members of the public, particularly routine correspondence conducted by local offices. It is worth mentioning them, and the original advice on which they were founded, partly to indicate that that advice did not fall on stony ground and partly to enable readers outside the Civil Service to consider whether there are any other organisations which might with advantage do the same sort of thing.

The practical rules cited above were originally formulated primarily for Government Departments and primarily for the writing of letters to members of the public. But they apply also to other forms of official writing and to forms of writing other than official. They are well tabulated in the following advice given to its staff by the Ministry of Housing and Local Government (now part of the Department of the Environment), which is directed to the composition of minutes and memoranda as well as letters of all kinds:

YOU MUST KNOW	Before you begin to write make sure that you:
Your subject	(a) have a clear understanding of the subject;
Your reason for writing	(b) know why you are writing – what does your correspondent want to know and why does he want to know it?
Your reader	(c) adapt your style and the content of the letter or minute to suit your correspondent's needs and his present knowledge of the subject.

YOU MUST BE	When writing you should:
Clear	(a) make your meaning clear; arrange the subject in logical order; be grammatically correct; not include irrelevant material;
Simple and brief	(b) use the most simple direct language; avoid obscure words and phrases, unnecessary words, long sentences; avoid technical or legal terms and abbreviations unless you are sure that they will be understood by the reader; be as brief as possible; avoid 'padding';
Accurate and complete	(c) be as accurate and complete as possible; otherwise further correspondence will follow, resulting in extra work and loss of time;
Polite and human	(d) in your letters to the public be sympathetic if your correspondent is troubled; be particularly polite if he is rude; be lucid and helpful if he is muddled; be patient if he is stubborn; be appreciative if he is helpful; and *never* be patronising;

Prompt	(e) answer promptly, sending acknowledgements or interim replies if necessary – delays harm the reputation of the Department, and are discourteous.

CHECK YOUR WRITING	Look critically at your written work. Can you answer 'yes' to the following questions about it?
Is it (a) clear?	(i) Can the language be easily understood by the recipient? (ii) Is it free from slang? (iii) Are the words the simplest that can carry the thought? (iv) Is the sentence structure clear?
(b) Simple and brief?	(i) Does it give only the essential facts? (ii) Does it include only essential words and phrases?
(c) Accurate?	(i) Is the information correct? (ii) Do the statements conform with rules, policy, etc.? (iii) Is the writing free from errors in grammar, spelling and punctuation?
(d) Complete?	(i) Does it give all the necessary information? (ii) Does it answer all the questions?
(e) Human?	(i) Is the writing free from antagonistic words and phrases? (ii) Is it, where appropriate, tactful, helpful, courteous, sympathetic, frank, forceful? (iii) Will the tone bring the desired response?

There is surely no writer, official or other, who will not write better if he follows this advice.

This chapter is called 'The Elements' because it suggests certain elementary rules ('be short, be simple, be human') with special reference to one of the elementary duties of an official –

to write an acceptable letter. But these are the elements only. They will be elaborated in Chapters 5 to 8, in which much of what has been said in this chapter will be expanded. There is nothing novel in this chapter's precepts. Similar precepts were laid down for the Egyptian Civil Service some thousands of years ago:

> Be courteous and tactful as well as honest and diligent.
> All your doings are publicly known, and must therefore
> Be beyond complaint or criticism. Be absolutely impartial.
> Always give a reason for refusing a plea; complainants
> Like a kindly hearing even more than a successful
> Plea. Preserve dignity but avoid inspiring fear.
> Be an artist in words, that you may be strong, for
> The tongue is a sword. . . .

If we may judge from the following letter, those brought up in this tradition succeeded in avoiding verbiage. The letter is from a Minister of Finance to a senior civil servant:

> Apollonius to Zeno, greeting. You did right to send the chickpeas to Memphis. Farewell.

4

CORRECTNESS

My Lord, I do here, in the name of all the learned and polite
persons of the nation, complain to Your Lordship as First
Minister, that our Language is extremely imperfect; that its
daily improvements are by no means in proportion to its daily
corruptions; that the pretenders to polish and refine it have
chiefly multiplied abuses and absurdities; and that in many
instances it offends against every part of grammar.

SWIFT

WE will now turn to the implications of the remark I made on
p. 16, 'Lapses from what for the time being is regarded as correct
irritate the educated reader, and distract his attention, and so
make him the less likely to be affected precisely as you wish.'
We shall have to add a fourth rule to the three with which we
finished the last chapter – be correct. It applies to both vocabulary and grammar; this chapter is concerned with vocabulary
only, and grammar will be the subject of Chapter 9.

Correctness of vocabulary seems once to have been enforced
more sternly on officials than it is now. More than two centuries
ago the Secretary to the Commissioners of Excise wrote this
letter to the Supervisor of Pontefract.

The Commissioners on perusal of your Diary observe that you
make use of many affected phrases and incongruous words, such as
'illegal procedure', 'harmony', etc., all of which you use in a sense
that the words do not bear. I am ordered to acquaint you that if you
hereafter continue that affected and schoolboy way of writing, and
to murder the language in such a manner, you will be discharged for
a fool.*

To us the punishment seems disproportionate to the offence,
though the same penalty today might prove gratifying to those
who think we have too many officials. But we can have nothing

*Quoted in *Humour in the Civil Service*, by John Aye (Universal
Publications, 1928).

but admiration for the sentiment of the letter or for the vigorous directness of its phrasing. It serves moreover to illustrate a difficulty presented by this precept. What is correctness and who is to be the judge of it? It cannot be the same now as it was then. A Collector of Customs and Excise today might certainly use the expression 'illegal procedure' without being called in question; he might even refer to the harmony of his relations with the Trade without running much risk. On the other hand it would not do for him to say, as the Supervisor of Pontefract might have said, that the Local Bench were an indifferent body, meaning that they performed their duties with impartiality, or that he prevented the arrival of his staff at his office, meaning that he always got there first.

English is not static – neither in vocabulary nor in grammar, nor yet in that elusive quality called style. The fashion in prose alternates between the ornate and the plain, the periodic and the colloquial. Grammar and punctuation defy all the efforts of grammarians to force them into the mould of a permanent code of rules. Old words drop out or change their meanings; new words are admitted. What was stigmatised by the purists of one generation as a corruption of the language may a few generations later be accepted as an enrichment, and what was then common currency may have become a pompous archaism or acquired a new significance.*

Eminent men with a care for the language, from Dean Swift † to Lord Wavell,‡ have from time to time proposed that an

* I have more to say in Chapter 11 about changes in usage and the constant development of the living language. In the rest of this chapter I have felt it necessary to change some of what Gowers wrote in three ways – adaptation, addition and subtraction; and, contrary to my general practice elsewhere in the book, I have here and there mentioned both what he said and what it now seems to me right to say, in order to illustrate how quickly judgments based on current usage may become out of date. But many of the judgments he made seem to me still sound and I have left them as he wrote them. B.D.F.

† *Proposal for correcting, improving and ascertaining the English Tongue.*

‡ Letter from Lord Wavell to Mr Ivor Brown quoted in *Ivor Brown's Book of Words.*

Authority should be set up to preserve what is good and resist what is bad. 'They will find', said Swift, 'many words that deserve to be utterly thrown out of the language, many more to be corrected, and perhaps not a few long since antiquated, which ought to be restored on account of their energy and sound.' 'They should issue', said Lord Wavell, 'a monthly journal of words that required protection and a pillory of misused words, and so on.' Swift's plea, which was made in the form of a letter to the Lord Treasurer, came to nothing. This, Lord Chesterfield drily observed, was not surprising, 'precision and perspicuity not being in general the favourite objects of Ministers'. Dr Johnson thought the task hopeless:

Academies have been instituted to guard the avenues of the language, to retain fugitives and to repulse invaders; but their vigilance and activity have been vain; sounds are too volatile and subtile for legal restraints; to enchain syllables and to lash the wind are equally the undertakings of pride, unwilling to measure its desires by its strength.

In recent years we have seen a Society for Pure English, with leaders as eminent as Henry Bradley, Robert Bridges and Logan Pearsall Smith, inviting the support of all those who 'would preserve all the richness of differentiation in our vocabulary, its nice grammatical usages and its traditional idioms, but would oppose whatever is slipshod and careless and all blurring of hard-won distinctions, and oppose no less the tyranny of schoolmasters and grammarians, both in their pedantic conservatism and in their enforcing of new-fangled rules'. But it is now defunct.

Dr Johnson was right, as usual. One has only to look at the words which Swift wanted to expel to realise how difficult, delicate and disappointing it is to resist new words and new meanings. He condemns, for instance, *sham*, *banter*, *mob*, *bully* and *bamboozle*. A generation later Dr Johnson called *clever* a 'low word' and *fun* and *stingy* 'low cant'. Should we not have been poorer if Swift and Johnson had had their way with these? There is no saying how things will go. The fight for admission to the language is quickly won by some assailants and long resistance is maintained against others. The word that excited Swift to greatest fury was *mob*, a contraction of *mobile vulgus*. Its victory was rapid and complete. So was that of *banter* and *bamboozle*, which he found hardly less offensive. And if *rep* for *reputation* proved ephemeral, and *phiz* for *physiognomy* never emerged from slang status, and is now dead, that is not because Swift denounced them, but because public opinion disliked them or got tired of them. *Reliable* was long opposed on the curious ground that it was an impossible construction; an adjective formed from *rely* could only be *reli-on-able*. This objection was a survival of the theory, widely held in pre-Fowler days, and not yet wholly exorcised, that no sentence could be 'good grammar', and no word a respectable word, if its construction violated logic or reason. (I shall have more to say about this reign of pedantry when we consider grammar in Chapter 9.) It is not the habit of the English to refrain from doing anything merely because it is illogical; in any case it was less illogical to accept *reliable* than to strain at it after swallowing *available* and *objectionable*.

Some words gatecrash irresistibly because their sound is so appropriate to the meaning they are trying to acquire. *Spiv* is now well established. *Blurb*, Professor Weekley tells us, was described by Robert Bridges as 'an admirable word, quite indispensable'. *Haver* does not mean *vacillate* (it means *blather*), but almost everyone south of the Border thinks it does: there is no withstanding its suggestion of simultaneous hovering and wavering.* Vidkun Quisling won instant admission to the company of the immortals, who, like the Earl of Sandwich, Mr Joseph Aloysius Hansom, General Shrapnel and Captain Boycott, have given their names to enrich the language. There has been stout resistance against certain words that attacked the barrier in the nineteenth century with powerful encouragement from Dickens

---

*So wrote Gowers, though he recorded in a footnote the wrath of a Scottish friend at his 'weak-kneed acquiescence'. As a Scot, I am always pained by the Englishman's misuse of *haver* and I cannot condone it. It may in time be universally accepted, but not before my death. B.D.F.

– *mutual*, *individual*, *phenomenal* and *aggravate*. *Mutual* in the sense of *common*, pertaining to both parties, as in *Our Mutual Friend*, goes back to the sixteenth century, according to the *OED*, but is 'now regarded as incorrect'. Perhaps the reason why it is so difficult to restrain the word to its 'correct' meaning is the ambiguity of *common*. 'Our common friend' might be taken as a reflection on the friend's manners or birth. On the other hand it would be a great pity if *mutual* became so popular in its 'incorrect' sense that we could no longer rely on it when we need it for its correct one. The use of *individual* that is unquestionably correct is to distinguish a single person from a collective body, as it is used in the Income Tax Acts to distinguish between a personal taxpayer and a corporate one. But its use as a facetious term of disparagement (like the French *individu*) used to be common and still lingers. That was how Mr Jorrocks understood it when Mr Martin Moonface described him as an 'unfortunate individual', and provoked the retort 'You are another indiwidual'. *Phenomenal* to the purists means nothing more that 'perceptible to the senses', and a *phenomenon* is an occurrence so perceptible. But the purists have lost at least half this battle. It is still unusual to use *phenomenon* by itself to denote something striking or rare: it still tends to need a descriptive adjective or adjectival clause (such as 'striking' or 'rare'). But *phenomenal* in the sense of *prodigious* is now common. Over *aggravate* the long-drawn-out struggle still continues between those who, like Dickens, use it in the sense of *annoy* and those who would confine it to its original sense of *make worse*. The Dickens team seems now to be winning, in the writing of good authors as well as in speech; but here too their victory must not be allowed to disqualify the word for its original purpose.

Today the newcomers are mostly from the inventive and colourful minds of the Americans. We have changed our outlook since Dean Alford declared nearly a hundred years ago that the way the Americans corrupted our language was all of a piece with the character of that nation 'with its blunted sense of moral obligation and duty to men'. But we have not yet accepted H. L. Mencken's suggestion that since Americans far outnumber Britons American English should be regarded as the norm and British English as a mere dialect. We therefore still have defenders of our tongue who scrutinise these immigrants very closely. That is as it should be, for some of them are certainly undesirables. But we ought not to forget how greatly our language has been enriched by the vigorous word-making habit of the Americans. Bridges' tribute to *blurb* might be applied to other more recent acquisitions, *gatecrasher*, *debunk*, *cold war*, *baby-sitter*, *stockpile*, *bulldoze*, *teenager*, *commuter* and many others. For more about the influence of America see Chapter 11.

It is around new verbs that the battle now rages most hotly. New verbs are ordinarily formed in one of three ways, all of which have in the past been employed to create useful additions to our vocabulary. The first is the simple method of treating a noun as a verb; it is one of the beauties of our language that nouns can be so readily converted into adjectives or verbs. This was the origin, for instance, of the verb *question*; and there are many other such verbs, such as *function*, *condition*, *experience* and *mention*. The second is what is called 'back-formation', that is to say, forming from a noun the sort of verb from which the noun might have been formed if the verb had come first. In this way the verb *diagnose* was formed from *diagnosis* and the verb *televise* from *television*. The third is to add *ise** to an adjective, as *sterilise* has been formed from *sterile*.

All these methods are being used today with no little zest. New verbs for something that is itself new (like *pressurise*) cannot be gainsaid. *Service* is a natural and useful newcomer in an age when almost everyone keeps a machine of some sort that needs periodical attention. But it provides an interesting example of the way these new verbs take an ell, once you give them an inch. *Service* is already trying to oust *serve*, as in:

A large number of depots of one sort or another will be required to service the town.
To enable a Local Authority to take advantage of this provision it is essential that sites should be available, ready serviced with roads and sewers.

*On the question whether this should be *ise* or *ize* see p. 237.

A Welsh secretariat should be established in Brussels to service the needs of Welsh organisations.

The verb *to contact*, described by Sir Alan Herbert many years ago as 'loathsome', has now made its way into the language, perhaps because, as Ivor Brown said, 'there is no word which covers approach by telephone, letter and speech, and *contact* is self-explanatory and concise'. Earlier editions of this book recorded some people as still strongly objecting to the use as verbs of *feature*, *glimpse*, *position*, *sense* and *signature*, though all had long since found their way into the dictionaries. All have now won their way, except perhaps *signature* (which indeed does not deserve to). The verbs *loan*, *gift* and *author* were verbs centuries ago and are now trying to come back again after a long holiday, spent by *loan* in America, by *gift* in Scotland and by *author* in oblivion. Whatever may be the fate of these, we shall not be disposed to welcome such a word as *reaccessioned*, used by a librarian of a book once more available to subscribers. To *underground* (of electric cables) seems at first sight an unnecessary addition to our vocabulary of verbs when *bury* is available, but an editor to whom a protest was made retorted that *bury* would not have done because the cables were 'live'.

But these words are merely skirmishers. The main body of the invasion consists of verbs ending in *ise* (and their accompanying nouns ending in *isation*). Earlier editions of this book noted that 'among those now nosing their way into the language' were *casualise* (employ casual labour), *civilianise* (replace military staff by civilian), *diarise* (enter in a diary), *editorialise* (make editorial comments on), *finalise* (finally settle), *hospitalise* (send to hospital), *publicise* (give publicity to), *servicise* (replace civilian staff by military), *cubiclise* (equip with cubicles), *randomise* (shuffle). Of these I would say that to-day no one raises an eyebrow at *finalise* or *publicise*, that *civilianise* and *hospitalise* are often used, but still with some distaste, that *randomise* is still nosing its way, but not in the sense of 'shuffle', and that the other noses have retreated somewhat. But *decasualise* has done better than *casualise*. *Decasualisation* is the regular, if unlovely, word for the process of abolishing a system of casual labour. Recent advances in technology have produced, reasonably enough, such newcomers as *miniaturise, containerise, computerise* and, less reasonably perhaps, *denuclearisation*. I am not sure whether *palletisation* can sneak in under the same colours. The usual reason for inventing such words is that they enable us to say in one word what would otherwise need several. Whether that will prove a valid passport time alone can show.* If the words I have listed were all, they might eventually be swallowed, though with some wry faces. But they are by no means all; a glut of this diet is being offered to us (*trialise, itinerise, reliableise* and *extemporisation* are among the least palatable), and we are showing signs of nausea. It is perhaps significant that at the Coronation of Queen Elizabeth II the word *Inthroning* was substituted for the first time for the word *Inthronisation*, used in all previous Coronations. This may have been symptomatic of a revolt against the ugliness of *ise* and still more of *isation*, which Sir Alan Herbert has compared to lavatory fittings, useful in their proper place but not to be multiplied beyond what is necessary for practical purposes.

Another popular way of making new words is to put *de, dis* or *non* at the beginning of a word in order to create one with an opposite meaning. *De* and *dis* are termed by the *OED* 'living prefixes with privative force'. 'Living' is the right word; they have been living riotously of late. Anyone, it seems, can make a new verb by prefixing *de* to an existing one. Some years ago Sir Alan Herbert made a collection of some remarkable creations of this sort, and included them in his list of 'septic verbs'. Among them were *debureaucratise, decontaminate, dedirt, dehumidify, deinsectize, deratizate, derestrict, dewater, dezincify*.

Some of these, happily, have proved to be freaks of an occasion and are seen no more. But there is a class which will always have a strong claim to survival, whether we like it or not. It

*A remarkable experiment in this direction is the American verb to *nolle prosse*, meaning to enter a writ of *nolle prosequi*. Will this in time acquire over here the same status as is already enjoyed by the verb to *sub-poena*?

includes *decontaminate, derestrict, derequisition* and *deschedule*.
Their origin is the same: they all denote the undoing of something the doing of which called for – or at any rate was given –
a special term. If to affect with gas is to *contaminate*, to enforce
a speed limit is to *restrict*, to commandeer a house is to *requisi-
tion*, and to mark an area of the country as qualifying for special
development grants is to *schedule*, then the cancellation of those
things will inevitably be *decontaminate, derestrict, derequisition*
and *deschedule*; and it is no use saying that they ought to be
cleanse, exempt, release and *disqualify*, or any other words that
are not directly linked with their opposites. Some people may
still wince on reading that the authorities have decided to de-
trunk a road, as though it were an elephant, and on hearing that
witnesses in a postponed trial have been dewarned. But they
must learn to be brave. An interesting word on the fringes of
this class is *debrief*. One might think it meant telling the recipient of a brief that his brief is withdrawn, but in fact it means
asking him how he got on in carrying it out; and it is as well
established in this meaning for space pilots in the 1970s as it
was for aircraft pilots in the 1940s. It is not yet in use in the
legal profession.

Most of the new *dis*-words since the war have been invented
by economists (several by *The Economist* itself). *Disincentive*
and *disinflation*, received at first with surprised disapproval,
have quite settled down. It is recognised that the old-fashioned
opposites of *incentive* and *inflation* – *deterrent* and *deflation* –
will not do; we need special words for that particular form of
deterrent that discourages men from working hard, and for that
process of checking inflation which is something less than deflation. On the heels of these new arrivals came *diseconomy* and
dissaving.

It would yield economies that would far outweigh the diseconomies that are the inevitable price of public ownership and giant size.

Some 13·4 million of the 22 million income earners . . . kept their
spending in such exact step with their incomes that they saved or
dissaved less than £25 in that year.

These have also been accepted on the ground that in the first no positive word – neither *extravagance* nor *waste* nor *wastefulness* – would express the writer's meaning so well as *diseconomies*, and that in the second *dissaved* is the only way of expressing the opposite of *saved* without a clumsy periphrasis that would destroy the nice balance of the sentence. These words can certainly claim to have sprung from deliberate and provocative choice and not from mental indolence. What is deplorable is that so many of those who go in for the invention of opposites by means of 'living prefixes with privative force' do not know when to stop. It becomes a disease. *Disincentive* replaces *deterrent*; then *undisincentive* ousts *incentive*, and then *disincentive* itself has to yield to *non-undisincentive*. This tendency is well parodied by George Orwell; in the 'newspeak' which he pictured as the language imposed by a despotic government in 1984 *very bad* has become *doubleplusungood*.

The same warning is needed about the prefix *non*. To put *non* in front of a word is a well-established way of creating a word with the opposite meaning. *Non-appearance*, *non-combatant*, *nonconformist* and *non-existent* are common examples. But the lazy habit of using *non* to turn any word upside-down, so as not to have the trouble of thinking of its opposite, is becoming sadly common. 'Institutions for the care of the *non-sick*' presumably means something different from 'institutions for the care of the healthy', but the difference is not apparent. *Non-total* appears where *partial* is meant and *non-professional* is sometimes unnecessarily preferred to *unprofessional*, *lay*, or *amateur*. This is not to say that new words with *non* are always to be condemned. They are sometimes needed because of a certain ambiguity in the prefix *un*. Thus, your coat may be described as 'unbuttoned' either when you have undone the buttons or when you have never done them up. Similarly with *uncovered*, *undone*, *undressed*, *unfastened* and many others. For this reason certain countries may prefer to be described as 'non-aligned' rather than 'unaligned' so as to avoid any possible implication that they were once aligned. Our social security system makes a valid distinction between *unemployed* and *non-employed*. Even when the adjective has *un* the noun is often

happier with *non*. If you wish to remain uninvolved, uncooperative or undiscriminating you will adopt a policy of non-
involvement, non-cooperation or non-discrimination.

Yet another favourite device for making new words is the
suffix *ee*. This is an erratic suffix, not conforming wholly to any
rule. But in its main type it serves to denote the object of a verb,
either the indirect object, as in *assignee*, *referee* and *trustee*, or
the direct object, as in *examinee*, *trainee* and *employee*. It therefore makes for confusion of language if the suffix is used to
form a word meaning the subject of the verb. *Escapee* is a
foolish word for one who escapes. Nor is a new *ee* word justified
if a perfectly good word is already on the job; *prosecutee* is not
needed when we have *defendant*. Apart from misuses such as
these, it would be idle to object to new *ee* words on principle;
their purpose is often the same as that of many of our new verbs
– to enable us to use one word instead of several. I do not object,
as some people do, to *amputee*, *interviewee* or *promotee*, nor to
the more recent (and slightly illogical) *parolee* for an offender
allowed out on parole. Sometimes, again, they are intended to
be mildly facetious, and there is no great harm in that. But
many *ee* words are ugly and we should not invent new ones
unless they are really necessary.

While the age-long practice of creating new words has quick-
ened its tempo, so has the no less ancient habit of extending the
meaning of established words. Here again we ought to examine
the novelties on merits, without bias. The main test for both is
whether the new word, or the new meaning, fills a need in the
vocabulary. If it is trying to take a seat already occupied – as the
new verbs *decision* and *suspicion* are squatting in the places of
decide and *suspect*, and the enlarged meanings of *anticipate* and
claim in those of *expect* and *assert* – they are clearly harming
the language by 'blurring hard-won distinctions'. Still more are
words like *overall* and *involve* open to that charge: they are
claiming the seats of half a dozen or more honest words. But
those that claim seats hitherto empty may deserve admittance.
Stagger, for example, has enlarged its meaning both logically
and usefully in such a phrase as *staggered holidays*. *Deadline*

(originally a line around a military prison beyond which a prisoner might be shot) has done the same in taking over the task of signifying a limit of any sort beyond which it is not permissible to go. Nor do I see why purists should condemn the use of *nostalgia* not only for a feeling of homesickness but also for the emotion aroused by thinking of days that are no more. An appeal to etymology is not conclusive.

Sophisticated was once an uncomplimentary word implying sophistry and even artfulness (*unsophisticated* being its opposite). But it is now commonly used either as the opposite of *naive* with no uncomplimentary implication, or in the sense of *complicated*, particularly in technological contexts. A computer is a more sophisticated tool than an abacus, a ballistic missile a more sophisticated weapon than a musket; and the old connexion with sophistry has quite disappeared. There is neither hope nor good sense in resisting this enlargement of meaning. If we want to accuse a man of sophistry *sophistical* is still available. *Prestigious* is a more recent example. Most dictionaries still define it by reference to *prestidigitation*, or sleight of hand, but it has come to be used as the adjective from *prestige* (which has the same etymological origin.) A prestigious person is now a VIP, not a conjuror, and a prestigious project one undertaken to enhance the promoter's prestige, though not necessarily his bank balance. There is no other word which does this job. *Prestigious* passes. *Swinging*, in its new sense of bright, up-to-date and care-free, has hardly yet made its way into literary use but may well do so before long.

When a word starts straying from its derivative meaning it may often be proper, and sometimes even useful, to try to restrain it; there are many now who would like to restrain the wanderlust of *alibi* and *shambles*. The ignorant misuse of technical terms excites violent reactions in those who know their true meanings. The popular use of *to the nth degree* in the sense of *to the utmost* exasperates the mathematician, who knows that strictly the notion of largeness is not inherent in *to the nth* at all. The use of *by and large* in the sense of *broadly speaking* exasperates the sailor, who knows that the true meaning of the phrase – alternately close to the wind and with the wind abeam or aft – has not the faintest relation to the meaning given to it by current usage. But there is a point where it becomes idle pedantry to try to put back into their etymological cages words and phrases that escaped from them many years ago and have settled down firmly elsewhere. To do that is to start on a path on which there is no logical stopping-point short of such absurdities as insisting that the word *anecdote* can only be applied to a story never told before, whereas we all know that it is more likely to mean one told too often. As Sir Clifford Allbutt used to remind his students, 'the word *apostate* means for us far more than an *absentee* or a *dissenter*, and a *muscle* more than a *little mouse*; *monks* rarely live alone; *rivals* contend for more than water rights, and *hypocrites* are no longer confined to the theatre.'

Sometimes words appear to have changed their meanings when the real change is in the popular estimate of the value of the ideas they stand for. Only very recently have the dictionaries recognised that *appeasement* can be anything but praiseworthy. *Imperialism*, which Lord Rosebery defined as 'a greater pride in Empire, a larger patriotism', has fallen from its pedestal. *Academic* has suffered a similar debasement owing to the waning of love of learning for its own sake and the growth of mistrust of intellectual activities that have no immediate utilitarian results. It is frequently used to mean *irrelevant, theoretical* or *impractical*. In music, according to the music critic of *The Times*, the word 'has descended from the imputation of high esteem to being a withering term of polite abuse', in spite of Stanford's attempt to stop the rot by defining the word as 'a term of opprobrium applied by those who do not know their business to those who do'. *Elite* and *paternal* are going the same way: *élitist* is a term of abuse in many modern mouths and *paternalism* implies bossiness or interference rather than kindliness or protectiveness.

Public opinion decides all these questions in the long run; there is little that individuals can do about them. Our national vocabulary is a democratic institution, and what is generally accepted will ultimately be correct. I have no doubt that if anyone should read this book in fifty years' time he would find current objections to the use of certain words in certain senses as curious as we now find Swift's denunciation of *mob*.

The duty of the official is, however, clear. Just as it has long been recognised that, in salaries and wages, the Civil Service must neither walk ahead of public opinion nor lag behind it, but, in the old phrase, be 'in the first flight of good employers', so it is the duty of the official in his use of English neither to perpetuate what is obsolescent nor to give currency to what is novel, but, like a good servant, to follow what is generally regarded by his masters as the best practice for the time being. Among his readers will be vigilant guardians of the purity of English prose, and they must not be offended. So the official's vocabulary must contain only words that by general consent have passed the barrier and he must not give a helping hand to any that are still trying to get through, even though he may think them deserving.

> For last year's words belong to last year's language
> And next year's words await another voice.

The sentence that is right, adds Eliot, is one

> ... where every word is at home,
> Taking its place to support the others,
> The word neither diffident nor ostentatious,
> An easy commerce of the old and the new,
> The common word exact without vulgarity,
> The formal word precise but not pedantic,
> The complete consort dancing together.*

I will end this chapter on correctness in words with a list of some words and phrases often used in senses generally regarded as incorrect. At the end of Chapters 7 and 8 are lists of other words and phrases that are apt to be used unsuitably rather than incorrectly. It is not easy to decide which words should be assigned to the 'incorrect' category and which to the 'unsuitable', and I do not suppose that all readers will agree with my classification: so many words are trying to arrogate new meanings

*T. S. Eliot, *Little Gidding* (Faber & Faber, 1943).

that opinions may well differ about which have succeeded and which not. Even if my choice is right now, it will almost certainly be out of date before long.

ABROGATE, ARROGATE

Abrogate means *repeal* or *cancel*; *arrogate* means *claim for oneself* (usually unjustifiably or arrogantly). They are sometimes confused with each other and sometimes with other words such as *abdicate* or *derogate*. The correct use of *arrogate* is illustrated just above ('so many words are trying to arrogate new meanings'). The incorrect use of *abrogate* is illustrated by

... the manager will abrogate his responsibility by giving the same increase to all.

The writer meant *abdicate*.

ALIBI

The Victorians allowed great scope to individuality and masculinity, strong passions and high spirits, and other alibis for overweening egomania, insecurity and aggression.

Members of the timber trade, like members of any other trade, are glad of any alibi to explain any particular increases in price.

Either we accept the bare facts or we go down to a lower standard of living. The day of alibis is gone.

Alibi is used in these examples in the sense of *excuse*, or of an admission of guilt with a plea of extenuating circumstances, or of throwing the blame on someone else. But *alibi* is the Latin for *elsewhere*. To plead an alibi is to rebut a charge by adducing evidence that the person charged was elsewhere at the time of the act alleged against him. The vogue of detective stories may have stimulated the corruption. So many of them rely on an alibi for their plot that ignorant readers think the word will do for any means of rebutting a charge. The mischief is that if the enlarged use establishes itself language will lose precision; we shall be left without a word to signify the true meaning of *alibi*,

ALTERNATE(LY) and ALTERNATIVE(LY)

These are sometimes confused. *Alternate(ly)* means by turns.
Alternative(ly) means in a way that offers a choice. 'The journey
may be made by rail or alternately by road' means, if it means
anything, that every other journey may be made by road. It does
not mean, as the writer intended, that for every journey the
traveller has a choice between the two means of transport. Conversely 'alternatively they sat and walked in the moonlight,
talking of this and that' cannot have been intended to mean that
they sat and walked in the moonlight as an alternative to doing
something else; what must have been intended is that they sat
and walked alternately. *Alternate* can also be a verb meaning,
in popular language, to 'take it in turns'.

APPRAISE and APPRISE

To *appraise* is to form a judgment about the value of something. You can appraise a candidate for a job by interviewing
him, or a race-horse from his appearance in the paddock. It is
sometimes confused with *apprise*, which means *inform*. Both
the following are wrong:

Mr Heath has been anxious to appraise himself of the developments in various Ministries since Parliament rose for the Christmas
recess.
Being appraised of the proposals for an oil refinery at Longhaugh
we wrote to the Secretary of State to express our deep concern.

A PRIORI

Do not say *a priori* when you mean *prima facie*.

Services in the bottom of Table 2 seem *a priori* to be suited to
traditional bureaucratic organization.
Several countries most advanced from a medical point of view
have for the last 20 years done without this drug, 'a fact', says the

Board, 'which is sufficient to show that there is an *a priori* case for its total abolition'.

No – it does not. To argue *a priori* is to argue from assumed axioms and not from experience. The argument here rests on the 20-year experience of several countries, and so is an argument *a posteriori*.

Prima facie, which is what the writer probably had in mind, means on a first impression, before hearing fully the evidence for and against. In fact you can probably get on without either phrase. In the first of the above examples *at first sight* would do very well: in the second *a strong case* or *an arguable case* would be an improvement.

BEG THE QUESTION

This does not mean, as is commonly supposed, to evade a straight answer to a question. It means to form a conclusion by making an assumption which is as much in need of proof as the conclusion itself. Logicians call this *petitio principii*. 'Thus to say that parallel lines will never meet because they are parallel is simply to assume as a fact the very thing you profess to prove' (Brewer). A single word can be used in a question-begging way. *Reactionary*, *victimisation*, *aggression*, *imperialism* and *warmonger* are examples.

BEHOVES

It is now slightly old-fashioned, but not yet affectedly so, to write that it behoves a driver to take care rather than that he must, should or ought to take care. This verb can have no subject but *it*. *The fog behoved the driver to take care* is wrong. For some odd reason it is sometimes confused with *becomes*, even (as in the following) by prominent politicians writing to the Press:

It ill behoves any man responsible for defence policy to think of how best to make political propaganda.

COMPOUND (verb)

This word is often misused. It means *to mix together* into a composite whole, or *to settle* by mutual agreement, or *to condone* for a consideration. Thus, a mixture is compounded of its ingredients; you may compound an annual liability by paying a lump sum; or you may compound a felony if you have a private motive for not wanting the felon prosecuted. It does not mean *to multiply* or *to complicate* as some people suppose (perhaps from a woolly mental association with *compound interest* or *compound fracture*). Here are two examples of misuse:

The percentage figure was wrongly calculated and applying it to the wrong total only compounded the mistake.
[A certain city's] parking problems are as serious as any in the world; and they are compounded by frequent strikes on the public transport system.

The first of these is particularly unfortunate because *to compound a mistake* is a useful phrase in its proper meaning.

Instead of misusing *compound*, try *multiply*, *complicate*, *aggravate*, *increase*, *add to* or the like.

COMPRISE

A body comprises (or consists of) the elements of which it is composed (or constituted); in the first example, for instance, Op. 77 comprises the quartets, not the other way round. *Compose* or *constitute* or *form* should have been used in these examples.

The two quartets comprising Haydn's Op. 77.
The smaller Regional Hospitals which comprise a large proportion of those available to Regional Boards.
The twelve Foreign Ministers who comprise the Atlantic Treaty Council.

The *OED* recognises *comprise* in the sense of *compose*, but calls it 'rare'. In the interests of precision it should remain so,

The difference between *comprise* and *include* is that *comprise* is better when all the components are enumerated and *include* when only some of them are.

CONSEQUENTIAL

Consequential has now only two meanings in common use. It retains that of *self-important*, and in legal language it signifies a secondary and incidental result, especially in the phrases *consequential damages* and *consequential amendments*. For all other purposes *consequent* is the adjective of *consequence*. Thus a Minister might say, 'This amendment is consequent on a promise I gave on second reading' and 'This amendment is consequential on one accepted yesterday'.

CREDENCE, CREDIBILITY, CREDULITY

These words are sometimes confused. *Credence* means belief or trust, *credibility* the quality of being believable and *credulity* the quality of being ready to believe anything.

In order to give some credence to the viability of the proposals made in this report an attempt has been made to . . .

Here *credence* should be *credibility* (though *plausibility* would be better). True, *credibility to the viability of* would be an ugly phrase, but the proper remedy is to omit *the viability of* altogether. The vogue word *viability* has been unnecessarily dragged in.

DEFINITIVE

This word differs from *definite* by importing the idea of finality. A definite offer is an offer precise in its terms. A definitive offer is an offer which the person making it declares to be his last word.

DESIDERATE

Desiderate is a rather pedantic word. It is not, as some think, a formal synonym of *desire* or *ask for*.

One influential deputation desiderated State management [of licensed premises in New Towns].

Desiderate means more than *desire*. It means to feel the want of, to miss, to think long for, as the Irish say. Mrs Gummidge desiderated the old 'un. But the influential deputation cannot have been feeling like that about something that existed only in their hopes.

DISINTERESTED

Disinterested means 'unbiased by personal interest' (*OED*). It is sometimes used wrongly for *uninterested* (i.e. not interested), as when a Minister said in Parliament:

I hope that [what I have said] will excuse me from the charge of being disinterested in this matter.

A public man dealing with public business can never be 'charged' with being disinterested, as if it were a crime. It is his elementary duty always to be so.

DIVERGE, DIVERGENT

If two paths diverge they get further away from each other. *Diverge* and *divergent* do not mean the same as *differ* and *different*. Their meanings differ, but they do not diverge.

These are all matters of considerable complexity on which BOAC and BEA held divergent views.

If this were true there would be little hope of reconciliation. But in fact the writer only meant *different*. (You can tell that he is a bad writer, because he preferred *matters of considerable complexity* to *complex matters*.)

The interests of clients, administrators and the public at large may diverge, and this should be recognised in the theoretical basis of research.

If this were true it would be hard to see how the research could ever progress from the theoretical to the practical.

ECONOMIC

There is no excuse for confusing the adjectives *economical* and *economic*, though confusion is seen sometimes in unexpected places. (For example, a Minister recently prided himself on 'the more effective and economic organisation that will result from these changes'.) The first is now associated only with economy and the second only with economics. A tenant may protest with truth that what is admittedly an economic rent is not for him an economical one.

ENABLE

This word means to make able, not to make possible. You may say that your courage enables you to win or makes your victory possible, but not that it enables your victory.

The following examples come from the same 'Explanatory and Financial Memorandum' published with a Parliamentary Bill:

Clause 6 will enable reciprocal agreements with countries outside the United Kingdom to apply to . . . as well as . . .
The provisions of the Bill are estimated to enable a net saving of about 80 staff.

The first is right, the second wrong.
An academic member of the Joint Matriculation Board should know better than to write:

Objective testing . . . enables examination in a wide range of subjects.

FACTITIOUS

Factitious means 'engineered' in the derogatory sense of that word, i.e. not naturally or spontaneously created. It is easily confused with *fictitious*, which means sham, counterfeit, unreal. A factitious thing may be genuine; a fictitious thing cannot.

FEASIBLE

This word means *practicable, capable of being done.* It should not be used as a synonym for *probable* or *plausible.*

HISTORIC

Historic means noted in history; *historical* means belonging to history. This useful differentiation should not be blurred by the use of one for the other.

For largely historic reasons the bulk of new town residents are tenants.

The third word is wrong and the first two are in the wrong order. *Largely* is not intended to qualify *historic.* We need 'Largely for historical reasons'.

But we must allow accountants to continue to use *historic costs* and *historic rates of interest.* This practice may be illogical, in more senses than one, but in both senses it is hallowed by long custom.

I.E.

This is sometimes used (by confusion with *e.g.*) to introduce an example. It stands for *id est* ('that is') and introduces a definition, as one might say 'we are meeting on the second Tuesday of this month, i.e. the tenth'. *E.g.* (*exempli gratia*) means 'for the sake of example' and introduces an illustration, as one might say 'let us meet on a fixed day every month, e.g. the second Tuesday'.

ILK

Ilk is a Scots word meaning *same*. It is not a noun meaning *kind*, *sort* or *kidney*. 'James Sporran of that ilk' means 'James Sporran of Sporran'; it shows that he lives on the estate that bears the family name and distinguishes him from his cousins, the Sporrans of Glenhaggis, and his distant kinsmen, the Sporrans of Upper Tooting. The schoolmaster who wrote to *The Times* about the damage done to the BBC by 'Mrs Whitehouse and her ilk' should write out fifty times 'I must not use words I do not understand'.

INFER

It is a common error to use *infer* for *imply*:

Great efforts were made to write down the story, and to infer that the support was normal. . . . I felt most bitter about this attitude . . . for . . . it inferred great ignorance and stupidity on the part of the enemy.

A writer or speaker *implies* what his reader or hearer *infers*. The difference is illustrated thus by Sir Alan Herbert:

If you see a man staggering along the road you may infer that he is drunk, without saying a word; but if you say 'Had one too many?' you do not infer but imply that he is drunk.

There is authority for *infer* in the sense of *imply*, as there is for *comprise* in the sense of *compose*. But here again the distinction is worth preserving in the interests of the language.

INTERVAL

One would not suspect this word of obscurity, but it is sometimes misused to denote merely a space or a period of time, rather than a space or a period between two things or events.

. . . the training period was still 3 years, an interval widely regarded in the industry as being unrealistically long.

This writer has more to answer for than the misuse of *interval*. He must tell us why he prefers *unrealistically* to *too*.

Some people object to the common phrase *at frequent intervals* on the ground that it is the frequency of the occurrences in question, not of the intervals between them, that matters. This is pedantry. But it is not pedantry to suggest that

It is expected that the Committee will meet at three or four monthly intervals, but more frequently if necessary

would have been better without the *intervals*. 'Every three or four months' or 'three or four times a year' is what is meant.

LEADING QUESTION

This does not mean, as is widely supposed, a question difficult to answer, or the most important of a series of questions, or a question designed to embarrass the person questioned. On the contrary, it means a question designed to help him by suggesting the answer – a type of question not permitted when a witness is being examined by the counsel who called him.

MITIGATE

Mitigate for *militate* is a curiously common malapropism. An example is:

I do not think that this ought to mitigate against my chances of promotion.

ORAL, VERBAL

Oral has to do with the mouth; *verbal* has to do with words. To use *verbal* where *oral* is meant is another surprisingly common mistake. It is not very helpful to describe a message or an agreement as *verbal*; most messages and agreements are in words rather than, say, figures or smoke-signals. But an *oral* message or agreement is one expressed by word of mouth, not in writing. A *verbal* misunderstanding or argument is one about words rather than substance, and the words may have been either written or spoken: an *oral* misunderstanding is due, as like as not, to a faulty telephone line.

One need not know Latin to remember which is which. No one chooses wrong in *oral contraceptive* or *verbal diarrhoea*.

PRACTICAL and PRACTICABLE

Practical, with its implied antithesis of *theoretical*, means useful in practice. *Practicable* means capable of being carried out in action.

That which is practicable is often not practical. Anything that is possible of accomplishment by available means may be called practicable. Only that which can be accomplished successfully or profitably under given circumstances may be called practical.

(WESEEN, *Words Confused and Misused*)

PRESCRIPTIVE RIGHT

This does not mean the same as indefeasible right. *Prescriptive right* is a technical term of the law. It means a right founded on 'prescription', that is to say on long and unchallenged custom. It has no greater sanctity than any other sort of right; on the contrary, it is likely to be more questionable than most.

PROTAGONIST

This word is not the opposite of *antagonist* (one who contends with another); the pair must not be used as synonyms of *supporter* and *opponent*, the *pros* and the *antis*. *Protagonist* has nothing to do with the Latin word *pro*: its first syllable is derived from a Greek word meaning *first*, and it means literally the principal actor in a play; hence it is used for the most prominent personage in any affair. It is not necessarily associated with the advocacy of anything, although it often happens to be so in fact. I have been given many examples of this blunder, which is common even in reputable quarters. It is briefly and comprehensively exemplified by this political comment in a high-class periodical:

> Inevitably, either protagonist or antagonist must fail.

Instead of misusing *protagonist*, try *advocate*, *champion* or *proposer* if *supporter* is not quite what you want.

REDUNDANT

This is an imposing word and, no doubt for that reason, is used in senses that it will not bear. The idea of *too much* is inseparable from it: 'superabundant, superfluous, excessive', is what the dictionary says. To treat it as meaning merely *inappropriate* is wrong. *Redundancy* now has a special meaning in relation to employment, when some of the present work-force becomes unnecessary either because the work is being reduced or because new methods or machinery enable it to be done by fewer people. But when a Trade Union official insists that there must be 'no redundancy' he does not necessarily mean that no steps must be taken which will make any of the work-force redundant: he means rather that no one must be dismissed as a result.

REFUTE

Refute should be confined to the sense of proving falsity or error, and not used loosely as a synonym for *deny* or *repudiate*, as in:

> The local authority refute the suggestion that their proposal is extravagant, but their arguments are wholly unconvincing.

RESOURCE

There is much pardonable confusion between *resource, recourse* and *resort*. The most common mistake is to write 'have resource to' instead of 'have recourse to' or 'have resort to'. The correct usage can be illustrated thus:

They had recourse (or had resort, or resorted) to their reserves; it was their last resource (or resort); they had no other resources.

Resources is at present a vogue word; more will be found about it on pp. 127–8.

TRANSPIRE

It is a common error to use *transpire* as if it meant *happen* or *occur*. It does not. It means *become known*. An example of its wrong use is:

Your letter arrived at my office while I was in Glasgow, attending what transpired to be a very successful series of meetings.

WASTAGE

There is a difference that ought to be preserved between *waste* and *wastage*; *wastage* should not be used as a more dignified alternative to *waste*. The ordinary meaning of *waste* is 'useless expenditure or consumption, squandering (of money, time, etc.)'. The ordinary meaning of *wastage* is 'loss by use, decay, evaporation, leakage, or the like'. You may, for instance, properly say that the daily wastage of a reservoir is so many gallons. But you must not say that a contributory factor is the wastage of water by householders if what you mean is that householders waste it.

Waste has recently come to be used as a verb, signifying 'convert into waste paper'. This is quite unnecessary (*destroy* or *throw away* will generally do) and may be misleading. One hopes, at least, that *waste* does not carry its normal meaning in the following official instructions.

Departments are asked to ensure that as many documents as possible are wasted at the earliest possible date.
On receipt of [this leaflet] previous prints are to be wasted.

5

THE CHOICE OF WORDS: INTRODUCTORY

> The craftsman is proud and careful of his tools: the surgeon
> does not operate with an old razor-blade; the sportsman fusses
> happily and long over the choice of rod, gun, club or racquet.
> But the man who is working in words, unless he is a profes-
> sional writer (and not always then), is singularly neglectful of
> his instruments.
>
> IVOR BROWN

> What appears to be a sloppy or meaningless use of words may
> well be a completely correct use of words to express sloppy or
> meaningless ideas.
>
> ANONYMOUS DIPLOMAT

HERE we come to the most important part of our subject.
Correctness is not enough. The words used may all be words
approved by the dictionary and used in their right senses; the
grammar may be faultless and the idiom above reproach. Yet
what is written may still fail to convey a ready and precise
meaning to the reader. That it does so fail is the charge brought
against much of what is written nowadays, including much of
what is written by officials. Matthew Arnold once said that the
secret of style was to have something to say and to say it as
clearly as you can. This is over-simple, but it will do well enough
as a first principle for the kind of writing in which emotional
appeal plays no part. The most prevalent disease in present-day
writing is a tendency to say what one has to say in as complicated a way as possible. Instead of being simple, terse and
direct, it is stilted, long-winded and circumlocutory; instead of
choosing the simple word it prefers the unusual; instead of the
plain phrase the cliché.

The forms most commonly taken by the disease will be examined in the following three chapters. In this one we are
concerned (if I may borrow a bit of jargon from the doctors)
with its aetiology and with prescribing some general regimen

for the writer that will help him to avoid catching it. It is largely a matter of acquiring good habits and eschewing bad ones; for very few people are incurably bad writers by nature, just as very few are congenitally diseased or deformed.

Why do so many writers prefer complexity to simplicity? Officials are far from being the only offenders. It seems to be a morbid condition contracted in early manhood. Children show no signs of it. Here, for example, is the response of a child of ten to an invitation to write an essay on a bird and a beast:

The bird that I am going to write about is the owl. The owl cannot see at all by day and at night is as blind as a bat.

I do not know much about the owl, so I will go on to the beast which I am going to choose. It is the cow. The cow is a mammal. It has six sides – right, left, an upper and below. At the back it has a tail on which hangs a brush. With this it sends the flies away so that they do not fall into the milk. The head is for the purpose of growing horns and so that the mouth can be somewhere. The horns are to butt with, and the mouth is to moo with. Under the cow hangs the milk. It is arranged for milking. When people milk, the milk comes and there is never an end to the supply. How the cow does it I have not yet realised, but it makes more and more. The cow has a fine sense of smell; one can smell it far away. This is the reason for the fresh air in the country.

The man cow is called an ox. It is not a mammal. The cow does not eat much, but what it eats it eats twice, so that it gets enough. When it is hungry it moos, and when it says nothing it is because its inside is all full up with grass.

The writer had something to say and said it as clearly as he could, and so has unconsciously achieved style. But why do we write, when we are ten, 'so that the mouth can be somewhere' and perhaps when we are thirty 'in order to ensure that the mouth may be appropriately positioned environmentally'? I will hazard a few possible reasons.

The first affects only the official. It is a temptation to cling too long to outworn words and phrases. The British Constitution, as everyone knows, has been shaped by retaining old forms and putting them to new uses. Among the old forms that we are reluctant to abandon are those that have long been traditional in State documents and the accepted language of administration, Parliamentary government and diplomacy. In their proper place these words and phrases do no harm because no one ever reads them attentively; they are no longer intended to convey thought from one brain to another. But the official, living in this atmosphere, properly proud of the ancient traditions of his service, sometimes allows his style of letter-writing to be affected by it – *adverting* and *acquainting* and *causing to be informed*. There may even be produced in his mind a feeling that all common words lack the dignity that he is bound to maintain. As suggested on pp. 266–7, the tendency to preserve governmental dignity is not to be wholly derided; but there is no doubt that it is too often overdone.

Another possible reason is that many people retain in maturity the adolescent's love of the long word. Most of us can remember how delighted we were at discovering the meaning of lovely long words like *irrelevant, disenchantment, confrontation, intractable, discriminatory, opportunistic* and so on, how proud we were of these additions to our schoolboy vocabulary, and how eagerly we sought opportunities of showing off our new toys. All young people of sensibility feel the lure of rippling and reverberating polysyllables. So it is perhaps because the writer has not quite grown up that he finds a satisfaction in 'transferred to an alternative location' which cannot be got from 'moved to another site'; that 'ablution facilities' strike a chord which does not vibrate to 'wash-basins'. Far-fetched words are by definition 'recherché' words, and are thought to give distinction; thus such words as *allergic, ambivalent, catalyst* and *viable* acquire their vogue. A newly-discovered metaphor shines like a jewel in a drab vocabulary; thus *blueprint, escalation, ceiling* and *target* are eagerly seized, and the dust settles on their discarded predecessors – *plan, growth, limit* and *objective*. But it will not do. Official writing is essentially of the sort of which Horace said: 'Ornatum res ipsa vetat, contenta doceri' – the very subject matter rules out ornament; it asks only to be put across.

There is another reason that affects mainly the official – he hears a call to the instinct of self-preservation. It is sometimes dangerous to be precise. 'Mistiness is the mother of safety', said Newman. 'Your safe man in the Church of England is he who steers his course between the Scylla of "Aye" and the Charybdis of "No" along the channel of "No meaning".' Ecclesiastics are not in this respect unique. Politicians have long known the dangers of precision of statement, especially at election time.

'And now for our cry,' said Mr Taper.

'It is not a Cabinet for a good cry', said Tadpole; 'but then, on the other hand, it is a Cabinet that will sow dissension in the opposite ranks, and prevent them having a good cry.'

'Ancient institutions and modern improvements, I suppose, Mr Tadpole.'

'Ameliorations is the better word; ameliorations. Nobody knows exactly what it means.'*

That was written well over a hundred years ago, but no student of modern politics will say that it is out of date. Policies of 'dynamic realism', 'imaginative pragmatism' or 'purposive abrasiveness' would have appealed to Mr Tadpole in exactly the same way.

When the official does not know his Minister's mind, or his Minister does not know his own mind, or the Minister thinks it wiser not to speak his mind, the official must sometimes cover his utterance with a mist of vagueness. Civil Service methods are often contrasted unfavourably with those of business. But to do this is to forget that no Board of Directors of a business concern have to meet a committee of their shareholders every afternoon, to submit themselves daily to an hour's questioning on their conduct of the business, to get the consent of that committee by a laborious process to every important step they take, or to conduct their affairs with the constant knowledge that there is a shadow board eager for the shareholders' authority to take their place. The systems are quite different and are bound to produce different methods. Ministers are under daily attack, and their reputations are largely in the hands of their staff. Only if he has full and explicit authority from his Minister

* Disraeli's *Coningsby*.

can a civil servant show in an important matter that promptness and boldness which are said to be the attributes of men of business.

The words which he writes will go on record, possibly for all time, certainly for a great many years. They may have to be published, and may have a wide circulation. They may even mean something in international relationships. So, even though mathematical accuracy may in the nature of things be unattainable, identifiable inaccuracy must at least be avoided. The hackneyed official phrase, the wide circumlocution, the vague promise, the implied qualification are comfortingly to hand. Only those who have been exposed to the temptation to use them know how hard it is to resist. But with all the sympathy that such understanding may mean, it is still possible to hold that something might be done to purge official style and caution, necessary and desirable in themselves, of their worst extravagances.

This is a quotation from a leading article in *The Times*. It arose out of a correspondent's ridicule of this extract from a letter written by a Government Department to its Advisory Council:

> In transmitting this matter to the Council the Minister feels that it may be of assistance to them to learn that, as at present advised, he is inclined to think that, in existing circumstances, there is, *prima facie*, a case for. . . .

It is as easy to slip into this sort of thing without noticing it as to see the absurdity of it when pointed out. One may surmise that the writer felt himself to be in a dilemma: he wanted the Advisory Council to advise the Minister in a certain way, but did not want them to think that the Minister had made up his mind before getting their advice. But he might have done this without piling qualification on qualification and reservation on reservation; all that he needed to say was that the Minister thought so-and-so but wanted to know what the Advisory Committee thought before taking a decision.

This quotation illustrates another trap into which official writing is led when it has to leave itself a bolt-hole, as it so often has. Cautionary clichés are used automatically without thought of what they mean. There are two of them here: *inclined to think* and *as at present advised*. Being *inclined to think,* in the sense of inclining to an opinion not yet crystallised, is a reasonable enough expression, just as one may say colloquially *my mind is moving that way*. But excessive use of the phrase may provoke the captious critic to say that if being inclined to think is really something different from thinking, then the less said about it the better until it has ripened into something that can be properly called thought. We can hardly suppose that the writer of the following sentence really needed time to ponder whether his opinion might not be mistaken:

> We are inclined to think that people are more irritated by noise that they feel to be unnecessary than by noise that they cause themselves.

As at present advised should be used only where an opinion has been formed on expert (e.g. legal) advice, never, as it is too often, as the equivalent of saying: 'This is what the Minister thinks in the present state of his mind but, as he is human, the state of his mind may change'. That may be taken for granted.

There is often a real need for caution, and it is a temptation to hedging and obscurity. But it is no excuse for them. A frank admission that an answer cannot be given is better than an answer that looks as if it meant something but really means nothing. Such a reply exasperates the reader and brings the Service into discredit.

Politeness plays its part too: what is vague is less likely to give offence. Politeness often shows itself in euphemism, a term defined by the dictionary as 'the substitution of a mild or vague expression for a harsh or blunt one'. It is prompted by the same impulse as led the Greeks to call the Black Sea the Euxine (the hospitable one) in the hope of averting its notorious inhospitableness, and the Furies the Eumenides (the good-humoured ladies) in the hope that they might be flattered into being less furious. For the Greeks it was the gods and the forces of nature that had to be propitiated; for those who govern us today it is the electorate. Hence the prevalence of what the grammarians call *meiosis* (understatement) and the use of qualifying adverbs such as *somewhat* and *rather* and the popularity of the *not un-* device. This last is useful in its place. There are occasions when a writer's meaning may be conveyed more exactly by (say) *not unkindly, not unnaturally* or *not unjustifiably* than by *kindly, naturally* or *justifiably*. But the 'not un-' habit is liable to take charge, with disastrous effects, making the victim forget all straightforward adjectives and adverbs. When an Inspector of Taxes writes 'This is a by no means uncomplicated case', we may be pretty sure that he is employing meiosis. And 'I think the officer's attitude was not unduly unreasonable' seems a chicken-hearted defence of a subordinate. George Orwell recommended that we should all inoculate ourselves against the disease by memorising this sentence: 'A not unblack dog was chasing a not unsmall rabbit across a not ungreen field'.

Similarly, 'less than truthful' is a euphemism for 'lying' and 'no little' a meiosis for 'great'. But the writer of the following pays so much more attention to avoiding the stark than to conveying his meaning that he ends by conveying exactly the opposite.

In communicating these data to your organisation after fullest consultation with all my colleagues also concerned, I would certainly be less than truthful if I were to say that this has occasioned the Ministry (and this Section in particular) no little difficulty but that the delay is nevertheless regretted.

He might more easily have said 'I am sorry we could not send you this information sooner, but we have found this a very difficult case': what he has succeeded in saying is that the case was easy and that he does not regret the delay.

Or a vague word may be preferred to a precise one because the vague is less alarming; or the natural word may be rejected because it has acquired unpleasant associations. The poor have become the lower income brackets, backward countries are developing countries, unsuccessful teachers (and others) are described as coming from the lower end of the achievement range. Even a prison is now sometimes a correctional facility. There are

no stupid, backward or troublesome children; they are intellec-
tually unendowed or maladjusted or disturbed – and as like as
not underprivileged and socially disadvantaged as well. There
are contexts in which we cannot use the word *race* because of its
overtones of racial discrimination or colour prejudice; we have
to use *ethnic origin* instead. Black is coloured, idiots are sub-
normal, war is armed conflict, a deficit is a borrowing requirement. This sort of substitution may be natural and sometimes
useful, but it has its limitations. If the unpleasantness, or the
supposed unpleasantness, attaches to the thing itself it will taint
the new name; in course of time yet another will have to be
found, and so *ad infinitum*. Homosexuals are working their way
through our vocabulary at an alarming rate: for some time now
we have been unable to describe our more eccentric friends as
queer, or our more lively ones as *gay*, without risk of misunderstanding, and we have more recently had to give up calling
our more nimble ones *light on their feet*. We do not seem to
have done ourselves much good when we assigned the blameless
but unsuitable word *lavatory* to a place where there is nowhere
to wash; we merely blunted the language; and now *toilet* and
powder-room are blunted in their turn.*

Another reason is the love of showing off. There are several
different manifestations of this, all of which are dealt with
more fully elsewhere in this book. The writer wants to parade
his knowledge of long or unfamiliar or foreign words; or he
wants to show that he is familiar with the latest fashion (that
he is, in the current phrase, 'with it'); or he wants to impress
by his use of language lest he should fail to do so by what he is
saying – in other words he is afraid of being damned as superficial or amateur. All these may combine to produce such flatu-
lent writing as appears in the examples below.

*For a neat commentary on the tendency to use language which is at
once polysyllabic, euphemistic and fashionable – three of the types mentioned in this chapter – I cannot improve on the drawing of a small girl
pointing to her young brother and shouting 'Mummy! Johnny's polluted
his environment again'. But in a few years this drawing may not even
raise a smile: the caption may be what everyone says in these circumstances.

There remains one more reason – laziness. As I observed in Chapter 1, clear thinking is hard work. A great many people go through life without doing it to any noticeable extent. And as George Orwell, from whom I then quoted, has pointed out, sloppy and ready-made phrases 'will construct your sentences for you and even think your thoughts for you to a certain extent'. It is as though the builder of a house did not take the trouble to select with care the materials that he thought most suitable for his purpose, but collected chunks of masonry from ruined houses built by others and stuck them together anyhow. That is not a promising way to produce anything significant in meaning, attractive in form, or of any practical use.

So much for what I have termed the 'aetiology' of the disease. Before turning to treatment it may be useful to illustrate the symptoms. To show that the British official is not the only (nor the worst) sufferer from the disease, I have gone for my examples to various sources, including writings by doctors and social workers, and drawing on the United States as well as our own country. I have added translations of the first four; the fifth seems to me to defy translation.

EXAMPLE	TRANSLATION
(Quoted by *The Economist*) 'NATO has expressed its fundamental change of policy as "evolving in place of the overriding medium-term defence hypothesis to which all economic planning was functionally subordinate, an antithesis of balancing *desiderata*, such as the politico-strategical necessity against the economico-social possibility and further these two components against the need for a maximum of flexibility" '.	'What this really means [says *The Economist*] is that, whereas a national defence programme has been taken hitherto as something imposed from above which could not be altered, now the military requirements of NATO will be made to match the economic achievements of the individual countries.'

EXAMPLE

TRANSLATION

The attitude of each, that he was not required to inform himself of, and his lack of interest in, the measures taken by the other to carry out the responsibility assigned to such other under the provision of plans then in effect, demonstrated on the part of each lack of appreciation of the responsibilities vested in them, and inherent in their positions.

Neither took any interest in the other's plans, or even found out what they were. This shows that they did not appreciate the responsibilities of their positions.

(Quoted in *The Lancet*, from which the translation also is taken.) Experiments are described which demonstrate that in normal individuals the lowest concentration in which sucrose can be detected by means of gustation differs from the lowest concentration in which sucrose (in the amount employed) has to be ingested in order to produce a demonstrable decrease in olfactory acuity and a noteworthy conversion of sensations interpreted as a desire for food into sensations interpreted as a satiety associated with ingestion of food.

Experiments are described which demonstrate that a normal person can taste sugar in water in quantities not strong enough to interfere with his sense of smell or take away his appetite.

It is suggested that although there is not necessarily any need for any form of welfare referral – that would depend on all the circumstances – officers can, through greater understanding of these universal phenomena, firstly behave more sensitively at

Although welfare help may not be wanted staff should, by a better understanding of human behaviour, be aware that the claimant is going through a particularly difficult time; they should avoid jumping to conclusions which might lead either

EXAMPLE

a time when the claimant is especially vulnerable and, secondly, avoid making precipitate judgments on the basis of temporary reactions – judgments which could lead to inappropriate referral on the one hand, or irritated reactions to uncooperative behaviour on the other.*

To reduce the risk of war and establish conditions of lasting peace requires the closer co-ordination in the employment of their joint resources to underpin these countries' economies in such a manner as to permit the full maintenance of their social and material standards as well as to adequate development of the necessary measures.

TRANSLATION

to an unwanted referral or to a charge of un-cooperative behaviour.

We can now turn to the question whether some general advice can be given to fortify the writer against infection. Several distinguished men have tried their hands at this. This is what Fowler said:

Anyone who wishes to become a good writer should endeavour, before he allows himself to be tempted by more showy qualities, to be direct, simple, brief, vigorous and lucid.

This general principle may be translated into general rules in the domain of vocabulary as follows:

Prefer the familiar word to the far-fetched.
Prefer the concrete word to the abstract.
Prefer the single word to the circumlocution.

*Unlike the other examples, this one never saw the light of day. It is taken from the first draft of a training instruction in a Government Department; the translation shows how it was redrafted before being issued. The ugly word *referral*, which appears in both versions, is in this context legitimate 'departmental shorthand' (see pp. 24–6).

The Choice of Words: Introductory

Prefer the short word to the long.
Prefer the Saxon word to the Romance.

'These rules', he added, 'are given in order of merit; the last is also the least.'

He also pointed out that

all five rules will often be found to give the same answer about the same word or set of words. Scores of illustrations might be produced; let one suffice: *In the contemplated eventuality* (a phrase no worse than anyone can pick for himself out of his paper's leading article for the day) is at once the far-fetched, the abstract, the periphrastic, the long and the Romance, for *if so*. It does not very greatly matter by which of the five roads the natural is reached instead of the monstrosity, so long as it *is* reached. The five are indicated because (1) they differ in directness, and (2) in any given case only one of them may be possible.

Later authorities have not allowed Fowler to have the last word; and indeed his rules would have absurd results if applied too rigidly. The best that could be said for prose containing nothing but familiar, concrete, single, short, Saxon words is that it would be less intolerable than prose which always opted the other way. His fourth and fifth rules have attracted most disagreement, and rightly so; for we cannot fully exploit the richness of the English language if we are frightened of all words that are Latin in origin or more than two or three syllables in length. The advice to prefer the Saxon word to the Romance also raises the practical difficulty that it is not given to many of us always to be sure which is which. Any virtue there may be in these two rules is really already implicit in the rule to prefer the familiar word to the far-fetched; and most people are likely to think that what Bradley had written, before Fowler formulated his rules, is all that need be said on the subject:

The cry for 'Saxon English' sometimes means nothing more than a demand for plain and unaffected diction, and a condemnation of the idle taste for 'words of learned length and thundering sound' which has prevailed at some periods of our literature. So far it is worthy of all respect; but the pedantry that would bid us reject the word

79

fittest for our purpose because it is not of native origin ought to be strenuously resisted.

What we are concerned with is not a quest for a literary style as an end in itself, but to study how best to convey our meaning without ambiguity and without giving unnecessary trouble to our readers. This being our aim, the essence of the matter may be expressed in the following three rules, and the rest of what I have to say in the domain of vocabulary will be little more than an elaboration of them.

> Use no more words than are necessary to express your meaning, for if you use more you are likely to obscure it and to tire your reader. In particular do not use superfluous adjectives and adverbs and do not use roundabout phrases where single words would serve.
> Use familiar words rather than the far-fetched, if they express your meaning equally well; for the familiar are more likely to be readily understood.
> Use words with a precise meaning rather than those that are vague, for they will obviously serve better to make your meaning clear; and in particular prefer concrete words to abstract, for they are more likely to have a precise meaning.

As Fowler pointed out, rules like these cannot be kept in separate compartments; they overlap. But in the next three chapters we will follow roughly the order in which the rules are set out and examine them under the headings 'Avoiding the superfluous word', 'Choosing the familiar word' and 'Choosing the precise word'.

6

THE CHOICE OF WORDS: AVOIDING THE SUPERFLUOUS WORD

> A reader of Milton must be always upon duty; he is surrounded with sense, it arises in every line, every word is to the purpose; there are no lazy intervals, all has been considered, and demands and merits observation. Even in the best writers you sometimes find words and sentences which hang on so loosely you may blow 'em off; Milton's are all substance and weight; fewer would not have serv'd the turn, and more would have been superfluous.
>
> JONATHAN RICHARDSON, quoted by F. E. HUTCHINSON
> in *Milton and the English Mind*, p. 137

THE fault of verbiage (which the *OED* defines as 'abundance of words without necessity or without much meaning') is too multiform for analysis. But certain classifiable forms of it are specially common, and in this chapter we will examine some of these, ending with an indeterminate class which we will call 'padding', to pick up what has been left outside the others.

VERBOSITY IN ADJECTIVES AND ADVERBS

Palmerston* wrote of one of Her Majesty's Ministers abroad who had neglected an admonition to go through all his despatches and strike out all words not necessary for fully conveying his meaning: 'If Mr Hamilton would let his substantives and adjectives go single instead of always sending them forth by twos and threes, his despatches would be clearer and easier to read'.

It has been wisely said that the adjective is the enemy of the noun. If we make a habit of saying 'The true facts are these', we shall come under suspicion when we profess to tell merely 'the facts'. If a *crisis* is always *acute* and an *emergency* always *grave*, what is left for those words to do by themselves? If *active*

*Quoted by Sir C. K. Webster in *Politica*, August 1934.

constantly accompanies *consideration*, we shall think we are being fobbed off when we are promised bare consideration. If a decision is always qualified by *definite*, a decision by itself becomes a poor filleted thing. If conditions are customarily described as *prerequisite* or *essential*, we shall doubt whether a *condition* without an adjective is really a condition at all. An *unfilled vacancy* may leave us wondering whether a mere vacancy is really vacant. If a part is always an *integral part* or a *component part* there is nothing left for a mere part except to be a spare part.

Cultivate the habit of reserving adjectives and adverbs to make your meaning more precise, and suspect those that you find yourself using to make it more emphatic. Use adjectives to denote kind rather than degree. By all means say an *economic crisis* or a *military disaster*, but think well before saying an *acute crisis* or a *terrible disaster*. Say if you like 'The proposal met with noisy opposition and is in obvious danger of defeat'. But do not say 'The proposal met with considerable opposition and is in real danger of defeat'. If that is all you want to say it is better to leave out the adjectives and say 'The proposal met with opposition and is in danger of defeat'.

Official writers seem to have a curious shrinking from certain adjectives unless they are adorned by adverbs. It is as though they were naked and must hastily have an adverbial dressing-gown thrown around them. The most indecent adjectives are, it seems, those of quantity or measure such as *short* and *long*, *many* and *few*, *heavy* and *light*. The adverbial dressing-gowns most favoured are *unduly*, *relatively* and *comparatively*. These adverbs can only properly be used when something has been mentioned or implied which gives a standard of comparison. But we have all seen them used on innumerable occasions when there is no standard of comparison. They are then meaningless. Their use is merely a shrinking from the nakedness of an unqualified statement. If the report of an accident says that about a hundred people were taken to hospital but comparatively few were detained, that is a proper use of the adverb. But when a circular says that 'our diminishing stocks will be expended in a relatively short period', without mentioning any other period with which to compare it, the word signifies nothing.

Sometimes the use of a dressing-gown adverb actually makes the writer say the opposite of what he intended. The writer of the circular which said, 'It is not necessary to be unduly meticulous in . . .' meant to say 'you need not be meticulous', but what he actually said was 'you may be meticulous but need not be unduly so', leaving the reader to guess when the limit of dueness in meticulousness has been reached.

Undue and *unduly* seem to be words that have the property of taking the reason prisoner. 'There is no cause for undue alarm' is a phrase I have seen used in all sorts of circumstances by all sorts of people, from a Government spokesman about the plans of the enemy to a headmistress on the occurrence of a case of poliomyelitis. It is, I suppose, legitimate to say 'Don't be unduly alarmed', though I should not myself find much reassurance in it. But 'there is no cause for undue alarm' differs little, if at all, from 'there is no cause for alarm for which there is no cause', and that hardly seems worth saying. *Undue hardship* is another phrase which makes its appearance far more often than it makes sense.

The following is an example, not of *undue* superfluous, but of *undue* nonsensical:

It does not require undue prescience to anticipate that the enlarged EEC will soon be an effective member of the 'big league'.

Nothing that is undue can ever be required. Reason demands some such word as *unusual*. (See also pp. 118–19 for this use of *anticipate*.)

Undue and *unduly* have of course their own proper job to do, as in 'The speech was not unduly long for so important an occasion'.

As some adjectives seem to attract unnecessary adverbs, so do some nouns unnecessary adjectives. I have mentioned *consideration*'s fondness for the company of *active*, but it often walks out with other charmers too, such as *careful, sympathetic* and *thorough*, whose tendency to cling does it little good; it has recently become dissatisfied with *careful* and taken up with *in depth* instead. *In depth* is also in great demand as a companion for *study*, *review*, *research* and others, and seems quite capable of ruining all of them. *Danger* is another word that is often given support it does not need, generally *real* or *serious*.

The special needs of children under 5 require as much considera-tion as those of children aged 5–7, and there is a serious danger that they will be overlooked in these large schools. . . . There is a real danger . . . that the development of the children would be un-duly forced. . . .

Here we have *serious, real* and *unduly* all used superfluously. *Serious* is prompted by a feeling that *danger* always needs adjec-tival support, and *real* is presumably what grammarians call 'elegant variation' * to avoid repeating the same word. *Unduly* is superfluous because the word *forced* itself contains the idea of undue. *Real* danger should be reserved for contrast with imaginary danger, as, for instance, 'Some people fear so-and-so but the real danger is so-and-so'. These things may seem trivial, but nothing is negligible that is a symptom of loose thinking.

Vague adjectives of intensification like *considerable, appreci-able* and *substantial* are too popular. None of these three should be used without three questions being asked. Do I need an adjective at all? If so, would not a more specific adjective suit better? Or, failing that, which of these three (with their different shades of meaning) is most apt? If those who write 'This is a matter of considerable urgency' were to ask themselves these questions, they would realise that 'This is urgent' serves them better; and those who write 'A programme of this magnitude will necessarily take a considerable period' will find it more effective to say 'a long time'. Strong words like *urgent, danger, crisis, disaster, fatal, grave, overriding, prime, paramount* and *essential* lose their force if used too often. Reserve them for strong occasions, and then let them stand on their own legs, without adjectival or adverbial support. Otherwise you may find yourself writing like this extract from a ministerial speech:

*See p. 192.

Although it is overriding obviously that the prime responsibility of the ballistic missile early warning system must remain paramount at all times ...

It would be a fairly safe bet that *respective* (or *respectively*) is used unnecessarily or wrongly in legal and official writings more often than any other word in the language. It has one simple straightforward use, and that is to link up subjects and objects where more than one is used with a single verb. Thus, if I say 'Men and women wear trousers and skirts' you are left in doubt which wears which – which indeed is no more than the truth nowadays. But if I add the word *respectively* I allot the trousers to the men and the skirts to the women. It can also be used harmlessly in a distributive sense, as in the sentence 'Local Authorities should survey the needs of their respective areas'. But it contributes nothing to the sense; there is no risk of Local Authorities thinking that they are being told to survey one another's areas. Anyway it is neater to write 'Each Local Authority should survey the needs of its area'. *Respective* and *respectively* are used wrongly or unnecessarily far more often than they are used rightly, and I advise you to leave them alone. You can nearly always get on without them. Even in the example I gave you just now you can say 'Men wear trousers and women skirts', which has the advantage of being crisper and therefore better English. Here is a sentence in which the writer has fallen into one of the many traps set by this capricious word. He has tried to make it distribute two things among three, and so left the reader guessing.

The Chief Billeting Officer of the Local Authority, the Regional Welfare Officer of the Ministry of Health, and the Local Officer of the Ministry of Labour and National Service will be able to supplement the knowledge of the Authority on the needs arising out of evacuation and the employment of women respectively.

It is as though one were to say 'Men and women wear trousers and skirts and knickers respectively'. Who has the knickers?

Here is an example, taken from a departmental circular, of the magnetism of this word:

Owing to the special difficulty of an apportionment of expenditure between (1) dinners and (2) other meals and refreshments respectively . . .

Having taken elaborate care so to arrange the sentence as to make *respectively* unnecessary, the writer found the lure of it irresistible after all.

Definite and *definitely* must be a good second to *respective* and *respectively* in any competition for the lead in adjectives and adverbs used unnecessarily. It can hardly be supposed that the adverb in the injunction – 'Local Authorities should be definitely discouraged from committing themselves' – would make any difference to the official who has to carry it out; the distinction between discouraging a Local Authority definitely and merely discouraging it is too fine for most of us. Other examples are:

This is definitely harmful to the workers' health.

The recent action of the committee in approving the definite appointment of four home visitors.

This has caused two definite spring breakages to loaded vehicles.

It is wise to be sparing of *very*. If it is used too freely it ceases to have any meaning; it must be used with discrimination to be effective. Other adverbs of intensification, like *necessarily* and *inevitably*, are also apt to do more harm than good unless you want to lay stress on the element of necessity or inevitability. An automatic *inevitably*, contributing nothing to the sense, is common:

The Committees will inevitably have a part to play in the development of the service.

The ultimate power of control which flows inevitably from the agency relationship.

And there can never be any excuse for *must inevitably* or *must necessarily*. The adverbs throw an unwarrantable aspersion on *must*'s ability to do its job.

Other intrusive words are *incidentally*, *specific* and *particular*. In conversation, *incidentally* (like *actually* and *definitely*) is often a noise without meaning; in writing it is an apology for irrelevance, sometimes expedient but often unnecessary or even ambiguous:

The Concert will include horn concertos by Haydn and Mozart, both incidentally written to order.

Incidentally to the announcer's announcement or to the composer's career?

Particular intrudes (though perhaps more in a certain type of oratory than in writing) as an unnecessary reinforcement of a demonstrative pronoun:

No arrangements have yet been made regarding moneys due to this particular country.

We would point out that availabilities of this particular material are extremely limited.

On the same day on which you advised the Custodian of the existence of this particular debt.

VERBOSITY IN PREPOSITIONS

In all utility writing today, official and commercial, the simple prepositions we have in such abundance tend to be forgotten and replaced by groups of words more imposing perhaps, but less precise. The commonest of these groups are:

> As regards
> As to
> In connexion with
> In regard to
> In relation to
> In respect of
> In terms of
> In the case of
> In the context of
> Relative to
> With reference to
> With regard to

They are useful in their proper places, but they are generally made to serve merely as clumsy devices to save a writer the labour of selecting the right preposition. In the collection that follows the right preposition is added in brackets:

A firm timetable *in relation to* the works to be undertaken should be drawn up (for).

It has been necessary to cause many dwellings to be disinfested of vermin, particularly *in respect* of the common bed-bug (of).

The Authority are fully conscious of their responsibilities *in regard to* the preservation of amenities (for).

It will be necessary to decide the priority which should be given to nursery provision *in relation to* other forms of education provision (over).

The rates vary *in relation to* the age of the child (with).

The Concorde is not needed *in the context of* the ordinary man's holidaymaking (for).

We must be realistic *in terms of* recruitment possibilities in determining the overall manpower figure for the civil service (about). (But see also p. 157 for *realistic* and pp. 152–5 for *overall*.)

Denuclearisation *in respect of* war-like purposes (of?).

This may impose severe restrictions *as to* Britain's food imports from the old Commonwealth (on).

The extra expenditure made little difference *in terms of* the extra employment created (to).

There may be difficulties *with regard to* the provision of suitable staff (in).

Similar considerations apply *with regard to* application for a certificate (to).

The best possible estimate will be made at the conference *as to* the total number of houses which can be completed in each district during the year (of).

The Lord Chancellor should give a clear indication *as to* his intentions (of).

Sometimes more drastic treatment is needed than the substitution of a single preposition:

A series of changes in the structure of inclusive tour control prices, which have already borne fruit *in terms of* increased traffic (have already produced more traffic).

As to deserves special mention because it leads writers astray in other ways besides making them forget the right preposition. It may tempt them into a more elaborate circumlocution:

> The operation is a severe one as to the after-effects. (The after-effects of the operation are severe.)
> It is no concern of the Ministry as to the source of the information. (The source of the information is no concern of the Ministry.)

As to also has a way of intruding itself where it is not wanted, especially before such words as *whether*, *who*, *what*, *how*. All the following examples are better without *as to*:

> Doubt has been expressed as to whether these rewards are sufficient.
> I have just received an enquiry as to whether you have applied for a supplement to your pension.
> I am to ask for some explanation as to why so small a sum was realised on sale.
> I will look into the question as to whether you are liable.

As to serves a useful purpose at the beginning of a sentence by way of introducing a fresh subject:

> As to your liability for previous years, I will go into this and write further to you.

VERBOSITY IN ADVERBIAL AND OTHER PHRASES

Certain words beget verbosity. Among them are the following.

Case and *instance*. The sins of *case* are well known; it has been said that there is perhaps no single word so freely resorted to as a trouble-saver and consequently responsible for so much flabby writing.

Here are some examples to show how what might be a simple and straightforward statement becomes enmeshed in the coils of phrases formed with *case*:

> The cost of maintenance of the building would be higher than was the case with a building of traditional construction. (The building would be more expensive to maintain than a building of traditional construction.)

That country is not now so short of sterling as was formerly the case. (. . . as it used to be.)

Since the officiating president in the case of each major institute takes up his office on widely differing dates. (Since the officiating presidents of the major institutes take up office on widely differing dates.)

The National Coal Board is an unwieldy organisation, in many cases quite out of touch with the coalfields. (Often)

This trick use of *case* is even worse when the reader might be misled, if only momentarily, into thinking that a material case was meant:

Cases have thus arisen in which goods have been exported without the knowledge of this Commission.

Water for domestic use is carried by hand in many cases from road standpipes.

There are, of course, many legitimate uses of the word, and writers should not be frightened away from it altogether by Quiller-Couch's much-quoted and rather overdone onslaught. There are, for instance (to borrow from Fowler):

> A case of measles.
> You have no case.
> In case of need, or fire, or other emergency.
> A case of burglary or other crime.
> A law case of any sort.
> Circumstances alter cases.

But do not say 'That is not the case' when you mean 'That is not so', or 'It is not the case that I wrote that letter', when you mean 'It is not true that I wrote that letter', or merely 'I did not write that letter'.

Instance beguiles writers in the same way as *case* into round-about ways of saying simple things:

In the majority of instances the houses are three-bedroom. (Most of the houses are three-bedroom.)

Most of the factories are modern, but in a few instances the plant is obsolete. (In a few of them)

In the first instance can generally be replaced by *first*,

Another such word is *concerned* in the phrase *as* (or *so*) *far as . . . is concerned*. It is perhaps putting the case too high to say that this phrase could always be replaced by a single preposition. I do not think that the phrase can be dispensed with by those who wish to emphasise that they have blinkers on, and are concerned only with one aspect of a question. 'So far as I am concerned you may go home' implies that someone else has a say too. Or again:

So far as the provisions of the Act are concerned, the sum so released may . . . be utilised to reimburse you for expenses . . .

There is no other equally convenient way of making clear that the writer is removing only the impediment created by the Act and is not concerned with any other impediment there may be. (But this does not excuse him for writing *utilised* instead of *used*. See p. 129.)

Possibly, though less certainly, this sentence might claim the same indulgence:

The effect of the suggested system, so far as the pharmaceutical industry is concerned, would be to ensure rewards for research and development work until the new preparations were absorbed into the B.P.

It might be argued that we should not get quite the same meaning from 'on the pharmaceutical industry'; this destroys the suggestion that there may be other effects, but the writer is not concerning himself with them.

But these are exceptions. There is no doubt that the phrase is generally a symptom of muddled thinking:

Some were opposed to hanging as a means of execution where women were concerned. (. . . as a means of executing women.)

The administration of the improvement grant scheme as far as works to privately owned dwellings are concerned. (The administration of improvement grants to private dwellings.)

Wood pulp manufacture on a commercial scale is a very recent development so far as time is concerned. (Omit the last six words.)

The punishments at their disposal may not be of very serious effect so far as the persons punished are concerned. (. . . on the persons punished.)

That is a matter which should be borne in mind because it does rule out a certain amount of consideration so far as the future is concerned.

I cannot translate this with any confidence. Perhaps it means 'That is a matter which should be borne in mind because it circumscribes our recommendations for the future'.

The fact that is an expression sometimes necessary and proper, but sometimes a clumsy way of saying what might be said more simply. When it is preceded by *in view of* or *owing to* or *in spite of* it may be merely an intricate way of saying *because* or *although*.

Owing to the fact that the exchange is working to full capacity. (Because the exchange . . .)
The delay in replying has been due to the fact that it was hoped to arrange for a representative to call upon you. (I delayed replying because I hoped to arrange for a representative to call on you.)

So too *until such time as* is usually merely a verbose way of saying *until*. It may be useful to convey a suggestion that the event contemplated is improbable or remote or has no direct connexion with what is to last until it occurs. But it cannot do so in

You will be able to enjoy these facilities until such time that he terminates his agreement.

If the phrase is used, it should be *such time as*, not, as here, *such time that*.

There cannot, I think, ever be any justification for preferring the similar phrase *during such time as* to *while* or *so long as*.

As has other sins of superfluity imputed to it, besides the help it gives in building up verbose prepositions and conjunctions. (See pp. 87–9.)

There is reason in saying, of a past date, 'these allowances will be payable as from the 1st January last', but there is none in saying, of a future date, 'these allowances will cease to be payable as from the 1st July next'. 'On the 1st July' is all that is needed. The phrase 'as and from', not unknown, is gibberish.

As such is sometimes used in a way that seems to have no meaning:

> The statistics, as such, add little to our information.

If they do not do so as statistics, in what capacity do they? The writer probably meant 'by themselves'.

> There is no objection to the sale of houses as such.

Here the context shows the writer to have meant that there was no objection of principle to the sale of houses.

Certain pairs of words have a way of keeping company without being able to do any more together than either could have done separately. *Save and except* seems to have had its day, but we still have with us *as and when*, *if and when* and *unless and until*. *As and when* can perhaps be defended when used of something that will happen piecemeal ('Interim reports will be published as and when they are received'). Nothing can be said for the use of the pair in such a sentence as:

> As and when the Bill becomes an Act guidance will be given on the financial provisions of it as they affect hospital maintenance.

Bills cannot become Acts piecemeal.

If and when might plead that both are needed in such a sentence as 'Further cases will be studied if and when the material is available', arguing that *if* alone will not do because the writer wants to emphasise that material becoming available will be studied immediately, and *when* alone will not do because it is uncertain whether the material ever will be available. But this is all rather subtle, and the wise course will almost always be to decide which conjunction suits you better, and to use it alone. I have not been able to find (or to imagine) the use of *unless and until* in any context in which one of the two would not have sufficed alone.

Point of view, *viewpoint*, *standpoint* and *angle*, useful and legitimate in their proper places, are sometimes no more than a refuge from the trouble of precise thought, and provide clumsy ways of saying something that could be said more simply and effectively. They are used, for instance, as a circumlocution for a simple adverb, such as 'from a temporary point of view' for 'temporarily'. Here are a few examples:

He may lack the most essential qualities from the viewpoint of the Teaching Hospitals. (He may lack the most essential qualities for work in a Teaching Hospital.)

I can therefore see no reason why we need to see these applications, apart from an information point of view. (. . . except for information.)

This may be a source of embarrassment to the Regional Board from the viewpoint of overall planning and administration. (This is a particularly bad one. The plain way of putting it is: 'This may embarrass the Regional Board in planning and administration'.)

Bare boards are unsatisfactory from every angle. (. . . in every respect.)

From a cleaning point of view there are advantages in tables being of a uniform height. (For cleaning . . .)

Each of these issues is examined from the standpoint of its background. (Perhaps this means 'with its history in mind': or perhaps not.)

This development is attractive from the point of view of the public convenience. (This, I am told, provoked a marginal comment: 'What is it like looking in the opposite direction?')

Aspect is the complement of *point of view*. As one changes one's point of view one sees a different aspect of what one is looking at. It is therefore natural that *aspect* should lead writers into the same traps as do *point of view, viewpoint* and *standpoint*. It induces writers, through its vagueness, to prefer it to more precise words, and it lends itself to woolly circumlocution. I cannot believe that there was any clear conception in the head of the official who wrote 'They must accept responsibility for the more fundamental aspects of the case'. *Aspect* is one of the words that should not be used without deliberation, and it should be rejected if its only function is to make a clumsy paraphrase of an adverb.

VERBOSITY IN AUXILIARY VERBS

Various methods are in vogue for softening the curtness of *will not* or *cannot*. The commonest are *is not prepared to, is not in a position to, does not see his way to* and *cannot consider*. Such phrases as these are no doubt dictated by politeness, and therefore deserve respect. But they must be used with discretion. The recipient of a letter may feel better – though I doubt it – if he is told that the Minister 'is not prepared to approve' than he would have done if the letter had said 'the Minister does not approve'. But there is not even this slender justification for the phrase if what he is told is that the Minister *is* prepared to approve.

> In view of this further information the Board are prepared to admit your claim in respect of . . . A payable order for £535 is enclosed accordingly.

Are prepared to admit should be *have admitted*. Since the money is enclosed the preparatory stage is clearly over.

But there is a legitimate use of *prepared to*, as in the following:

> In order to meet the present need, the Secretary of State is prepared to approve the temporary appointment of persons without formal qualifications.

Here the Secretary of State is awaiting candidates, prepared to approve them if they turn out all right. But the phrase should never be used in actually giving approval; it is silly, and if the habit takes hold it will lead to such absurdities as:

> I have to acknowledge your letter of the 16th June and in reply I am prepared to inform you that I am in communication with the solicitors concerned in this matter.

There are other dangers in these phrases. They may breed by analogy verbiage that is mere verbiage and cannot call on politeness to justify its existence. You may find yourself writing that the Minister *will take steps to* when all you mean is he *will*, or that he will *cause investigation to be made with a view to ascertaining*, when what you mean is that he will *find out. Take steps to* is not always to be condemned. It is a reasonable way of expressing the beginning of a gradual process, as in:

Steps are now being taken to acquire this land.

But it is inapposite, because of its literal incongruity, in such a sentence as:

All necessary steps should be taken to maintain the present position.

There is a danger that some of these phrases may suggest undesirable ideas to the flippant. To be told that the Minister is 'not in a position to approve' may excite a desire to retort that he might try putting his feet on the mantelpiece and see if that does any good. The retort will not, of course, be made, but you should not put ideas of that sort about your Minister into people's heads. Pompous old phrases must be allowed to die if they collapse under the prick of ridicule. Traditional expressions such as 'I am to request you to move your Minister to do so-and-so' and 'The Minister cannot conceal from himself' owed their death partly to the risible pictures they conjured up – the one of physical pressure applied to a bulky and inert object and the other of an honest man's prolonged and painful struggle in unsuccessful self-deception.

VERBOSITY IN PHRASAL VERBS

The English language likes to tack an adverbial particle to a simple verb and so to create a verb with a different meaning. Verbs thus formed have been called by Logan Pearsall Smith, following Bradley, 'phrasal verbs'. This habit of inventing phrasal verbs has been the source of great enrichment of the language. Pearsall Smith says:

From them we derive thousands of vivid colloquialisms and idiomatic phrases by means of which we describe the greatest variety of human actions and relations. We can take *to* people, take them *up*, take them *down*, take them *off* or take them *in*; keep *in* with them, keep them *down* or *off* or *on* or *under*; get *at* them or *round* them or *on with* them; do *for* them, do *with* them or *without* them, and do them *in*; make *up to* them; set them *up* or *down* or hit them *off* – indeed there is hardly any action or attitude of one human being to another which cannot be expressed by means of these phrasal verbs.

But there is today a tendency to form phrasal verbs to express a meaning no different from that of the verb without the parti-cle. To do this is to debase the language, not to enrich it. *Drown out, sound out, lose out, rest up, miss out on*, are examples of phrasal verbs used in America in senses no different from that of the unadorned verb. We have rightly welcomed the newcomer *measure up to* in the sense of to be adequate to an occasion: it conforms to our own practice of adding particles to give a verb a different meaning. But *pay off*, *try out* and *start up* are often used in contexts where the particles do not seem to contribute anything to the sense. See also pp. 185, 269.

POMPO-VERBOSITY

A very common cause of verbosity is the desire to be grand. The dividing line between dignity and pomposity is not always well marked. Something depends on the subject matter, for language that is aptly used to describe affairs of grave national concern will be merely pompous if applied to the trivial or the hum-drum. But there is no doubt that pompo-verbosity is a persistent and insidious danger, both to official writers and to others. I have already (p. 78) quoted the phrase *making precipitate judg-ments on the basis of temporary reactions*, which is pompo-verbosity for *jumping to conclusions*. Here are a few more examples:

They will have to work with unusually distant time-horizons. (They will have to look unusually far ahead.)
This would make a major contribution to increased efficiency in its own right. (This would in itself do much to increase efficiency.)
The decorating as well as the making processes [in the pottery

industry] have been subjected to intensive simplification. (Have been greatly simplified.)

To the extent that [this] is held not to be practicable an obstacle is of course created in the path of successful completion of [the] scheme. (If this is not practicable it will be difficult to complete the scheme.)

The existing Immigration Regulations occasionally – only a very limited number of cases have come to my attention – produce undue hardship as a result of the very strict interpretation. (The strict interpretation of the existing Immigration Regulations occasionally causes hardship, though I know of only very few cases.)

Long passages have visual unattractiveness. (Long passages look ugly *or* are not beautiful.)

The Council has decided to inform your Department that no adverse observations are offered on planning grounds to the proposed redevelopment. (The Council sees no objection on planning grounds to the proposed redevelopment.)

PADDING

All forms of verbosity might be described as padding, and the topic overlaps others we shall come to in the chapters on choosing the familiar word and choosing the precise word. I use *padding* here as a label for the type of verbosity Sir Winston Churchill referred to in a memorandum entitled 'Brevity' that he issued as Prime Minister on the 9th August 1940. He wrote:

Let us have an end of such phrases as these:

'It is also of importance to bear in mind the following considerations . . .' or 'consideration should be given to the possibility of carrying into effect. . . .' Most of these woolly phrases are mere padding, which can be left out altogether, or replaced by a single word. Let us not shrink from using the short expressive phrase even if it is conversational.

'Padding' then, in the sense in which Sir Winston used the word, consists of clumsy and unobtrusive stitches on what ought to be a smooth fabric of consecutive thought. No doubt it comes partly from a feeling that wordiness is an ingredient of politeness, and blunt statement is crude, if not rude. There is an

element of truth in this : an over-staccato style is as irritating as
an over-sostenuto one. But it is a matter of degree; and official
prose is of the sort that calls for plainness rather than elegance.
Moreover the habit of 'padding' springs partly from less meri-
torious notions – that the dignity of an official's calling demands
a certain verbosity, and that naked truth is indecent and should
be clothed in wrappings of woolly words.

Padding can easily creep into official letters if each paragraph
is thought to need introductory words – 'I am to add'; 'I am further to observe'; 'I am moreover to remark'; 'Finally I am to
point out'; and so forth. This form of padding is not as prevalent in official letters as it used to be, but is quite common
elsewhere.

In addition it is perhaps relevant to mention that . . .

is not, as you might think, from a civil servant's letter in the
1940s. It comes from a formal memorandum submitted by a
local authority to a House of Commons Select Committee in
1970.

Here is the same phenomenon in a circular sending a form for
a statistical return :

  (i) *It should be noted that* the particulars of expenditure . . .
    relate to gross costs.
  (ii) *It is appreciated that* owing to staffing difficulties Local Auth-
    orities may not find it possible on this occasion to complete
    Tables. . . .
  (iii) *It will be noted that* in Tables . . . the only overhead ex-
    penditure . . . which the Authorities are asked to isolate is. . . .
  (iv) Table 4 . . . is intended to provide a broad picture.

The words italicised in the first three paragraphs are padding.
They are no more needed there than in paragraph (iv), where
the writer has wisely done without them. Perhaps he felt that he
had run out of stock.

Other examples :

I am prepared to accept the discharge of this account by payment
in instalments, but *it should be pointed out that* no further service
can be allowed until the account is again in credit.

The opportunity is taken to mention that it is understood . . .

I regret that the wrong form was forwarded. *In the circumstances* I am forwarding a superseding one.

It should be noted that there is a possibility of a further sale.

This form of padding deserves special mention both because the temptation affects officials more than most people and because it is comparatively easy to resist. It shows itself more plainly than other more subtle temptations to pad. For the rest, padding can be defined as the use of words, phrases and even sentences that contribute nothing to the reader's perception of the writer's meaning. Among those that seem to be specially tempting are *in this connexion* and *for your information*. These have their proper uses, but are more often found as padding clichés. In none of the following examples do they serve any other purpose.

I am directed to refer to the travelling and subsistence allowances applicable to your Department, and in this connexion I am to say . . .

Mr X is an applicant for appointment as a clerk in this Department and in this connexion I shall be glad if you will complete the attached form.

The Minister's views in general in this connexion and the nature and scope of the information which he felt would assist him in this connexion was indicated at a meeting. . . .

For your information this machine is required for the abovementioned power station.

For your information I should perhaps explain that there is still a shortage of materials.

For your information I would inform you that it will be necessary for you to approach the local Agricultural Executive Committee.

Of course is another adverbial phrase that needs watching lest it should creep in as padding. In journalism, especially of the gossip kind, *of course* is used to impress readers by showing the writer's familiarity with an out-of-the-way piece of information or with the families of great personages. The official, if he overworks the phrase, is more likely to do so from genuine humility. He puts it in so as not to seem didactic: 'Don't think that I suppose you to be so stupid that you don't already know or infer what I am telling you, but I think I ought to mention it'. Sometimes *of course* is wisely used for this purpose – if, for instance, the writer has good reason to say something so obvious as to make a touchy reader feel that he is being treated like a fool. It is better in such circumstances to say 'of course' than its pompous variant 'as you are doubtless aware'. *Of course* might with advantage have been used in:

It may be stated with some confidence that though it is possible for a blister-gas bomb to fall in a crater previously made by an HE bomb, the probability of such an occurrence is small.

In this example *It may be stated with some confidence that* is not only padding but also an absurdity. One might say with some confidence that this will not happen, or with complete confidence that it is improbable. But to feel only some confidence about its improbability is carrying intellectual timidity almost to imbecility.

The following extracts from two documents issued by the same Ministry about the same time are instructive.*

The first is:

I am to add that, doubtless, local authorities appreciate that it is a matter of prime importance that information about possible breaches of Defence Regulation . . . should reach the investigating officers of the Ministry . . . with the minimum of delay.

The second is:

After six years of war almost every building in this country needs work doing to it. The whole of the building labour force could be employed on nothing else but repairs and maintenance. Yet there are hundreds of thousands of families who urgently need homes of their own and will keep on suffering great hardship until houses can be provided for them.

* These extracts, as their subject matter shows, date from about 1945. I was therefore minded to omit them, with Gowers' commentary on them, as being irrelevant to the 1970s. But although Government officials today write like the first extract much more seldom, and like the second much more often, than they did in 1945, contemporary examples to match the first extract can, unfortunately, be found, and it is impossible to say that Gowers' commentary is as yet wholly irrelevant. B.D.F.

The first of these is bad. It is the sort of thing that those who say civil servants write badly point to in support of their case. The first 18 of its 38 words are padding, and the last five are a starchy paraphrase of 'as soon as possible'. The second is excellent. It has no padding, and says what it has to say in brisk businesslike English. Why this difference of style within the same Department? We can only guess, but I do not think the guess is difficult. The first was written for the guidance of Local Government officials only. It was a routine matter and no special care was taken over it; its language is the sort that Local Authorities expect and understand. But the second was intended to impress the man in the street, and the writer was at pains to put his point in a way that would be grasped at once and would carry conviction. That is, I have no doubt, the explanation, but it is not a sufficient one. Whatever the purpose, the first is bad and the second good.

The following introductory sentence to a circular is, I think, wholly padding, but I cannot be sure, for I can find no meaning in it.

The proposals made in response to this request show differences of approach to the problem which relate to the differing recommendations of the Committee's Report, and include some modifications of those recommendations.

There are many types of padding other than the one we have been dealing with, and many padders other than Government Departments. Consider for instance these three passages:

The completed Research Report *now being prepared and* covering three years of intensive activity over the greater part of Scotland *with its factual matter, conclusions and recommendations* will be *an* invaluable *document* to the new statutory Tourist Board in planning *the provision of future* tourist facilities.

The Commission has been encouraged to look forward *in the future* to *a two-way process of* consultation with the Government before major policy decisions affecting its work are taken.

It is in any case important that senior management should at least involve itself in ensuring the existence of satisfactory policies and procedures for dealing with recruitment, induction, training and industrial relations.

In the first, all the italicised words are unnecessary, and we get quite a good sentence without them. In the second, we can start by omitting the italicised words, but more pruning is still needed. We shall probably finish with something like:

The Government have promised to consult the Commission before taking any important decisions affecting its work.

The third also carries a lot of surplus weight. The first 19 words are obviously heavily padded and should be replaced by something like *Senior management should insist on*. But the phrase *satisfactory policies and procedures for dealing with* also lacks litheness. We might try:

Senior management should always satisfy itself that the staff are being properly recruited and trained and industrial relations well handled.

But padding is too multifarious for analysis. It can only be illustrated, and the only rule for avoiding it is to be self-critical.

7

THE CHOICE OF WORDS:
CHOOSING THE FAMILIAR WORD

> Literary men, and the young still more than the old of this class, have commonly a good deal to rescind in their style in order to adapt it to business. But the young, if they be men of sound abilities, will soon learn what is not apt and discard it; which the old will not. The leading rule is to be content to be commonplace – a rule which might be observed with advantage in other writings, but is distinctly applicable to these.
>
> HENRY TAYLOR, *The Statesman*, 1836

BOSWELL tells of Johnson: 'He seemed to take pleasure in speaking in his own style; for when he had carelessly missed it, he would repeat the thought translated into it. Talking of the comedy of "The Rehearsal", he said, "It has not wit enough to keep it sweet". This was easy – he therefore caught himself and pronounced a more round sentence: "It has not vitality enough to preserve it from putrefaction".' The mind of another famous lover of the rotund phrase worked the opposite way. ' "Under the impression", said Mr Micawber, "that your peregrinations in this metropolis have not as yet been extensive, and that you might have some difficulty in penetrating the arcana of the Modern Babylon . . . in short", said Mr Micawber in a burst of confidence, "that you might lose your way . . .".' We should not hesitate which of these remarkable men to take as our model. We should cultivate Mr Micawber's praiseworthy habit of instinctively translating the out-of-the-way into the everyday.

Too many writers, official and other, incline rather towards the Johnsonian habit (which might be described as 'verbo-pomposity', a close relation to the 'pompo-verbosity' mentioned in the last chapter). They thus handicap themselves in achieving what we have seen must be the writer's primary object, to affect the reader precisely as he wishes. The simple reader is puzzled; the sophisticated one is annoyed.

The Choice of Words: Choosing the Familiar Word

The precept to choose the familiar word (which is also probably the short word) must of course be followed with discretion. Many wise men through the centuries, from Aristotle to Sir Winston Churchill, have emphasised the importance of using short and simple words. But no one knew better than these two authorities that sacrifice either of precision or of dignity is too high a price to pay for the familiar word. If the choice is between two words that convey a writer's meaning equally well, one short and familiar and the other long and unusual, of course the short and familiar should be preferred. But one that is long and unusual should not be rejected merely on that account if it is more apt in meaning. Sir Winston does not hesitate to prefer the uncommon word if there is something to be gained by it. If we were asked whether there was any difference in meaning between *woolly* and *flocculent* we should probably say no; one was commonplace and the other unusual, and that was all there was to it. But Sir Winston, in the first volume of his *Second World War*, uses *flocculent* instead of *woolly* to describe the mental processes of certain people, and so conveys to his readers just that extra ounce of contempt that we feel *flocculent* to contain, perhaps because the combination of *f* and *l* so often expresses an invertebrate state, as in *flop, flap, flaccid, flimsy, flabby* and *filleted*. Moreover there is an ugliness of shortness as well as an ugliness of length, and an ostentatious avoidance of long words can be just as irritating to the reader as an ostentatious resort to them. A literary artist like Ernest Hemingway can achieve wonderful force and poignancy by limiting himself almost entirely to words of one or two syllables, but if the rest of us try to write like that we give the impression of grunting.

But there are no great signs at present of any urgent need of a warning not to overdo the use of simple diction. The commonest ways in which failure to choose the simple word can offend the ordinary reader are the use of jargon and legal language and an addiction to showy words, including foreign words and phrases.

JARGON AND LEGAL LANGUAGE

When officials are accused of writing jargon, what is generally meant is that they affect a pompous and flabby verbosity. That is not what I mean. What I have in mind is that technical terms are used – especially conventional phrases invented by a Government Department – which are understood inside the Department but are unintelligible to outsiders. 'Departmental shorthand' (see Chapter 2) has escaped from its compound. A circular from the headquarters of a Department to its regional officers begins:

The physical progressing of building cases should be confined to . . .

Nobody could say what meaning this was intended to convey unless he held the key. It is not English, except in the sense that the words are English words. They are a group of symbols used in conventional senses known only to the parties to the convention. It may be said that no harm is done, because the instruction is not meant to be read by anyone unfamiliar with the departmental jargon. But using jargon is a dangerous habit; it is easy to forget that the public do not understand it, and to slip into the use of it in explaining things to them. If that is done, those seeking enlightenment will find themselves plunged in even deeper obscurity. A member of the Department has kindly given me this interpretation of the words quoted above, qualified by the words 'as far as I can discover':

' "The physical progressing of building cases" means going at intervals to the sites of factories, etc., whose building is sponsored by the Department and otherwise approved to see how many bricks have been laid since the last visit. "Physical" apparently here exemplifies a portmanteau usage (? syllepsis) and refers both to the flesh-and-blood presence of the inspector and to the material development of the edifice, neither of which is, however, mentioned. "Progressing", I gather, should have the accent on the first syllable and should be distinguished from pro*gres*sing. It means recording or helping forward the progress rather than going forward. "Cases" is the common term for units of work which consist of applying a given set of rules to a number of individual problems . . . "should be confined to" means that only in the types of cases specified may an officer leave his desk to visit the site.'

Legal diction, as we have seen, is almost necessarily obscure, and explanations of the provisions of legal documents must be translated into familiar words simply arranged.

With reference to your letter of the 12th August, I have to state in answer to question 1 thereof that where particulars of a partnership are disclosed to the Executive Council the remuneration of the individual partner for superannuation purposes will be deemed to be such proportion of the total remuneration of such practitioners as the proportion of his share in the partnership profits bears to the total proportion of the shares of such practitioner in those profits.

This is a good example of how not to explain. I think it means merely 'Your income will be taken to be the same proportion of the firm's remuneration as you used to get of its profits'. I may be wrong, but even so I cannot believe that language is unequal to any clearer explanation than the unfortunate correspondent received.

Here is another example of failure to shake off the shackles of legal language:

Separate departments in the same premises are treated as separate premises for this purpose where separate branches of work which are commonly carried on as separate businesses in separate premises are carried on in separate departments in the same premises.

This sentence is constructed with that mathematical arrangement of words which lawyers adopt to make their meaning unambiguous. Worked out as one would work out an equation, the sentence serves its purpose; as literature, it is balderdash. The explanation could easily have been given in some such way as this:

If branches of work commonly carried on as separate businesses are carried on in separate departments of the same premises, those departments will be treated as separate premises.

This shows how easily an unruly sentence like this can be reduced to order by turning part of it into an 'if' clause.

FOREIGN WORDS AND PHRASES

The safest rule about foreign words and phrases, as about legal tags or legal technical terms (whether in foreign or English words), is to avoid them if you can. This is partly because you may easily use them wrongly (Chapter 4 mentions the frequent misuse of the Latin phrase *a priori* and of the legal term *leading question*), and partly because even if your understanding and use of them are faultless your reader may be less learned than you and must not be made to feel inferior. Constant use even of familiar foreign expressions like *inter alia*, to say nothing of less common ones like *ratio decidendi*, gives the impression that the writer is trying to show off – which indeed is often just what he is doing.

I say 'if you can'; and you can very often. You can usually avoid *inter alia*, *per annum*, *prima facie*, *ceteris paribus*, *mutatis mutandis*, *con amore* and *carte blanche* by writing *among others*, *a year*, *at first sight*, *other things being equal*, *with the necessary changes*, *enthusiastically* and *blank cheque* (or *free hand*). But it would be pedantic to insist on a complete prohibition. Sometimes the foreigner, though still felt as foreign and still normally printed in italics, is well on the way to naturalisation and is already accepted and understood by nearly everyone. Perhaps *sub judice*, *recherché*, *fait accompli* and *ad infinitum* are now at the stage that *et cetera*, *agenda*, *garage* and *hotel* passed some time ago. Some foreigners have no wholly satisfactory English equivalents, and the near-equivalents, though good enough for many purposes, lack a nuance or a precision which can be conveyed only by the foreign word and may be important to the context. The foreign word, in short, may be the *mot juste*. Thus, there are near-equivalents to *dénouement*, *imbroglio*, *frisson*, *dolce vita* and *gravitas*, but sometimes none of them will quite do. If you are really certain that you need a particular foreign word to convey your meaning, and that your readers will take the meaning that you intend, you need not be frightened of that word. The important thing, particularly in official writing, is to put the reader's convenience before the writer's self-gratification.

When all this has been said (and there is much more that could be) the basic rule 'avoid them if you can' remains the safest guide.

OVERWORKED METAPHORS

Those who like showy words are given to overworking metaphors. There is no doubt about the usefulness and attractiveness of metaphors. They enable a writer to convey briefly and vividly ideas that might otherwise need tedious exposition. What should we have done, in our post-war economic difficulties, without our *targets*, *ceilings* and *bottlenecks*? But the very seductiveness of metaphors makes them dangerous, especially as we may be rather proud to have learned a new one and want to show off. Thus metaphors, especially new ones, tend to be used indiscriminately and soon get stale, but not before they have elbowed out words perhaps more commonplace but with meanings more precise. Sometimes metaphors are so absurdly overtaxed that they become a laughing-stock and die of ridicule. That has been the fate of 'exploring every avenue' and of 'leaving no stone unturned'.

Another danger in the use of metaphors is of falling into incongruity. So long at least as they are 'live'* metaphors, they must not be given a context that would be absurd if the words used metaphorically were being used literally. Nothing is easier to do; almost all writers fall occasionally into this trap. But it is

*A live metaphor is one that evokes in the reader a mental picture of the imagery of its origin; a dead one does not. If we write 'the situation is in hand' and 'he has taken the bit between his teeth', we are in both going to horsemanship for our metaphor. But to most readers the first would be a dead metaphor, and the sentence would have no different impact from 'the situation is under control'; the second would be a live one, calling up, however faintly and momentarily, the picture of a runaway horse.

worth while to take great pains to avoid doing so, because your reader, if he notices it, will deride you. So we should not refer to the biggest bottleneck when what we mean is the most troublesome one, for that will obviously be the narrowest. Possibilities more unpleasant than the writer can have intended are suggested by the warning to Civil Defence Workers that many persons who have experienced a nuclear explosion will have diarrhoea and vomiting and should not be allowed to swamp the medical services. The statesman who said that sections of the population were being squeezed flat by inflation was not then in his happiest vein, nor was the writer who claimed for American sociology the distinction of having always immersed itself in concrete situations, nor the enthusiastic scientist who announced the discovery of a virgin field pregnant with possibilities. The warning issued during a fuel shortage that gas rings might only be used by officers earmarked for the purpose suggests a curious method of identification, and the BBC did not choose their words felicitously when they said that every facet of negro music would be heard that night; facets, like children, should be seen not heard.

Among the metaphors specially popular at the present time the following deserve comment.

BACKGROUND

The *OED* recognises only two meanings for this word. One is 'the ground or surface lying at the back of or beyond the chief objects of contemplation'. The other is 'a less prominent position, where an object is not readily noticed'. The word has come into great favour, and is ranging a long way from the humble spheres assigned to it by the dictionary. Up to a point its extensions have been useful. To speak of examining the background of a proposal, in the sense of trying to find out what more there is in it than meets the eye, is a reasonable metaphor. So is what is called 'background training' to distinguish it from specialised training. And it is a reasonable extension of the metaphor to write:

The Choice of Words: Choosing the Familiar Word

Men and women with widely different backgrounds, ranging from graduates and trained social workers to a coalminer, a railway clerk and a clerk in an ironmongery store, had in fact succeeded.

But, like all these new favourites, it is beginning to get out of hand, and to displace more precise words:

From your particulars it would appear that your background is more suitable for posts in Government Departments employing quantity surveyors.

This does not seem to mean anything different from 'you are better qualified', the word *background* edging into the place of *experience* or *history*.

It is surprising to find more women than men, but local experience provides the background; during the war women left an area where there were no jobs for them.

Here it seems to be masquerading as *explanation*,

Further price increases, nevertheless, may be unavoidable against a background of rising costs.

Here the meaning seems nearer to *cause* than to *explanation*. *Against a background of* is equivalent to *because of*.

BLUEPRINT

This word has caught on as a picturesque substitute for *scheme* or *plan*, and the shine is wearing off it. It is not reasonable to ask that metaphors should be anchored at their points of origin, but it would make for accuracy of language if writers who use this one remembered that in the engineering industries, where it comes from, the blueprint marks the final stage of paper design.

BOTTLENECK

Bottleneck is a useful and picturesque metaphor to denote the point of constriction of something that ought to be flowing freely:

Even if the manufacturers could obtain ample raw material, the shortage of skilled labour would constitute a bottleneck in production.

For some years it led a hectic existence, being pressed into service in quite unsuitable contexts and often with absurd results (*a world-wide bottleneck, a vicious circle of interdependent bottle-necks,* and so on); but gross over-use brought it into disrepute, and it now seems to be settling down to a steady and sensible job – for example in describing traffic constriction on the roads – to which it is well suited.

BRACKETS and GROUPS

These words were put into currency by statisticians as synonyms for *class* or *category*, and they have been widely taken up. 'These are likely in the main to be bought by the lower income groups.' 'Will the Chancellor of the Exchequer move to set up a Select Committee to consider the financial hardships of the small income groups?' *Income group* has indeed become an official cliché. And we are told of what used to be called naughty children but are now juvenile delinquents:

It is some comfort to learn that the eight to thirteen bracket is the only one that involved more arrests.

It would be absurd to class *group* as a suspect word, but *bracket* is really rather silly as a synonym for it. The language is rich enough to do without it. Quite recently *cohort* has begun to appear, in sociological and other writing, as another synonym for *group*. This is perhaps precious rather than silly,

BREAKDOWN

It is fashionable, though not always apt, to use *breakdown* in a pseudo-scientific sense vaguely connoting analysis, subdivision, or classification of statistical matter. It is certainly inept when used of things that can be physically broken down:

The houses erected should be broken down into types. (. . . classified according to type.)

The breakdown of this number of houses into varying densities per acre. (The division . . .)

The Minister wishes to avoid fragmentation of the service by breaking down the two-tier system of administration provided for in the Act into a three-tier system.

Why *breaking down* in the last example? If the word *break* must be used at all *breaking up* would go better with *fragmentation*. But why not some ordinary word such as *changing*, *altering* or *converting*?

The fascination of this word may lead to quaint results.

Care should be taken that the breakdown of patients by the department under whose care they were immediately before discharge is strictly followed.

Unfortunately a complete breakdown of British trade is not possible.

Statistics have been issued of the population of the United States, broken down by age and sex.

CATALYST

Catalyst is a metaphor borrowed from chemistry. (The dictionaries define *catalysis* as the effect produced by a substance that without undergoing change itself aids a chemical change in other bodies, and *catalyst* as the agent in catalysis.) Its popularity is growing with suspicious rapidity, and there is some danger that what can clearly be a useful and expressive metaphor will be killed or blunted by over-use. To say that a particular event was 'the catalyst of change in the attitudes' of interested parties is reasonable enough; to say that 'the Church has been the catalyst for community development' is rather more doubtful; the temptation to make the metaphor play absurd antics can be illustrated by these two extracts from politicians' speeches (one Labour, one Conservative):

. . . a traumatic catalyst for a ferment of change.

Responsibility for implementing a binding agreement would automatically act as a catalyst for bridging the gap.

CEILING

Ceiling is a metaphor that has run wild for too long. Its respectable purpose is to provide a metaphorical equivalent to *maximum* or *limit*. But it is not a dead metaphor and it should not be used as if it were.

> The advisory Committee did not apply for a general increase in the ceilings.

> Any ceiling imposed under this rule may be increased or waived if the contributor agrees.

Ceiling here means *maximum prices* in the first example and *maximum benefits* in the second. The writers forgot that if one wants more headroom one does not increase the ceiling, still less perform the curious operation of waiving it; one raises it or, in the last resort, removes it.

> In determining the floor-space, a ceiling of 15,000 square feet should normally be the limit.

This is indeed a complicated way of saying that floor-space should not normally exceed 15,000 square feet. Why drag down the ceiling?

> There was no intention on the part of the Treasury of fixing an unrealistic ceiling which could not be held.

One wonders what sort of ceiling can. (For *unrealistic* in the sense of *unreasonable* see pp. 63–4.)

Unless you are accustomed to thinking of a ceiling as a blunt instrument that bites you will be surprised by:

> Manpower ceilings are a very blunt macro-instrument and will be either ineffective or unduly restrictive if not based on the results of management reviews and other 'micro' activities ... ceilings are biting, but this is what they were meant to do.

INTERFACE

Interface is a new metaphor which is becoming increasingly common in official writing. If one or two dimensions are enough

114

for you, you can make do with a *point of contact* or a *common frontier*. If you hanker after a third dimension you will feel the need of an *interface*. It is at present a vogue word and must be regarded as on probation. The fact that it is sometimes 'broad', sometimes 'virtual' and sometimes sat on ('I find myself sitting on a number of interfaces') suggests that it may need watching.

LIQUIDATE and LIQUIDATION

Liquidation is the process of ascertaining a debtor's liabilities and apportioning his assets to meet them – winding up his affairs in fact. The meaning has lately been enlarged so as to signify other sorts of winding-up, especially, with a sinister twist, the removal of opposition in a totalitarian state by methods possibly undisclosed but certainly unpleasant. The reason for this extension is no doubt to be found in the extension of the practices for which it stands. There are some who deprecate this enlargement of the word's meaning, but I do not think there is any use in doing that; it is well established, and can justly claim to be expressive and vivid and to fill a need. Sir Winston Churchill uses it in *The Gathering Storm*:

> Many of the ordinary guarantees of civilised society had been already liquidated by the Communist pervasion of the decayed Parliamentary Government.

But *liquidate* is one of the words which, having once broken out, run wild. The far-fetched word *terminate*, having superseded the familiar *end*, is itself being superseded by the more far-fetched *liquidate*. It is now apparently regarded as suitable for denoting the ending of anything, from massacring a nation to giving an employee notice. It should therefore be handled with care, and not put to such unsuitable duty as when a Local Authority writes:

> These still stand as examples of solid building construction, which

will stand the test of many more years of wear and tear before their usefulness has been finally liquidated.

PARAMETER

Parameter is a mathematical term with a precise meaning which, it is safe to say, not one in ten of those who use it understands. It is becoming increasingly common as a grand and showy synonym for *boundary*, *limit*, *framework* or *condition*. Sometimes one even suspects its users of confusing it with *perimeter*. The wise writer's attitude to *parameter*, as to *interface*, must at present be 'watch it'.

SYNDROME

Syndrome is another fairly new metaphor which is in danger of over-use. The medical meaning of the word is a group of symptoms or malfunctions which together suggest a particular disease or state of imbalance, either physical or mental. A syndrome is not itself a disease and the metaphor is wrongly used in such a sentence as 'His latest speeches suggest that on this topic he is suffering from an unfortunate syndrome.'

TARGET

Target has been so favourite a metaphor for so long that it might have been expected by now to be almost dead. But it is not, and there is still an air of absurdity about its use in ways unsuitable to its literal meaning. We cannot yet use it as if it were the same as *objective*, *goal*, *ambition* or *purpose*. We must still remember that to hit a target is to be successful and that to overshoot it is not. Yet we still find ourselves being urged, as we have been for years, not only to reach and attain our targets, but also to fight for them, to achieve them and to obtain them. We must not be lulled by a near target. It is discouraging to be a long way short of our target and (what seems to amount to the same thing) to be a long way behind it, but it is splendid to be a long way beyond it. The headline 'Target in danger' means that it is in no danger of being hit, and 'Target in sight' is intended to be exceptionally encouraging to those who are trying to hit it. A lecturer has recorded that, when he read in a speech by one of our Ministers of a 'global target' which, to the Minister's regret, could not be 'broken down', the picture that came into his mind was of a drunken reveller attacking a Belisha beacon. Nor should journalists say that only so many tons of coal are needed to 'top the year's bull's-eye', forgetting that bull's-eyes, like golf balls, give more satisfaction when hit in the middle than when topped. Nor can even the exigences of head-line language excuse the headline 'Export Target Hit' to intro-duce the news that, owing to a dock strike, the export target is unlikely to be hit.

So much for the perils of some of our more fashionable meta-phors. But it is not only in metaphors that a preference for the more showy word may lead a writer astray, and this chapter may fitly end with some common examples. All the words are good and useful words when properly used; my warning is only against the temptation to prefer them to other words which would convey better the meaning you want to express.

OTHER SEDUCTIVE WORDS

ACHIEVE

This word implies successful effort, and should not be treated as merely the equivalent of *getting* or *reaching*, as in the phrase, which I believe is not unknown, 'Officers achieving redundancy'. There is an air of dignity about *achieve* which may lead writers to prefer misguidedly such sentences as 'this was impossible of achievement' to the simpler 'this could not be done'. It is not sen-sible to say that a weapon 'has achieved good accuracy' instead of 'has proved to be (very) accurate' or to describe an unsuccess-ful student as 'a low achiever'.

ALLERGIC

Allergic is a useful word. 'I am allergic to Dr Fell' says in six words what it takes the famous quatrain 28 to say. It gives us a convenient alternative to the stilted 'I have a subconscious anti-pathy to' and the slang 'I have a thing about'. But it should not be allowed too often to displace common words that might be more suitable, such as *dislike*, *repugnance* and *aversion*.

AMBIVALENT

Ambivalent, like *allergic*, is overworked, and for the same reasons. It is sometimes even treated as if it meant *ambiguous*. It is a psychoanalytical term applicable to the simultaneous operation in the mind of two irreconcilable wishes. The word is new, but the condition it describes must be as old as humanity, and it would be a pity if so pretentious a usurper were allowed to displace the expression *mixed feelings*, which has served us so well and so long.

ANTICIPATE

The use of this word as a synonym for *expect* is now so com-mon, despite persistent opposition from lovers of the language, that some faint-hearts are beginning to give up the fight. But it is a gross example of the encroachment of a dignified word on the province of a simple one, and I am delighted to find that, in Government Departments at least, the fight is still being energe-tically carried on (though, as many examples in my collection show, the enemy still holds a strong position). It is, I think, still right and still worth while to urge that *anticipate* should be con-fined to its correct sense, that is to say, to convey the idea of forestalling an event, as in the time-honoured reply of Chancel-lors of the Exchequer, 'I cannot anticipate my budget statement'. A safe rule is to use it only with a substantive object, never with an infinitive or a *that*-clause. I give two examples, the first of its right use and the second of its wrong.

> Remember, in conducting, that your thought and gesture will almost certainly be too late rather than too early. Anticipate everything.
>
> It is anticipated that a circular on this and other matters will be issued at an early date.

As Sir Alan Herbert has pointed out, 'John and Jane anticipated marriage' is not likely to be interpreted as 'John and Jane expected to be married'.

Here is a remarkable example of its incorrect and correct use in consecutive sentences:

> The 'after-care' effort is concentrated on all large cases and cases where difficulty is anticipated. By this method most of the more serious problems are anticipated and action can be taken timeously.

In the odd sentence already quoted on p. 83,

> It does not require undue prescience to anticipate that the enlarged EEC will ...

anticipate cannot mean *expect* (as a matter of probability), for *prescience* admits of no doubt. It must mean *know* or *foresee* (as a matter of certainty) – though it is not impossible that this writer is misusing *prescience* as well as *undue* and *anticipate*.

APPROXIMATE(LY)

This means very close(ly). An approximate estimate is one that need not be exact, but should be as near as you can conveniently make it. There is no need to use *approximately* when *about* or *roughly* would do as well or even better, as in:

> It is understood that Mr X spent some time in America, approximately from 1939 to 1946.

Moreover the habit of using *approximate(ly)* leads to the absurdity of saying *very approximate* when what is meant is *very rough*, that is to say, *not* very approximate, as in:

An outline should be furnished to this Branch stating the relevant circumstances and a very approximate estimate of the expenditure involved.

COMPLEX (noun)

As a technical term in psychology, *complex* means a collection of suppressed tendencies, or the mental abnormality caused by them; and an *inferiority complex* is a state of mind that manifests itself in self-assertiveness, not diffidence. But in common usage it is now well established as meaning a consciousness, whether well founded or not, of inferiority.

In its other meaning of a *complex whole*, the noun *complex* is increasingly misused as a showy synonym of *collection* or *group*. It should be used only where there is something complex or complicated about the group referred to.

Parliamentary control of Government expenditure depends on a complex of constitutional principles, statutory requirements and Parliamentary conventions.
The sub-committee has considered the complex of recommendations in the Fulton Report relating to the status of employment.

In the first of these *complex* is rightly used; in the second it means no more than *group* and there is no justification for blunting its meaning in this way.

DEEM

This is an old-fashioned word which starches any letter in which it is used as a synonym for *think*. 'This method is deemed to be contra-indicated' is an unpleasant and obscure way of saying 'this method is thought unsuitable'. But the word is still useful in its technical sense of signifying the constructive or inferential as opposed to the explicit or actual. 'Everyone is deemed to have intended the natural and probable consequences of his actions'; 'Anyone who does not give notice of objection within three weeks will be deemed to have agreed'; 'Any expenditure incurred in the preparation of plans for any work . . .

shall be deemed to be included in the expenditure incurred in carrying out that work.'

DILEMMA

This word originally had a precise meaning which it would be a pity not to preserve. It should not therefore be treated as the equivalent of a difficulty, or, colloquially, of a fix or a jam. To be in a dilemma (or, if you want to show your learning, to be on the horns of a dilemma) is to be faced with two (and only two) alternative courses of action, each of which is likely to have awkward results.

ENVISAGE

There is a place for *envisage* to indicate a mental vision of something planned but not yet created, but not nearly such a big place as is given to it. Like *anticipate*, it is used more suitably with a direct object than with a *that*-clause.

Mr X said that he envisaged that there would be no access to the school from the main road (thought).

I would refer to your letter of the 26th February in which you envisaged the repairs would be completed by the end of this month (said that you expected).

Certain items will fall to be dealt with not by transfer to the Minister but in the way envisaged in Section 60 (described).

EVACUATE

This means to empty, and is a technical term of the military and medical sciences. As a military term it may be used (like *empty*) either of a place (*evacuate a fortress*) or of the people in it (*evacuate a garrison*). In the latter sense it was much used during the war to describe the process of moving people out of dangerous places, and they were given the convenient name of *evacuees*. Its inclination to encroach on the province of the simpler word *remove* needs watching.

121

EVENTUATE

See MATERIALISE.

EVOLVE

This is a useful word to denote a process of natural change or development which is gradual and perhaps self-generated. One thinks of the Darwinian theory of *evolution*. But it is sometimes used where the meaning does not require anything more than *change* or *develop*, and, like *involve*, it has a tendency to appear where nothing is needed at all, as in:

The Government accept the need for appropriate pricing policies to be evolved.

Here the last three words are either unnecessary or inappropriate, for pricing policies need to be invented, devised or developed by conscious effort; they will not evolve or be evolved by natural selection.

IDEOLOGY

This word offends some purists, but I do not see why it should, provided that its mesmeric influence is kept in check; the old-fashioned *creed* or *faith* may sometimes serve. But now that people no longer care enough about religion to fight, massacre and enslave one another to secure the form of its observance, we need a word for what has taken its place as an excitant of those forms of human activity, and I know of none better.

IMPLEMENT

This verb, meaning to carry out or fulfil, used to be hardly known outside the 'barbarous jargon of the Scottish Bar'.* In 1926 Fowler 'could not acquit of the charge of pedantry' a

* David Irving, quoted by Fowler.

writer who used the expression 'implementing Labour's promises to the electorate'. It is now too firmly established to be driven out, but the occasional use of *carry out*, *keep* or *fulfil* for a change would be refreshing.

INTEGRATE

This is a useful word in its proper place, to describe the process of combining different elements into a whole. But it has become too popular. It seems now to be the inevitable word for saying that anything has been joined, mixed, combined or amalgamated with anything else.

LIMITED (adjective)

It is pedantry to object to the use of *limited* in the sense of *restricted* on the ground that everything that is not unlimited must be limited. But the word should be used with discretion and should not be allowed to make a writer forget such words as *few* and *small*. Weseen says:

Limited is not in good use as a substitute for *small* or one of its synonyms. 'A man of limited (meagre) education and limited (inadequate) capital is likely to be limited to a limited (scant) income.'

To write *a limited number of* when you mean *a few* or *of limited use* when you mean *not very useful* is not perhaps a heinous crime, but if you find yourself doing it too often it is time to ask yourself whether you are forming pompous habits.

MAJORITY

The major part or *the majority* ought not to be used when a plain *most* would meet the case. They should be reserved for occasions when the difference between a majority and a minority is significant. Thus:

Most of the members have been slack in their attendance.
The majority of members are likely to be against the proposal.

MARGINAL(LY)

Marginal has a number of useful jobs to do. *Marginal notes* are notes written in the margin; *marginal cost* has an exact meaning in economics, which no other expression would convey so well; *marginal seats* provide half the excitement in a General Election. But in recent years *marginal* has come to be increasingly used to mean no more than *small*. This misuse has now reached the status of an epidemic and every writer should make a habit of crossing out *marginal* as soon as he has written it, restoring it only if satisfied that it is precisely the word he needs. He should do the same with *marginally*, and it is safe to say that he will never have to restore it at all. Here is a very small selection of passages where the epidemic has struck:

The second [point] is the marginal, but important, improvement in the detection rate of the police. (Slight)

The expenditure involved in restoring the building to its proper use was marginal. (Small)

The system is now only marginally capable of meeting the estimated demands upon it. (Barely)

It [the British system] will become marginally more likely to be improved if Britain joins the EEC. (Slightly)

The terms negotiated were marginally not as good as I could have wished. (Not quite as good)

[The building] is marginally within the danger zone. (Just)

MATERIALISE

Do not use this showy word, or the similar word *eventuate*, when a simpler one would do as well or better, e.g. *happen, occur, come about, take place* or even the colloquial *come off*.

It was thought at the time that the incoming tenant would take over the fixtures. This did not however materialise. (But he did not.)

The possibility of the boiler strike to which he had referred at the last meeting had not eventuated. (The boiler strike which he had said at the last meeting was possible had not occurred.)

Materialise has its own work to do as a transitive verb in the
sense of investing something non-material with material attributes, and as an intransitive verb in the sense of appearing in
bodily form.

MAXIMAL, MAXIMISE; MINIMAL, MINIMISE; OPTIMAL,
OPTIMISE

These words are all enjoying a vogue and are more often than
not signs of a writer who is muddled or showy or both. Here
are some extreme examples:

Junior staff in contact with clients cannot be involved only mini-
mally in their jobs without serious consequences for staff-client
relationships.

This seems a perversely obscure way of saying that if junior
staff are not much interested in their jobs they will not get on
well with their clients.

Unless the consultant's marginal productivity is greater than the
sum of all his patients', the optimisation of the consultant's time
is not identical to the maximisation of the community's resources.

This makes the excellent point that if a consultant keeps an
outpatient clinic waiting because he is on another job, the time
wasted by the patients is probably worth more in total than the
time he spent on that other job: so, on the whole, the community loses. Surely a writer who can score a good mark for
using *marginal* correctly should have been able to put it better.

The likelihood of such divergence is minimised where the clientele
includes all citizens at some time in their lives; it is maximised
where the clientele is a small minority, especially where this minority is regarded as in some way deviant *vis-à-vis* the rest of society.

There seems no good reason why *minimised* and *maximised*
should have been preferred to *smallest* and *greatest*. Perhaps
it was thought that these unpretentious words would be in some
way deviant *vis-à-vis* the rest of the sentence.

METICULOUS

Meticulous means, by derivation, 'full of little fears', and like its plebeian cousin *pernickety* still retains a flavour of fussiness over trifles. It is a useful word when the writer wants to suggest that carefulness is overdone, and it would be a great pity if it were rendered incapable of conveying that meaning because of its frequent use as a mere synonym for *careful*, *scrupulous* or *punctilious*. To confine it to its proper meaning is, I submit, the mark of a scrupulous, not a meticulous, writer.

OPTIMISTIC

Optimism is the quality of being disposed in all circumstances to hope for the best. The edge of the meaning of *optimistic* is being blunted by its being habitually used for *sanguine* or *hopeful*, when what is referred to is not a habit of mind, but an attitude towards particular circumstances.

Examples of its unsuitable use are:

The negotiations are making good progress, but it is too early to be either optimistic or pessimistic about them.

When an offender has shown positive interest in improving his skills ready for discharge, this is an optimistic sign.

OPTIMUM (adjective)

Do not treat *optimum* as a showy synonym for *best*. It should only be used of the product of conflicting forces. The optimum speed of a motor car is not the fastest it is capable of, but that which reconciles in the most satisfactory way the conflicting desires of its owner to move quickly, to economise petrol and to avoid needless wear and tear.

There is no great harm in preferring *optimal* to *optimum* as an adjective. But where *optimum* is wrong *optimal* will be wrong too.

ORIENT, ORIENTATE

These two verbs have the same meaning – to place so as to face east, or to determine how something stands in relation to the points of the compass. To orientate oneself is to get one's bearings, to see how one stands, and there is clearly plenty of scope for figurative uses. It is possible, though a little far-fetched, to say that if one is looking towards a particular objective one is figuratively oriented or orientated towards that objective, in the same way as a church is literally built with its chancel pointing due east. But the use of *oriented* or *orientated* in this figurative sense is passing all reasonable bounds. I have seen a social service described as 'client-orientated', a building as 'purpose-oriented', an aid project as 'non-population orientated', and I have received a booklet from a motoring organisation which tells me 'This booklet introduces you to a new safety-orientated service'. It is time to call a halt.

RENDITION

The original meaning, now archaic, was *surrender*, and, like *surrender* and *give up*, it could be used of either a garrison or a fugitive. The word is now less common in England than in America, where it is freely used in the sense of translation or version, and of musical or dramatic performance. For these we in Britain still prefer *rendering* though, with our usual disposition to imitate things American, we are giving *rendition* a run.

RESOURCES

Economists and others have increasingly stressed in recent years that when we are reckoning what some proposal will 'cost' it is often more realistic (particularly where public expenditure is concerned) to think of the use of 'resources' than of the expenditure of money – that is, to consider what materials, labour, foreign exchange and so on the project will need. There is nothing wrong in this, either economically or linguistically; *resources* aptly expresses what is meant. But the word has become altogether too fashionable. Because *management of resources* or *resource-allocation* are often (and even rightly) used where a generation ago we would have talked of financial control or authority for expenditure, some writers feel that they will appear fuddy-duddy unless they work *resources* into any sentence dealing with finance. Thus they will write 'This involves an unacceptable demand on resources' instead of 'We cannot afford this', and 'That would represent a misallocation of resources' instead of 'That would be wasteful'. Here are a couple of examples:

Where, however, particular [airline] services are cross-subsidised on a continuing basis, this indicates that there may be a misallocation of resources that should be rectified. (If some services are permanently subsidised by others, that suggests that some fares are too low and others too high.)

The timing of each successive stage will depend upon progress with the last and upon the resources that can be made available for the next. (For this sentence see also pp. 307–8. In the context *resources* here merely means staff.)

The instinctive substitution of *resources* for *finance* has led the writer of the following to use *resourceful* as the equivalent of *wealthy*:

Both [management and policy] must be in the hands of an authority at once local enough to understand people's needs and resourceful enough to afford the solutions.

UNILATERAL, MULTILATERAL, BILATERAL

These words are not for everyday use. They have long been part of the jargon of the diplomatist and the physiologist. And they have recently been admitted into that of the economist, where they are doing much hard work. But for ordinary purposes it is best to stick to *one-sided*, *many-sided* and *two-sided*. Under the influence of *unilateral* a sentiment that might have been plainly stated as 'we will not be the only country to disarm' is often expressed by politicians in the words 'we will not adopt a policy of unilateral disarmament', and the repudiation of a debt has been described (by a professor) as 'unilateral refusal to pay'.

USAGE and USER

These words are increasingly employed where *use* would be the right word. *Usage* does not mean *use*; it means either a manner of use (e.g. rough usage) or a habitual practice creating a standard (e.g. modern English usage). *User* (in its impersonal sense) is a legal term meaning the enjoyment of a right, and may be left to the lawyers. An example of *usage* wrongly employed for *use* is:

There is a serious world shortage of X-ray films due to increasing usage in all countries. In this country usage during the first six months of 1951 was 16 per cent greater than in the corresponding period of 1950.

See also p. 311.

UTILISE and UTILISATION

These words are rarely needed, for the simple word *use* will almost always serve. The official (not a Government official) who wrote 'This document is forwarded herewith for the favour of your utilisation' might have written 'please use this form'. That says what needed to be said in four syllables instead of 21.

Nor is there any reason for preferring the longer word in:

The sum so released may, upon receipt of same, be utilised to reimburse you for expenses.

Certainly *use* and *utilise* should not be employed merely by way of 'elegant variation' as they apparently are in:

It is expected that Boards will be able to utilise the accommodation now being used by the existing governing bodies.

VIABLE

Viable is a biological term denoting the capacity of a newly-created organism to maintain its separate existence. Its present vogue rivals that of *realistic*; its victims include *durable, lasting, workable, effective, practicable* and many others.

What is the alternative? I do not pretend to know the answer but who can doubt that no viable answer is possible unless and until the Commonwealth is strong and united within itself.

Here 'no viable answer is possible' seems to be merely a confused way of saying 'no alternative will work'.

It is legitimate to wonder whether a new business venture will prove economically viable (though some may prefer to wonder whether it will pay). But if one is considering how best to subject Zetland school teachers to Aberdeen University lectures there is no excuse for:

It may well be more economically viable to send a team of lecturers to Lerwick than to bring a group of teachers from Zetland to Aberdeen.

Here *more economically viable* merely means *cheaper*.

The following is a list of some more words that are over-worked in official documents, and beside them other words that might be used instead, if only, in some cases, as useful change-bowlers. I am not, of course, suggesting that they are necessarily synonyms of the words placed opposite to them or that those ought never to be used.

acquaint	inform; tell
adumbrate	sketch; outline; foreshadow
advert	refer
ameliorate	better; improve
apprise	inform
assist	help
commence	begin; start
consider	think

desire	wish
donate	give
evince	show; manifest; display
factor	fact; consideration; circumstance; feature; element; constituent; cause
function (verb)	work; operate; act
inform	tell
in isolation	by itself
initiate	begin; start
locality	place
practically	virtually; almost; nearly; all but
proceed	go
purchase	buy
purport (noun)	upshot; gist; tenor; substance
question (noun)	subject; topic; matter; problem
render	make
require	want; need
reside	live
residence	home
state	say
sufficient	enough
terminate	end
transmit	send; forward
visualise	imagine; picture

8

THE CHOICE OF WORDS:
CHOOSING THE PRECISE WORD

The search for the *mot juste* is not a pedantic fad but a vital
necessity. Words are our precision tools. Imprecision engen-
ders ambiguity and hours are wasted in removing verbal
misunderstandings before the argument of substance can begin.

ANONYMOUS CIVIL SERVANT

How popular and how influential is the practice [of personify-
ing abstract words] may be shown by such a list of words as the
following: Virtue, Liberty, Democracy, Peace, Germany,
Religion, Glory – all invaluable words, indispensable even,
but able to confuse the clearest issues unless controlled.

OGDEN and RICHARDS

THE LURE OF THE ABSTRACT WORD

THE reason for preferring the concrete to the abstract is clear.
Your purpose must be to make your meaning plain. Many
concrete words have a penumbra of uncertainty round them,
and an incomparably larger one surrounds all abstract words.
If you use an abstract word when you might use a concrete one
you are handicapping yourself in your task, difficult enough in
any case, of making yourself understood.

Unfortunately the very vagueness of abstract words is one
of the reasons for their popularity. To express one's thoughts
accurately is hard work, and to be precise is sometimes dangerous. We are tempted to prefer the safer obscurity of the abstract.
It is the greatest vice of present-day writing. Writers seem to
find it more natural to say 'Was this the realisation of an anticipated liability?' than 'Did you expect to have to do this?'; to
say 'Communities where anonymity in personal relationships
prevails' than 'Communities where people do not know one
another'. To resist this temptation, and to resolve to make your
meaning plain to your reader even at the cost of some trouble

to yourself, is more important than any other single thing if you would convert a flabby style into a crisp one. As Mr G. M. Young has said, an excessive reliance on the noun at the expense of the verb will, in the end, detach the mind of the writer from the realities of here and now, from when and how and in what mood the thing was done, and insensibly induce a habit of abstraction, generalisation and vagueness. To what lengths this can go may be illustrated by these three examples:

The desirability of attaining unanimity so far as the general construction of the body is concerned is of considerable importance from the production aspect.

The actualisation of the motivation of the forces must to a great extent be a matter of personal angularity.

Its practicability depends essentially on there being a mutuality of capability and interest.

The first, which relates to the building of vehicles, means, I suppose, that in order to produce the vehicles quickly it is important to agree on a standard body. The meaning of the second is past conjecture. The perpetrator of it is an economist, not an official. The third has something to do with defence and its meaning is perhaps befogged in the interests of national security (see also pp. 308–9).

Here are some less extreme examples of the habit of using abstract words to say in a complicated way something that might be said simply and directly:

There has been persistent instability in numbers of staff. (Staff has continually varied in numbers.)

The cessation of house-building operated over a period of five years. (No houses were built for five years. Note the infelicity of 'a cessation operated'. *Operate* is just what cessations cannot do.)

A high degree of carelessness, pre-operative and post-operative, on the part of some of the hospital staff, took place. (Some of the hospital staff were very careless both before and after the operation.)

The cessation of the present restrictions cannot be made. (The present restrictions cannot be ended.)

Intervention is contra-indicated. (We should not intervene.)

133

Sometimes abstract words are actually invented, so powerful is the lure of saying things this way.

[We are unwilling] to tolerate multilateralisation of the dialogue.

The following is not official writing, but as it appeared in a newspaper that never shrinks from showing up the faults of official writing, it deserves a place:

Initiation of a temporary organisation to determine European economic requirements in relation to proposals by Mr Marshall, American Secretary of State, was announced in the House of Commons this evening.

This way of expressing oneself seems to be tainting official speech as well as writing. 'We want you to deny indirect reception', said the goods clerk of my local railway station, telephoning to me about a missing case. 'What does that mean?' I asked. 'Why,' he said, 'we want to make sure that the case has not reached you through some other station.'

Exponents of the newer sciences are fond of expressing themselves in abstractions. Perhaps this is unavoidable, but I cannot help thinking that they sometimes make things unnecessarily difficult for their readers. Several examples are given elsewhere in this book (see in particular pp. 279–82). Here is one from psychology:

Reserves that are occupied in continuous uni-directional adjustment of a disorder are no longer available for use in the ever-varying interplay of organism and environment in the spontaneity of mutual synthesis.

In official writing the words *availability*, *lack* and *dearth* contribute much to the same practice, though they do not produce the same obscurity.

We would point out that the availabilities of this particular material are extremely limited. (. . . that this material is extremely scarce.)

The actual date of the completion of the purchase should coincide with the availability of the new facilities. (The purchase should not be completed until the new facilities are available.)

The lack of attraction in the three services is so deep that it has been found quite impossible to man them on a voluntary basis. (The three services are so unattractive. . .)

Lack is a useful word to denote a deficiency of something, and occasionally, though less commonly, the complete absence of something. But this word is being pressed too much into service. For instance, 'there is a complete lack of spare underground wire' is not the natural way of saying 'we have no spare underground wire' or 'There exists a considerable lack of knowledge about . . .' for 'We do not know much about . . .', or 'A dearth of information exists' for 'We have very little information'.

Here is a remarkable sentence in which *availability* is used to mean *lack*:

The availability of figures may indeed prove to be one of the obstacles in the efficiency of the whole of the proposed statistical content of the exercise.

This means 'Lack of figures may make it difficult to produce accurate statistics'. It is not unnatural that a man who writes *obstacles in* instead of *obstacles to* and who asks us to consider the efficiency of a content should now and again say exactly the opposite of what he means.

POSITION AND SITUATION

The words *position* and *situation* have a great fascination for those who are given to blurring the sharp outlines of what they have to say. A debate takes place in the House of Commons about a rise in unemployment. A speaker wants to say that he does not see how it would have been possible for the Government to make sure of there being enough work. Does he say so? No; the miasma of abstract words envelops him and he says, 'In view of all the circumstances I do not see how this situation could have been in any way warded off'. Later the spokesman for the Government wants to strike a reassuring note, and express his confidence that the rise is only temporary. He too takes refuge in vague abstractions. 'We shall', he says, 'ease through this position without any deleterious effect on the long-term situation.' On an historic occasion it fell to a master of words to make an announcement at a time of even graver crisis. Sir Winston Churchill did not begin his broadcast on 17 June 1940: 'The position in regard to France is extremely serious'. He began: 'The news from France is very bad'. He did not end it: 'We have absolute confidence that eventually the situation will be restored'. He ended: 'We are sure that in the end all will come right'.

Position and *situation*, besides replacing more precise words, have a way of intruding into sentences that can do better without them. These words should be regarded as danger-signals, and the writer who finds himself using one should think whether he cannot say what he has to say more directly.

It may be useful for Inspectors to be informed about the present situation on this matter. (. . . to know how this matter now stands.)

Unless these wagons can be moved the position will soon be reached where there will be no more wagons to be filled. (. . . there will soon be no more. . .)

Should the position arise where a hostel contains a preponderance of public assistance cases. . . . (If a hostel gets too many public assistance cases. . .)

All three sentences run more easily if we get rid of the *situation* and the *positions*.

It is common form for an Insurance Company, when asking for a renewal premium, to say:

No-claim bonus is shown subject to the position in this respect remaining unprejudiced until expiry.

This wraps up in verbiage the simple statement that the insured has a right to a no-claim bonus only if no claim is made before the expiry of the policy.

Position in regard to is an ugly expression, not always easy to avoid, but used more often than it need be. 'The position in

regard to invisible exports has deteriorated' seems to come more
naturally to the pen than 'invisible exports have dropped'. It is
not fair to put all the blame on officials. Even *The Times* is
capable of saying 'The question of the British position in regard
to the amount of authorisation' rather than 'the question how
much Britain is to get of the amount authorised'.

The position in regard to *situation* has certainly deteriorated
in recent years. This word has become something of an obses-
sion in certain sorts of writing. What, for instance, is a *motivat-
ing situation*? The following examples all come from a single
Report.

In some cases the church has been the catalyst for community
development in the total situation.

Not all educationists are converted to the idea of a separate
counsellor in the school situation.

... facilities for developing personal relationships and for creating
face-to-face situations.

The value of joint appointments as catalysts in the emerging
situation ...

There is a tendency for these groups to become static and their
members reluctant to pursue the activity in an adult situation.

... a considerable number of young people can be involved
in the youth work situation.

... a list of curriculum subjects which have the potential for
development in the after-school situation.

They are often strongly supported by young people in adult
education situations.

... the help that can be given by youth and community workers
in the industrial and commercial situation.

This is by no means an exhaustive list; after a time the reader
is ready to scream at each repetition of the word; and, as you
can judge from the extracts given, the style of writing gives
him much else to scream at too.

THE HEADLINE PHRASE

More serious is the harm that is being done to the language by
excessive use of nouns as adjectives. In the past, as I have said,

the language has been greatly enriched by this free-and-easy habit. We are surrounded by innumerable examples – Customs Officer, Highway Code, Nursery School, Community Centre, Trades Union Congress and so on. But something has gone wrong recently with this useful practice; its abuse is corrupting English prose. It has become natural to say 'World population is increasing faster than world food production' instead of 'The population of the world is increasing faster than the food it produces', 'The housing position will then be relieved' instead of 'More houses will then be available', 'The balance of payments position exceeds all expectation' instead of 'The balance of payments is more favourable than was expected.' It is old-fashioned to speak of the 'state of the world'; it must be the 'world situation'. The fact is, as Lord Dunsany once remarked, that 'too many *of*s have dropped out of the language, and the dark of the floor is littered with this useful word'. We meet daily, he adds, with things like 'England side captain selection' instead of 'Selection of captain of English eleven'; or even 'England side captain selection difficulty'. Nor would they stop nowadays at 'England side captain selection difficulty rumour'.

This sort of language is no doubt pardonable in headlines, where as many stimulating words as possible must be crowded into spaces so small that *treaties* have had to become *pacts*, *ambassadors envoys*, *investigations probes* and all forms of human enterprise *bids*. Headlines have become a language of their own, knowing no law and often quite incomprehensible until one has read the article that they profess to summarise. INSANITY RULES CRITIC and W. H. SMITH OFFER SUCCESS have quite different meanings from their apparent ones. Who could guess that the headline UNOFFICIAL STRIKES CLAIM introduces a report of a speech by a Member of Parliament who said that there was abundant evidence that unofficial strikes were organised and inspired by Communists as part of a general plan originating from abroad? I do not see how those three words by themselves can have any meaning at all; to me they convey a vague suggestion of the discovery of oil or gold by someone who ought not to have been looking for it. And if the announcement BULL GRANTS INCREASE is construed grammatically, it does not seem to deserve a headline at all: one would say that that was no more than was to be expected from any conscientious bull.

But what may be pardonable in headlines will not do in the text. *Nursery School* is a legitimate use of the noun-adjective, but *nursery school provision* is not to be preferred as a proper way of saying *the provision of nursery schools. Electricity crisis restrictions* and *world supply situation* may be all right as newspaper headlines but not in English prose. For instance:

An extra million tons of steel would buy our whole sugar import requirements. (. . . all the sugar we need to import.)

Food consumption has been dominated by the world supply situation. (People have had to eat what they could get.)

Delays must continue to occur because of the man-power situation. (. . . because there are not enough workers.)

An exceptionally choice example is:

The programme must be on the basis of the present head of labour ceiling allocation overall.

Here *head of labour* means *number of building operatives. Ceiling* means *maximum. Overall*, as usual, means nothing (see pp. 152–5). The whole sentence means 'The programme must be on the assumption that we get the maximum number of building operatives at present allotted to us'.

Everything is being done to expedite plant installation within the limiting factors of steel availability and the preparation of sites.

The only thing that can be said for the writer of this is that his conscience pulled him up before the end, and he did not write 'sites preparation'. The sentence should have run, 'So far as steel is available and sites can be prepared, everything is being done to expedite the installation of plant'.

The use of a noun as an adjective should be avoided where the same word is already an adjective with a different meaning. Do not, for instance, say 'material allocation' when you mean

139

'allocation of material', but reserve that expression against the time when you may want to make clear that the allocation you are considering is not a spiritual one. For the same reason this phrase is not felicitous:

> In view of the restrictions recently imposed on our capital economic situation. . . .

It is possible, of course, to go too far in condemning headline phrases. *Headline phrase* might itself be described as a headline phrase; and if so it is clearly a harmless one. But the constant use of such phrases is usually a sign either of unclear thinking or of unwillingness to say things as briskly and simply as possible. A headline phrase consisting of more than two words should be treated with suspicion, and things tend to get even more awkward if the phrase includes an adjective as well as a number of nouns; it is not always obvious on first reading which noun the adjective qualifies, and tiresome problems of hyphenation sometimes arise (see pp. 254–6). Few will think that the first sentence of this paragraph would have been better if it had read 'Excessive headline phrase condemnation is, of course, a possibility'; but few can deny that some people do write like this. Officials are by no means the only offenders. The following were produced by officials:

> The formulation of personnel management information requirements.
> Flexible resource allocation procedures.
> The conception of a major weapon system development.
> Water-cooled reactor design staff.
> Unnecessary file access difficulties.

But the following were not:

> The programming of transport facility development.

It seems a pity that this three-word phrase did not take the opportunity of entering the four-word class as *Transport facility development programming*. But even if it had it would have won no prizes.

A non-population oriented maternity service project

scores five, and

Surplus Government chemical warfare vapour detection kits

wins easily with seven.

Here are some other non-official headline phrase predilection examples:

I notice that planning permission condition trees never do get planted.

This means that when the planting of trees is a condition of the grant of planning permission they are not in the event planted. The next comes from a circular issued by a commercial firm.

This compulsion is much regretted, but a large vehicle fleet operator restriction in mileage has now been made imperative in meeting the demand for petrol economy.

This translated into English presumably means:

We much regret having to do this, but we have been obliged to restrict greatly the operation of our fleet of vehicles [or to restrict the operation of our fleet of large vehicles?] to meet the demand for economy in petrol.

This is from an article by a politician:

Avoiding technicalities . . . it might mean either mandatory (though flexible) minimum liquidity ratios, or a once-for-all sterilising of excess ban liquidity. . .

Here translation baffles me.

ABSTRACT ADJECTIVAL PHRASES

By this I mean using a phrase consisting of an abstract noun (e.g. *character*, *nature*, *basis*, *description*, *degree*) with an adjective, where a simple adjective would do as well. This too offends against the rule that you should say what you have to say as

141

simply and directly as possible in order that you may be readily understood.

These claims are of a very far-reaching character. (These claims are very far-reaching.)

The weather will be of a showery character. (It will be showery.)

A high degree of carelessness. (Great carelessness.)

New work of high priority which is of an inter-sectoral nature. (Urgent new work which is inter-sectoral. I leave to others the interpretation of *inter-sectoral*.)

The wages will be low owing to the unremunerative nature of the work.

The translation of the last example will present no difficulty to a student of Mr Micawber, who once said of the occupation of selling corn on commission: 'It is not an avocation of a remunerative description – in other words, it does *not* pay'. (Other examples of this type of abstract adjectival phrase will be found on p. 291.)

Proposition is another abstract word used in the same way.

Decentralisation on a regional basis is now a generally practical proposition. (. . . is now generally feasible.)

Accommodation in a separate building is not usually a practical proposition. (. . . is not usually feasible.)

The high cost of land in clearance areas makes it a completely uneconomic proposition to build cottages in those areas. (. . . makes it completely uneconomic to build cottages there.)

Proposition is becoming a blunderbuss word (see p. 34–5), constantly used for purposes for which *plan* or *project* would be better.

Basis is specially likely to lead writers to express themselves in roundabout ways. When you find you have written 'on a . . . basis' always examine it critically before letting it stand. You may well allow it to stand if you have written of staff paid on a weekly basis or of a house let on a monthly basis, but do not despise *by the week* or *by the month* as somewhat less pompous alternatives. The following examples would not escape so easily:

[Certain services are] cross-subsidised on a continuing basis by other more profitable services. (Permanently *or* year after year.)

Mr X's services will be available on a consulting basis. (Mr X will be available as a consultant *or* for consultation.)

The objective evidence that exists suggests that the building of large new hospitals on the basis of avoidance of duplicated facilities alone would represent suboptimisation. (. . . for the sole purpose of avoiding. . . But the sentence needs more extensive surgery than this.)

Such officer shall remain on his existing salary on a mark-time basis. (. . . shall mark time on his existing salary.)

The organisation of such services might be warranted in particular localities and on a strictly limited basis. (Scale.)

The machines would need to be available both day and night on a 24-hour basis. (. . . at any time of the day or night.)

Please state whether this is to be a permanent installation or on a temporary line basis. (. . . or a temporary line.)

A legitimate use of *basis* is:

The manufacturers are distributing their products as fairly as possible on the basis of past trading.

CLICHÉS

In the course of this book I have called numerous expressions clichés. A cliché may be defined as a phrase whose aptness in a particular context when it was first invented has won it such popularity that it has become hackneyed, and is used without thought in contexts where it is no longer apt. Clichés are notorious enemies of the precise word. To quote from the introduction to Eric Partridge's *Dictionary of Clichés*:

They range from fly-blown phrases (explore every avenue) through sobriquets that have lost all point and freshness (the Iron Duke) to quotations that have become debased currency (cups that cheer but not inebriate), metaphors that are now pointless, and formulas that have become mere counters (far be it from me to . . .).

A cliché then is by definition a bad thing, not to be employed by self-respecting writers. Judged by this test, some expressions are unquestionably and in all circumstances clichés. This is true

The Complete Plain Words

in particular of verbose and facetious ways of saying simple things (*conspicuous by its absence*, *tender mercies*, *durance vile*) and of phrases so threadbare that they cannot escape the suspicion of being used automatically (*leave no stone unturned*, *acid test*, *psychological moment*, *leave severely alone*). But a vast number of other expressions may or may not be clichés. It depends on whether they are used unthinkingly as reach-me-downs or deliberately chosen as the best means of saying what the writer wants to say. Eric Partridge's *Dictionary* contains some thousands of entries. But, as he says in his preface, what is a cliché is partly a matter of opinion. It is also a matter of occasion. Many of those in his dictionary may or may not be clichés; it depends on how they are used. Writers would be needlessly handicapped if they were never permitted such phrases as *cross the Rubicon*, *sui generis*, *swing of the pendulum*, *thin end of the wedge* and *white elephant*. These may be the fittest way of expressing a writer's meaning. If you choose one of them for that reason you need not be afraid of being called a cliché-monger. The trouble is that writers often use a cliché because they think it fine, or because it is the first thing that comes into their heads. It is always a danger-signal when one word suggests another and Siamese twins are born – *part and parcel*, *intents and purposes*, *this day and age* and the like. There is no good reason why *inconvenience* should always be said to be *experienced* by the person who suffers it and *occasioned* by the person who causes it. Single words too become clichés; they are used so often that their edges are blunted while more exact words are neglected. I have already said something in Chapter 7 about those whose popularity comes from the allure of novelty or sparkle; here I will give some examples of a few more that have no such claim to preference; some indeed seem to attract by their very drabness.

ACCOMMODATION

While we stay in the same place we can still call our house our house, or our flat our flat, or our lodgings our lodgings. But

144

if Authority arranges to move us, it will not be to another house, or a different flat, or new lodgings. It will always be to alternative accommodation. This cliché has run wild, and its versatility is astonishing. Sometimes it means no more than *houses*:

> The real cause of bad relations between landlord and tenant is the shortage of alternative accommodation.

Or it may mean something less than houses:

> Experience has shown that many applications have been received for exemption certificates [*sc.* from the obligation to provide sanitary conveniences] on the ground that alternative accommodation is available. . . Public sanitary conveniences should not be considered satisfactory alternative accommodation.

AFFECT

This word has won an undeserved popularity because it is colourless – a word of broad meaning that saves a writer the trouble of thought. It is a useful word in its place, but not when used from laziness. It may be easier to say 'The progress of the building has been *affected* by the weather, but it is better to use a more precise word – *hindered*, perhaps, or *delayed* or *stopped*.

ALTERNATIVE

The use of *alternative* for such words as *other*, *new*, *revised* or *fresh* is rife. Perhaps this is due to infection spread by the cliché *alternative accommodation*.

> The Minister regrets that he will not be able to hold the Conference arranged for the 15th March. Members will be informed as soon as alternative arrangements have been made.

Alternative must imply a choice between two or more things. *Other* is the right word here.

It is pedantry to say that, because of its derivation, *alternative* must not be used where the choices are more than two.

APPRECIATE

The ordinary meaning of *appreciate*, as a transitive verb, is to form an estimate of the worth of anything, to set a value on it, and hence to acknowledge with gratitude. In this last meaning it is used, much more often in America than in Britain, in such phrases as 'I should appreciate an early reply', 'I would appreciate your asking Mr X to explain . . .', 'My class would appreciate a discussion of . . .'

But it is sometimes used merely to make a piece of polite padding (see p. 98–9). And it is used far too often where it would be more suitable to use *understand*, *realise*, or *recognise*. When a request has to be refused, it may be laudable to attempt to soften the refusal by such phrases as 'I appreciate how hard it is on you not to have it', and 'you will appreciate the reasons why I cannot let you have it'. But in such phrases *appreciate* is faintly pompous (some would condemn it as incorrect). The laudable intention would be better served by *realise* in the first and *understand* in the second. An effective way of curbing over-use of the word might be to resolve never to use it with a *that* clause ('I appreciate that there has been delay'), but always give it a noun to govern ('I appreciate the trouble you have taken').

'It would be appreciated if' can usually be translated into 'I shall be glad (or grateful, or obliged, or even pleased) if. . .'. 'You will appreciate that . . .' can often be better expressed by 'you will realise that', or even 'of course'.

APPROPRIATE (adjective)

This is an irreproachable word. But so also are *right*, *suitable*, *fitting* and *proper*, and I do not see why *appropriate* should have it all its own way. In particular, the Whitehall cliché *in appropriate cases* might be confined more closely than it is now to cases in which it is appropriate.

The Choice of Words: Choosing the Precise Word

CLAIM

The proper meaning of *to claim* is to demand recognition of a right. But the fight to prevent it from usurping the place of *assert* has been lost in America and seems likely to be lost here also, especially as the BBC have surrendered without a struggle. Here are some recent examples from this country:

The police took statements from about forty people who claimed that they had seen the gunmen in different parts of the city.

The State Department claims that discrimination is being shown against the American film industry.

There are those who claim that the Atlantic Treaty has an aggressive purpose.

I have a friend who claims to keep in his office a filing tray labelled 'Too Difficult'.

The enlargement of *claim* ought to be deplored by all those who like to treat words as tools of precision, and to keep their edges sharp. Why should *claim*, which has its own useful job to do, claim a job that is already being efficiently done by others? Perhaps the idea underlying this usage is that the writer claims credence for an improbable or unverified assertion.

DECIMATE

To *decimate* is to reduce *by* one-tenth, not *to* one-tenth. It meant originally to punish mutinous troops by executing one man in ten, chosen by lot. Hence by extension it means to destroy a large proportion; the suggestion it now conveys is usually of a loss much greater than 10 per cent. Because of the flavour of exactness that still hangs about it, an adverb or adverbial phrase should not be used with it. We may say 'The attacking troops were decimated', meaning that they suffered heavy losses, but we must not say 'The attacking troops were badly decimated', and still less 'decimated to the extent of 50 per cent or more'.

147

DEVELOP

The proper use of this word is to convey the idea of a gradual unfolding or building up. Do not use it as a synonym for *arise*, *occur*, *happen*, *take place*, *come*. A typical example of its misuse is 'rising prices might develop' (for 'prices might rise').

ENTAIL

This word is given too much work to do. Often some other word such as *need*, *cause*, *impose*, *necessitate*, *involve*, might be more appropriate, or at least make a refreshing change. Sometimes *entail* intrudes where no verb is needed, a common habit of *involve*.

. . . a statement in writing that you are willing to bear the cost entailed of opening the case, withdrawing this amount and resealing.

If *entailed* must be used, the preposition should be *in*.

INVOLVE

The meaning of this popular word has been diluted to a point of extreme insipidity. Originally it meant *wrap up in something*, *enfold*. Then it acquired the figurative meaning *entangle a person in difficulties or embarrassment*, and especially *implicate in crime, or a charge*. Then it began to lose colour, and to be used as though it meant nothing more than *include*, *contain* or *imply*. It has thus developed a vagueness that makes it the delight of those who dislike the effort of searching for the right word. It is consequently much used, generally where some more specific word would be better and sometimes where it is merely superfluous.

This is no new phenomenon. Early in the twentieth century Sir Clifford Allbutt, writing about the English style of medical students at Cambridge, said:

To involve, with its ugly and upstart noun *involvement*, has to do duty for to *attack*, to *invade*, to *injure*, to *affect*, to *pervert*, to *encroach upon*, to *influence*, to *enclose*, to *implicate*, to *permeate*, to *pervade*, to *penetrate*, to *dislocate*, to *contaminate* and so forth.

Here are a few examples:

The additional rent involved will be £1. (Omit *involved*.)
There are certain amounts of the material available without permit, but the quantities involved are getting less. (Omit *involved*.)
It has been agreed that the capital cost involved in the installation of the works shall be included. (. . . that the capital cost of installing. . .)
It has been inaccurately reported that anything from eight sheep to eight oxen were roasted at the affair. The facts are that six sheep only were involved. (*Involved* here seems to be an 'elegant variation' for *roasted*.)
Much labour has been involved in advertising. (Much labour has been expended on advertising.)
The area of dereliction involved is approximately 85 acres. (The derelict area is about 85 acres.)

The following examples all occur in one paragraph of a memorandum, covering less than half a page, and strikingly illustrate the fascination this word exercises over undiscriminating writers:

The Ministry have indicated that they would not favour any proposal which would involve an increase in establishment at the present time. (*Involve* here is harmless, but in order to practise shaking off its yoke, let us substitute *mean* or *lead to*.)
The Company would oppose this application unless compensation involving a substantial sum were paid. (This one cannot get off so lightly. The writer should have said 'unless a substantial sum were paid in compensation'.)
We have been informed that the procedure involved would necessitate lengthy negotiation. . . (Here *involved* is doing no work at all and should be omitted.)

Such are some of the sadly flabby uses to which this word of character is put. Reserve it for more virile purposes and especially for use where there is a suggestion of entanglement or complication, as we use *involved* when we say 'this is a most involved subject'. Here are two examples of its reasonable use:

This experience has thrown into high relief the complications and delays involved in the existing machinery for obtaining approval.

Mr Menzies protested against the Australian Government's acceptance of the invitation to the conference at Delhi on the Indonesian dispute, holding that Australia ought not to be involved.

In this last example *involved* carries the meaning referred to above of entanglement in difficulties. Recently the word has undergone a further shift in meaning and it is now often used with the implication that getting involved is a desirable or a laudable thing rather than a worrying or an embarrassing one. This use is not to be objected to; it takes the word back nearer to its original meaning of *wrap up in something*. But from it has grown the current vogue of the noun *involvement*, which deserves an entry to itself. (Strictly, perhaps, it would have been better placed among the showy words listed in the last chapter, but it seems more convenient to consider it here.)

INVOLVEMENT

This is a vogue word which is becoming altogether too common for comfort. Its appeal is easy to understand: it says something that is not quite said by *co-operation*, *partnership*, *sympathy*, *sharing*, *contribution* or *responsibility*, though it is sometimes used where one of those less modish words would have done as well or better. Often it seems to be interchangeable with its fellow vogue word *participation*; indeed the two sometimes appear hand in hand. It is being reached for too often as a cosy substitute for exact meaning, and there are signs that it may before long become not merely tiresome but menacing to the language. Here are two of the innumerable examples I have collected:

Their involvement in, and response to, innovation is positive and refreshing.

The BBC should accept as a necessary and helpful development the [union's] policy of having more branch level participation in union decisions, in order to meet the desire of the [union's] rank and file for a greater sense of involvement in decision-making.

ISSUE (noun)

This word has a very wide range of proper meanings as a noun, and should not be made to do any more work – the work, for instance, of *subject, topic, consideration* and *dispute.*

ITEM

This word is a great favourite, especially in business letters. It is made to mean almost anything. It is safe to say that any sentence in which this omnibus use occurs will be improved either by omitting the word or by substituting a word of more definite meaning. The following is a typical instance; it refers to the condition of a set of batteries:

The accessory items, stands and other parts, are satisfactory, but the sediment approximates to 1-in. in depth and . . . this item can be removed conveniently when the renewals are effected.

Accessory items should be changed to *accessories* and *this item can be removed* to *this can be removed.*

The next example is from a notice of a meeting:

* I shall be able to attend the meeting.
* I shall not be able to attend the meeting.

* Please delete item not required.

Here what meant *sediment* in the first example appears to mean *words.*

MAJOR

This is a harmless word, unexceptionable in such company as *major road, major war, major railway accident.* But it is so much used that it is supplanting other more serviceable ones. Do not let *major* make you forget such words as *main, important*, *chief*, *principal*, *great* or *big*. For instance, *important* or *significant* might have been better than *major* in:

We do not expect to see any major change in the near future.

OVERALL (adjective)

The favour that this word has won during the past few years is astonishing. It is an egregious example of the process I described as boring out a weapon of precision into a blunderbuss. Indeed the word seems to have a quality that impels people to use it in settings in which it has no meaning at all.

Examples of its meaningless use are:

The independence of the Teaching Hospitals and their freedom from the overall control of the Regional Boards. . . .

The overall growth of London should be restrained.

Radical changes will be necessary in the general scheme of Exchequer grants in aid of local authorities, therefore, to secure that overall the policy of the Government in concentrating those grants as far as possible where the need is greatest is further developed. (Here, it will be observed, *overall* is an adverb.)

When an individual leaves an establishment, and his departure results in a net reduction of one in the overall strength. . . .

It looks as if the yield for the first fortnight . . . will be fewer than forty fresh orders, representing an overall annual output of no more than a thousand.

The Controller should assume a general overall responsibility for the efficient planning of all measures.

At national level, a Cabinet Minister has a general overall interest in the social services.

When *overall* is not meaningless, it is commonly used as a synonym for some more familiar word, especially *average*, *total* and *aggregate*.

For *aggregate*:

Compared with the same week a year ago, overall production of coal showed an increase of more than 100,000 tons. [i.e. deep-mined plus opencast.]

For *in all* or *altogether*:

Overall the broadcasting of 'Faust' will cover eight hours.

For *total*:

I have made a note of the overall demand of this company for the next year.

We must be realistic in terms of recruitment possibilities in determining the overall manpower figure for the civil service.

For *total of*:

In 1969–70 applicants for aid estimated that an overall 96,770 extra jobs will result, mostly from 1973 onwards.

For *average*:

The houses here are built to an overall density of three to the acre.

For *supreme*:

Vice-Admiral Duncan, of the United States Navy, was in overall command.

For *on the whole*:

The Secretary of State for the Colonies stated that the overall position in Malaya had greatly improved, although in some places it was still difficult.

For *generally*:

Small vital schemes of repair and adaptation which continually arise and must be dealt with irrespective of any attempt to improve overall hospital standards.

For *overriding*:

They came forward as witnesses because of the overall fear of being involved in a capital charge.

The plan should be given overall priority.

For *net*:

If users were charged for the extra service it would not result in any overall increase in the cost to the taxpayer.

For *gross*:

The overall deficit of £3,496,201 is partly offset by extra receipts of £794,269.

For *comprehensive*:

An overall plan for North Atlantic Defence measures was approved yesterday by the Defence Ministers at the Hague.
The absence of any overall national strategy is distressing but true.

For *perpetual* (or perhaps *besetting*):

Appreciating the overall difficulties concerned with the BBC's financial position, the Court nevertheless feels that financial stringency should not prevent the BBC from granting ...

For *whole*:

Mr C. said he could quite understand that the Conservative Party were unwilling to look at the overall picture.

For *bird's-eye*:

Our observer will be in the control tower, where he will have an overall view of the aerodrome.

For *complete*:

One volume was published, but the overall plan was never finished.

For *absolute*:

The Conservatives will have an overall majority in the new Parliament.

For *on balance*:

The purpose of the plan is to enable a larger initial payment to be made and correspondingly lower payments subsequently, entailing an overall saving to the customer.

For *Hip, hip, hooray*:

By their victory in the World Cup England clearly proved themselves the best team in the world overall.

Overall, according to the dictionaries, means 'including every-thing between the extreme points', as one speaks of the overall length of a ship. For this purpose it is useful, and it is so used in a trader's announcement:

> Overall floor space taken up by the machine is 24 by 24 inches.

But it is high time that its excursions into the fields of other words were checked. So pervasive has the word become that it is a pleasant surprise to come across an old-fashioned *general* in such sentences as:

> These reports may be used for obtaining a general picture of the efficiency of a given industry.
>
> Although Europe's general deficit with the outside world fell by over $2 billion during 1949, its deficit with the United States fell hardly at all.

Most writers today would say 'overall picture' and 'overall deficit' almost automatically.

PERCENTAGE, PROPORTION, FRACTION

Do not use the expression *a percentage* or *a proportion* when what you mean is *some*, as in:

> This drug has proved of much value in a percentage of cases.
>
> The London Branch of the National Association of Fire Officers, which includes a proportion of station officers . . .

Here *percentage* and *proportion* pretend to mean something more than *some*, but do not really do so. They do not give the reader any idea of the number or proportion of the successful cases or station officers. One per cent is just as much 'a percen-tage' as 99 per cent. So, for that matter, is 200 per cent.

Use *percentage* or *proportion* only if you want to express not an absolute number but the relation of one number to another, and can give at least an approximate degree of exactitude; so that, though you may not be able to put an actual figure on the percentage or proportion, you can at any rate say 'a high per-centage', 'a large proportion', 'a low percentage', 'a small proportion'. But never use such phrases merely for the sake of their impressive appearance. Remember the simple words *many*, *few* and *some* and do not desert them for proportions and percentages unless your meaning compels you to.

Fraction is different. It has become so common to use 'only a fraction' in the sense of 'only a small fraction' that it would be pedantry to object that $\dfrac{999}{1000}$ is as much a fraction as $\dfrac{1}{1000}$, just as it would certainly be pedantry to point out to anyone who says 'He has got a temperature' that 98 degrees is just as much 'a temperature' as 104.

REACTION

Reaction may be properly used as a technical term of chemistry (the response of a substance to a reagent), of biology (the response of an organ of the body to an external stimulus), or of mechanics ('to every action there is an equal and opposite reaction'). In its figurative sense ('What is your reaction?') it really ought to connote an automatic rather than an intellectual response. Yet it is increasingly used to replace such words as *opinion*, *view* or *impression*, whether or not reflection has preceded reaction. This offends many lovers of the language; they would say that though an *immediate reaction*, a *market reaction* and even *popular reaction* are admissible, a *considered reaction* is nonsense. *Reaction*'s extension of meaning may now be so firmly settled that to condemn it would be to risk a charge of pedantry. If so it is a pity, for exactitude of meaning has been blunted. But you need not fear such a charge if you choose yourself to use *reaction* only where you mean something automatic or 'off-the-cuff'. In its extended meaning it has plenty of natural synonyms.

The preposition after *reaction* must be *to*, not *on*. It is permissible to say 'His reaction to your letter was unfavourable'. But it is not permissible to say 'Your letter had an unfavourable reaction on him'. To say that is to imply a belief that one of the meanings of *reaction* is *effect*.

REALISTIC

This word has become exceedingly popular, perhaps because it has a question-begging flavour. What is realistic is what the writer agrees with.

Realistic is ousting words like *sensible, reasonable, practical, feasible, workmanlike, probable, likely, frank*. In some contexts it seems to mean merely *big*. For that is what a trade union official really means when he says that he will not start negotiations until he gets a 'realistic offer' from the employers. Here are a few examples to illustrate the versatility of the word:

The Corporation was morally bound to take up underwriting so long as the terms were realistic at the time of issue. (Reasonable)

Lord X made a most realistic observation when he suggested that the House of Lords should meet later. (Sensible)

This was a realistic speech which pulled no punches. (Frank)

We do not see as realistic any major expansion in the direct teaching of research methods. (Likely)

Grants towards the cost should be realistic. (Generous, *or* big enough)

We must be realistic in terms of recruitment possibilities in determining the overall manpower figure for the civil service. (We must not overestimate recruitment possibilities ...)

SIGNIFICANT(LY)

This is a good and useful word, but it has a special flavour of its own and it should not be thoughtlessly used as a mere variant of *important, considerable, appreciable* or *quite large* when one is dealing with numbers or quantities or other mathematical concepts. For one thing it has a special and precise meaning for mathematicians and statisticians which they are entitled to keep inviolate. For another, it ought to be used only where there is a ready answer to the reader's unspoken question 'Significant, is it? And what does it signify?' In 'A significant number of Government supporters abstained', 'There has been a significant rise in the Chancellor's popularity since his last Budget', 'There was no significant loss of power when the engine was tested with lower-octane fuel', this question can clearly be answered; but the writers of the following had no such significance in mind:

. . . knowledge about society will grow at a significantly slower pace than it is capable of achieving. (Much more slowly than it could)

Even after this . . . reduction the size of our labour force in [a particular factory] will remain significantly larger than it was a year ago. (Appreciably)

A significantly higher level of expenditure must be expected on libraries etc. (Considerably)

After the low proportion of commitments in respect of new dwellings during the fourth quarter there was a significant upturn in January. (Marked)

In the last example the upturn (or increase) might, it is true, have been significant; but the context shows that it was not, and no one is going to give the benefit of the doubt to a man who writes of a *low proportion of commitments in respect of new dwellings*.

9

THE HANDLING OF WORDS

Proper words in proper places make the true definition of
style.

SWIFT

If language is not correct, then what is said is not what is
meant; if what is said is not what is meant, then what ought
to be done remains undone.

CONFUCIUS

WE must now return to what I called in Chapter 4 'correctness', and consider what it means not in the choice of words but
in handling them when chosen. That takes us into the realm of
grammar, syntax and idiom – three words that overlap and are
often used loosely, with grammar as a generic term covering
them all.

Grammar has fallen from the high esteem that it used to
enjoy. A hundred and fifty years ago William Cobbett said that
'grammar perfectly understood enables us not only to express
our meaning fully and clearly but so to express it as to defy the
ingenuity of man to give our words any other meaning than
that which we intended to express'. The very name of grammar
school serves to remind us that grammar was long regarded as
the only path to culture and learning. But that was Latin grammar. When our mother-tongue encroached on the paramountcy
of the dead languages, questions began to be asked. Even at the
time when Cobbett was writing his grammar, Sydney Smith was
fulminating about the unfortunate boy who was 'suffocated by
the nonsense of grammarians, overwhelmed with every species
of difficulty disproportionate to his age, and driven by despair
to pegtop and marbles'. Very slowly over the past hundred years
the idea seems to have gained ground that the grammar of a
living language, which is changing all the time, cannot be fitted
into the rigid framework of a dead one; nor can the grammar
of a language such as Latin, which changes the forms of its

words to express different grammatical relations, be profitably applied to a language such as English, which has got rid of most of its inflexions, and expresses grammatical relations by devices like prepositions and auxiliary verbs and by the order of its words. It is about seventy years since the Board of Education itself declared: 'There is no such thing as English grammar in the sense which used to be attached to the term'. George Saintsbury denounced the futility of trying to 'draw up rules and conventions for a language that is almost wholly exception and idiom'. Jespersen preached that the grammar of a language must be deduced from a study of how good writers of it in fact write, not how grammarians say it ought to be written. George Orwell went so far as to say that 'correct grammar and syntax are of no importance so long as one makes one's meaning clear'.

The old-fashioned grammarian certainly has much to answer for. He created a false sense of values that still lingers. I have ample evidence in my own correspondence that too much importance is still attached to grammarians' fetishes and too little to choosing the right words. But we cannot have grammar jettisoned altogether; that would mean chaos. There are certain grammatical conventions that are, so to speak, a code of good manners. They change, but those current at the time must be observed by writers who wish to express themselves clearly and without offence to their readers. In this chapter, then, I shall concern myself with some points of current usage on which I have noticed guidance to be needed.

Strictly, idiom is different from grammar: the two are often in conflict. Idiom is defined by the *OED* as 'a peculiarity of phraseology approved by usage and often having a meaning other than its logical or grammatical one'. When anything in this book is called 'good English idiom' or 'idiomatic', what is meant is that usage has established it as correct. Idiom does not conflict with grammar or logic as a matter of course; it is usually grammatically and logically neutral. Idiom requires us to say *capable of doing*, not *capable to do*, and *able to do*, not *able of doing*. Logic and grammar do not object to this, but they would be equally content with *capable to do* and *able of doing*. At the same time idiom is, in Jespersen's phrase, 'a tyrannical, capricious, utterly incalculable thing', and if logic and grammar get in its way, so much the worse for logic and grammar. It is idiomatic – at least in speech – to say 'I won't be longer than I can help' and 'it's me'. That the first is logically nonsense and the second a grammatical howler is neither here nor there; idiom makes light of such things. Yet during the reign of pedantry attempts were constantly made to force idiom into the mould of logic. We were not to speak of a *criminal being executed*, for 'a sentence can be executed but not a person'; we were not to say *vexed question* for 'though many a question vexes none is vexed'; nor *most thoughtless* for 'if a person is without thought there cannot be degrees of his lack of that quality'; nor *light the fire*, for 'nothing has less need of lighting'; nor *round the fireside*, for 'that would mean that some of us were behind the chimney'. So argued Landor,* a stout and undiscriminating defender of his language against the intrusion of the illogical. In spite of Fowler and Jespersen, some trace still lingers of the idea that what is illogical or ungrammatical 'must' be wrong, such as condemnation of *under the circumstances* and of the use of a plural verb with *none*. The truth is, as Logan Pearsall Smith says:

Plainly a language which was all idiom and unreason would be impossible as an instrument of thought; but all languages permit the existence of a certain number of illogical expressions: and the fact that, in spite of their vulgar origin and illiterate appearance, they have succeeded in elbowing their way into our prose and poetry, and even learned lexicons and grammars, is proof that they perform a necessary function in the domestic economy of speech.†

In this chapter advice will be given about common troubles in the handling of words. After an opening section on the arrangement of words, these troubles will be classified under those with Conjunctions (p. 167): Negatives (p. 175): Number

* Imaginary Conversations between Horne Tooke and Dr Johnson and the Author and Archdeacon Hare.

† *Words and Idioms* (Constable & Co., 5th ed., 1943).

(p. 179): Prepositions (p. 185): Pronouns (p. 190): Verbs (p. 206). The chapter will end with sections on Some points of idiom (p. 220): Some common causes of confused expression (p. 231): and A few points of spelling (p. 236).

TROUBLES IN ARRANGEMENT

Of these three – grammar, syntax and idiom – it is syntax, in its strict sense of 'orderly arrangement', that is of the greatest practical importance. The quotation that heads this chapter says that proper words in proper places make the true definition of style. But something more than 'style' depends on putting words in their proper places. In a language like ours, which, except in some of its pronouns, has got rid of its different forms for the subjective and objective cases, your very meaning may depend on your arrangement of words. In Latin, the subject of the verb will have a form that shows it is 'in the nominative', and the object one that shows it is 'in the accusative'; you may arrange them as you like, and the meaning will remain the same. 'Amor vincit omnia' means exactly the same as 'Omnia vincit amor' (Love conquers all things). But English is different. In the two sentences 'Cain killed Abel' and 'Abel killed Cain' the words are the same, but when they are reversed the meaning is reversed too.

If all you want to say is a simple thing like that, there is no difficulty. But you rarely do. You probably want to write a more complicated sentence telling not only the central event but also its how, why and where. The Americans have a useful word, *modifier*, by which they mean 'words or groups of words that restrict, limit or make more exact the meaning of other words'. The 'modifiers' bring the trouble.

The rule is easy enough to state. It is, in the words of an old grammarian, 'that the words or members most nearly related should be placed in the sentence as near to each other as possible, so as to make their mutual relation clearly appear'. But it is not so easy to keep. We do not always remember that what is clear to us may be far from clear to our readers. Sometimes it is not clear even to us which 'words or members' are 'most nearly related', and if there are many 'modifiers' we may be confronted with difficulties of the jig-saw type.

The simplest type of faulty arrangement, and the easiest to fall into, is illustrated by the following examples. Their offence is that they obscure the writer's meaning, if only momentarily, and usually make him appear to be guilty of an absurdity.

There was a discussion yesterday on the worrying of sheep by dogs in the Minister's room.

The official statement on the marriage of German prisoners with girls made in the House of Commons. . . .

It is doubtful whether this small gas company would wish to accept responsibility for supplying this large area with all its difficulties.

More examples will be found on pp. 305–6.

Faulty arrangement of this sort is not unknown even in model regulations issued by Government Departments to show local authorities how things ought to be done:

No child shall be employed on any weekday when the school is not open for a longer period than four hours.

'For a longer period than four hours' qualifies *employed*, not *open*, and should come immediately after *employed*.

I shall have something more to say on this subject (pp. 246–7) in pointing out the danger of supposing that disorderly sentences can be set right by vagrant commas. But one cause of the separation of 'words or members most nearly related' is so common that, although I have already touched on it (p. 31), an examination of some more examples may be useful. That is the separation of the subject from the verb by intervening clauses, usually defining the subject.

Officers appointed to permanent commissions who do not possess the qualifications for voluntary insurance explained in the preceding paragraphs and officers appointed to emergency commissions direct from civil life who were not already insured at the date of appointment (and who, as explained in para. 3, are therefore not required to be insured during service) may be eligible. . . .

In this example the reader is kept waiting an unconscionable time for the verb. The simplest way of correcting this will generally be to change the order of the words or to convert relative clauses into conditional, or both. For instance:

Officers appointed to permanent commissions may be eligible though they do not possess the qualifications for voluntary insurance explained in the preceding paragraphs. So may officers appointed to emergency commissions direct from civil life who . ; ; etc.

Sometimes the object allows itself to be driven a confusing distance from the verb. In the following example the writer has lumbered ponderously along without looking where he was going and arrived at the object (*officers*) of the verb *are employing* with a disconcerting bump:

One or two of the largest Local Authorities are at present employing on their staff as certifying officers and as advisers to the Mental Deficiency Act Committees officers having special qualification or experience in mental deficiency.

He would have given himself little more trouble, and would have saved his reader some, if he had turned the sentence round and written:

Officers having special qualification or experience in mental deficiency are at present being employed on the staff of one or two of the largest Local Authorities as certifying officers and as advisers to the Mental Deficiency Act Committees.

Other common errors of arrangement likely to give the reader unnecessary trouble, if they do not actually bewilder him, are letting the relative get a long way from its antecedent and the auxiliary a long way from the main verb. Examples:

(Of relative separated from antecedent.)

Enquiries are received from time to time in connection with requests for the grant of leave of absence to school children during term time for various reasons, which give rise to questions as to the power to grant such leave.

What is the antecedent of *which*? *Enquiries*, *requests* or *reasons*? Probably *enquiries*, but it is a long way off. In this sentence it matters little, but in other sentences similarly constructed it might be important for the antecedent to be unmistakable. The surest way of avoiding ambiguity, when you have started a sentence like this, is to put a full stop after *reasons*, and begin the next sentence *These enquiries*, or *These requests* or *These reasons*, whichever is meant.

(Of verb separated from auxiliary.)

The Executive Council should, in the case of approved institutions employing one doctor, get into touch with the committee.

The Council should accordingly, after considering whether they wish to suggest any modifications in the model scheme, consult with the committee . . .

It is a bad habit to put all sorts of things between the auxiliary and the verb in this way; it leads to unwieldy sentences and irritated readers.

Adverbs sometimes get awkwardly separated from the words they qualify. 'They should be so placed in a sentence as to make it impossible to doubt which word or words they are intended to affect.' If they affect an adjective or past participle or another adverb their place is immediately in front of it (*accurately placed, perfectly clear*). If they affect another part of a verb, or a phrase, they may be in front or behind. It is usually a matter of emphasis: *he came soon* emphasises his promptitude; *he soon came* emphasises his coming.

The commonest causes of adverbs going wrong are the fear, real or imaginary, of splitting an infinitive (see pp. 216–20) and the waywardness of the adverbs *only* and *even*. *Only* is a capricious word. It is much given to deserting its post and taking its place next the verb, regardless of what it qualifies. It is more natural to say 'he only spoke for ten minutes' than 'he spoke for only ten minutes'. The sport of pillorying misplaced *onlys* has a great fascination for some people, and *only*-snooping seems to have become as popular a sport with some purists as split-infinitive-snooping was a generation ago. A recent book, devoted to the exposing of errors of diction in contemporary writers, contained several examples such as:

He had only been in England for six weeks since the beginning of the war.

This only makes a war lawful: that it is a struggle for law against force.

We can only analyse the facts we all have before us.

These incur the author's censure. By the same reasoning he would condemn Sir Winston Churchill for writing in *The Gathering Storm*:

Statesmen are not called upon only to settle easy questions.

Fowler took a different view. Of a critic who protested against 'he only died a week ago' instead of 'he died only a week ago' Fowler wrote:

There speaks one of those friends from whom the English language may well pray to be saved, one of the modern precisians who have more zeal than discretion . . .

But it cannot be denied that the irresponsible behaviour of *only* does sometimes create real ambiguity. Take such a sentence as:

His disease can only be alleviated by a surgical operation.

We cannot tell what this means, and must rewrite it either:

Only a surgical operation can alleviate his disease (it cannot be alleviated in any other way),

or:

A surgical operation can only alleviate his disease (it cannot cure it).

Again:

In your second paragraph you point out that carpet-yarn only can be obtained from India, and this is quite correct.

The writer must have meant 'can be obtained only from India', and ought to have so written, or, at the least, 'can only be obtained from India'. What he did write, if not actually ambiguous (for it can hardly be supposed that carpet-yarn is India's only product), is unnatural, and sets the reader puzzling for a moment.

So do not take the *only*-snoopers too seriously. But be on the alert. It will generally be safe to put *only* in what the plain man feels to be its natural place. Sometimes that will be its logical position, sometimes not. When the qualification is more important than the positive statement, to bring in the *only* as soon as possible is an aid to being understood; it prevents the reader from being put on a wrong scent. In the sentence 'The temperature will rise above 35 degrees only in the south-west of England', *only* is carefully put in its right logical place. But the listener would have grasped more quickly the picture of an almost universally cold England if the announcer had said, 'the temperature will only rise above 35 degrees in the south-west of England'. What is often still better in such cases is to avoid *only* by making the main statement a negative: 'the temperature will not rise above 35 degrees, except in the south-west of England'.

Even has a similar habit of getting into the wrong place. The importance of putting it in the right one is aptly illustrated in the *ABC of English Usage* thus:

Sentence: 'I am not disturbed by your threats'.
 (i) Even I am not disturbed by your threats (let alone anybody else).
 (ii) I am not even disturbed by your threats (let alone hurt, annoyed, injured, alarmed).
 (iii) I am not disturbed even by your threats (*even* modifies the phrase, the emphasis being on the threats).

It is also possible, though perhaps rather awkward, to put *even* immediately before *your*, and so give *your* the emphasis (your threats, let alone anybody else's).

TROUBLES WITH CONJUNCTIONS*

(i) *And*. There used to be an idea that it was inelegant to begin a sentence with *and*. The idea is now dead. And to use *and* in this position may be a useful way of indicating that what

---

*This is an elastic heading. It may for instance be said that neither *both* nor *like* is strictly a conjunction. But their caprices make it convenient to include them in this section.

you are about to say will reinforce what you have just said. But do not do this so often that it becomes a mannerism. One occasionally sees *And* used to begin a paragraph; this has a slightly affected air. *But*, on the other hand, may be freely used to begin either a sentence or a paragraph.

(ii) *And which.* There is a grammarians' rule that it is wrong to write *and which* (and similar expressions such as *and who, and where, but which, or which,* etc.) except by way of introducing a second relative clause with the same antecedent as one that has just preceded it. The rule is unknown in French and may be destroyed eventually by usage, but for the present its observance is expected from those who would write correctly. According to this rule, Nelson was wrong grammatically, as well as in other more important ways, when he wrote to Lady Nelson after his first introduction to Lady Hamilton:

> She is a young woman of amiable manners and who does honour to the station to which he has raised her.

To justify the *and who* grammatically a relative is needed in the first part of the sentence, for example:

> She is a young woman whose manners are amiable and who, etc.

Conversely, the writer of the following sentence has got into trouble by being shy of *and which*:

> Things which we ourselves could not produce and yet are essential to our recovery.

Here, says the grammarian, *which* cannot double the parts of object of *produce* and subject of *are*. To set the grammar right the relative has to be repeated just as it would have to be if it were an inflective one (e.g. 'Men whom we forget but who should be remembered').

> Things which we ourselves could not produce and which are, etc.

The wisest course is to avoid the inevitable clumsiness of *and which*, even when used in a way that does not offend the purists. Thus these two sentences might be written:

She is a young woman of amiable manners who does honour to the station to which he has raised her.

Things essential to our recovery which we ourselves could not produce.

(iii) *As* must not be used as a preposition, on the analogy of *but*. (See next page.) You may say 'no one knows the full truth but me', but you must not say 'no one knows the truth as fully as me'. It must be 'as fully as I'. The first *as* is an adverb and the second a conjunction.

We say 'as good *as* ever' and 'better *than* ever'. But should we use *as* or *than*, or both, if we say 'as good or better'? The natural thing to say is 'as good or better than ever', ignoring the *as* that *as good* logically needs, and you commit no great crime if that is what you do. But if you want both to run no risk of offending the purists and to avoid the prosy 'as good as or better than', you can write 'as good as ever or better'. Thus you could change:

Pamphlets have circulated as widely, and been no less influential, than those published in this volume.

into:

Pamphlets have circulated as widely as those published in this volume, and have been no less influential.

(For the superfluous *as* see p. 92.)

(iv) *Both*. When using *both . . . and*, be careful that these words are in their right positions and carry equal weight. Nothing that comes between the *both* and the *and* can be regarded as carried on after the *and*. If words are to be carried on after the *and* they must precede the *both*; if they do not precede the *both* they must be repeated after the *and*. For instance:

He was both deaf to argument and entreaty.

Since *deaf to* comes after *both* it cannot be 'understood' again after *and*. We must adjust the balance in one of the following ways:

He was both deaf to argument and unmoved by entreaty.
He was deaf both to argument and to entreaty.
He was deaf to both argument and entreaty.

Here is a sentence where the unbalanced *both* puts the reader off the scent:

Staff may seek rewards and satisfaction from both their superiors and from their clients.

This seems to say that there are two superiors, from both of whom, as well as from their clients, the staff may seek rewards. But that is not what the writer meant: he should have written 'both from their superiors ...'

An extreme example of the unbalanced *both* is:

The proposed sale must be both sanctioned by the Minister and the price must be approved by the District Valuer.

The need for proper balancing of *both ... and* applies also to such pairs as *either ... or, neither ... nor, not only ... but also, not so much ... as, between ... and*.

Do not use *both* where it is not necessary because the meaning of the sentence is no less plain if you leave it out:

Both of them are equally to blame. (They are equally to blame.)
Please ensure that both documents are fastened together. (... that the documents are fastened together.)

(v) *But*, in the sense of *except*, is sometimes treated as a preposition, but more commonly as a conjunction. Mrs Hemans would not have been guilty of 'bad grammar' if she had written 'whence all but him had fled', but in preferring *he* she conformed to the usual practice. That is the worst of personal pronouns: by retaining the case-inflexions that nouns have so sensibly rid themselves of they pose these tiresome and trivial questions. (See also *I and Me* pp. 194–5 and *Who and Whom* pp. 203–5.) If the sentence could have been 'whence all but the boy had fled' no one could have known whether *but* was being used as a conjunction or a preposition, and no one need have cared.

In using *but* as a conjunction an easy slip is to put it where there should be an *and*, forgetting that the conjunction that you want is one that does not go contrary to the clause immediately preceding but continues in the same sense.

It is agreed that the primary condition of the scheme is satisfied, but it is also necessary to establish that your war service interrupted an organised course of study for a professional qualification comparable to that for which application is made, *but*, as explained in previous letters, you are unable to fulfil this condition.

The italicised *but* should be *and*. The line of thought has already been turned by the first *but*; it is now going straight on. A similar slip is made in:

The Forestry Commission will probably only be able to offer you a post as a forest labourer, or possibly in leading a gang of forest workers, but there are at the moment no vacancies for Forest Officers.

Either *only* must be omitted or the *but* must be changed to *since*.

(vi) *If*. The use of *if* for *though* or *but* may give rise to ambiguity or absurdity. It is ambiguous in such a sentence as:

This case, if not proved, is arguable.

Its absurdity is demonstrated in Sir Alan Herbert's imaginary example:

Milk is nourishing, if tuberculous.

Care is also needed in the use of *if* in the sense of *whether*, for this too may cause ambiguity.

Please inform me if there is any change in your circumstances.

Does this mean 'Please inform me now whether there is any change' or 'If any change should occur please inform me then'? The reader cannot tell. If *whether* and *if* become interchangeable, unintentional offence may be given by the lover who sings:

> What do I care,
> If you are there?

(vii) *Inasmuch as*. This is sometimes used in the sense of *so far as* and sometimes as a clumsy way of saying *since*. It is therefore ambiguous, and might well be dispensed with altogether.

(viii) *Like*. Colloquial English admits *like* as a conjunction, and would not be shocked at such a sentence as 'Nothing succeeds like success does'. In America they go even further, and say 'It looks like he was going to succeed'. But in English prose neither of these will do. *Like* must not be treated as a conjunction. So we may say 'nothing succeeds like success'; but it must be 'nothing succeeds *as* success does' and 'it looks *as if* he were going to succeed'.

But the convention forbidding *like he does*, where *like* is a conjunction, should not frighten writers away from *like him*, where it is a prepositional adverb, and make them lean over backwards with such a sentence as 'The new Secretary of State, as his predecessor, is an Etonian'. Shakespeare knew better than to write 'I am no orator like Brutus is' but felt no qualms about 'it is tyrannous to use it like a giant'.

(ix) *Provided* (*that*). This form of introduction of a stipulation is better than *providing*. The phrase should be reserved for a true stipulation, as in:

He said he would go to the meeting provided that I went with him.

and not used loosely for *if* as in:

I expect he will come tomorrow, provided that he comes at all.

Sometimes this misuse of *provided that* creates difficulties for a reader:

Such emoluments can only count as qualifying for pension provided that they cannot be converted into cash.

The use of *provided that* obscures the meaning of a sentence that would have been clear with *if*.

(x) *Than* tempts writers to use it as a preposition, like *but* (see p. 170), in such a sentence as 'he is older than me'. Examples can be found in good writers, including a craftsman as scrupulous as Mr Somerset Maugham. But some grammarians will not have it. According to them we must say 'he is older than I' (i.e. than I am). We may say 'I know more about her than him' if what we mean is that my knowledge of her is greater than my knowledge of him, but if we mean that my knowledge of her is greater than his knowledge of her, we must say 'I know more about her than he (does)'. Fowler, more tolerant, merely says that, since the prepositional *than* may cause ambiguity, it is to that extent undesirable. But it is so common a colloquialism that those who observe the stricter ruling risk the appearance of pedantry unless they add the verb.

But even the stricter grammarians recognise one exception – *whom*. We must say 'than whom', and not 'than who', even though the only way of making grammatical sense of it is to regard *than* as a preposition. But that is rather a stilted way of writing, and can best be left to poetry:

Beelzebub ... than whom, Satan except, none higher sat.

Be careful not to slip into using *than* with words that take a different construction. *Other*, *otherwise*, *else* and *elsewhere* are the only words besides comparatives that take *than.** *Than* is sometimes mistakenly used in place of *as*:

Nearly twice as many people die under 20 in France than in Great Britain, chiefly of tuberculosis.

(xi) *That.* For *that* (conjunction) see pp. 202–203.
(xii) *When.* It is sometimes confusing to use *when* as the equivalent of *and then*.

Let me have full particulars when I will be able to advise you. (Please let me have full particulars. I shall then be able to advise you.)
Alternatively the Minister may make the order himself when it has the same effect as if it has been made by the Local Authority.

*Other than is an oddity, originating perhaps in false analogy (as if *other* were a comparative like *better*). But in modern English it is the only acceptable construction. *Else* can take *than* but prefers *but*, whereas *elsewhere* prefers *than*. There is no logical accounting for any of this.

(. . . the Minister may make the order himself, and it then has the same effect, etc. . . .)

(xiii) *While*. It is safest to use this conjunction only in its temporal sense ('Your letter came while I was away on leave'). That does not mean that it is wrong to use it also as a conjunction without any temporal sense, equivalent to *although* ('While I do not agree with you, I accept your ruling'). But in this sense it can sometimes be ambiguous, as in:

While he is short of experience, he will do the job quite adequately.

And it should certainly not be used in both senses in the same sentence, as in:

While appreciating your difficulties while your mother is seriously ill. . . :

Moreover, once we leave the shelter of the temporal sense, we are on the road to treating *while* as a synonym for *and*:

Nothing will be available for some time for the desired improvement, while the general supply of linoleum to new offices may have to cease when existing stocks have run out.

There is no point in saying *while* when you mean *and*, and it is much better not to use it for *although* either.* If you are too free with *while* you are sure sooner or later to land yourself in the absurdity of seeming to say that two events occurred simultaneously which could not possibly have done so.

The first part of the concert was conducted by Sir August Manns . . . while Sir Arthur Sullivan conducted his then recently composed *Absent Minded Beggar*.

Careful screening by appraisal interviews would help to . . . while later interviews would provide a means . . .

*Some people make a distinction between *while* and *whilst*, using *while* only in its temporal sense and *whilst* for *and* or *although*. I see little harm in this; but *whilst* is an unnecessary word and many people pass blamelessly from cradle to grave without ever using it.

TROUBLES WITH NEGATIVES

(i) *Double negatives*. It has long been settled doctrine among English grammarians that two negatives cancel each other and produce an affirmative. As in mathematics $-(-x)$ equals $+x$, so in language 'he did not say nothing' must be regarded as equivalent to 'he said something'.

It is going too far to say, as is sometimes said, that this proposition is self-evident. The ancient Greeks did not think that two negatives made an affirmative. Nor do the modern French. Nor did Chaucer think so, for, in a much-quoted passage, he wrote:

> He never yit no vileineye ne sayde
> In al his lyf, unto no maner wight.
> He was a verray parfit gentil knyght.

Nor did Shakespeare, who made King Claudius say:

> Nor what he said, though it lacked form a little,
> Was not like madness.

Nor do the many thousands of people who find it natural today to deny knowledge by saying 'I don't know nothing at all about it'.

Still, the grammarians' rule should be observed in English today. This extract from a formal memorandum to a Select Committee of the House of Commons must be condemned as illiterate:

The time is not being used neither adequately nor efficiently.

Breaches of the rule are commonest with verbs of surprise or speculation ('I shouldn't wonder if there wasn't a storm.' 'I shouldn't be surprised if he didn't come today'). Indeed this is so common that it is classed by Fowler among his 'sturdy indefensibles'. A recent speech in the House of Lords affords a typical instance of the confusion of thought bred by double negatives:

Let it not be supposed because we are building for the future

175

rather than the present that the Bill's proposals are not devoid of significance.

What the speaker meant, of course, was 'Let it not be supposed that the Bill's proposals *are* devoid of significance'.

Another example is:

There is no reason to doubt that what he says in his statement ; ; ; is not true.

Here the speaker meant, 'There is no reason to doubt that his statement *is* true'.

And another:

It must not be assumed that there are no circumstances in which a profit might not be made.

Avoid multiple negatives when you can. Even if you dodge the traps they set and succeed in saying what you mean, you give your reader a puzzle to solve in sorting the negatives out. Indeed it is wise never to make a statement negatively if it could be made positively.

The elementary ideas of the calculus are not beyond the capacity of more than 40 per cent of our certificate students.

All our overseas posts do not report to this Division except for part of their work.

It is hard to say whether the first assertion is that two-fifths or three-fifths of the class could make something of the ideas. If the writer had said that the ideas were within the capacity of at least sixty per cent, all would have been clear. It is harder still to say what the second assertion is – perhaps it is that some overseas posts report only part of their work to this Division (whereas others report all of it); but whatever the meaning is there can be little doubt that it would have been clearer if expressed in positive rather than negative form.

The meaning of the following two examples is, in the end, quite clear, but only after more unravelling than the reader ought to be forced to undertake:

Few would now contend that too many checks cannot be at least as harmful to democracy as too few.

The Opposition refused leave for the withdrawal of a motion to annul an Order revoking the embargo on the importation of cut glass.

(ii) *Neither . . . nor.* Some books tell you that *neither . . . nor* should not be used where the alternatives are more than two. That is, you may write 'Neither blue nor red' but must not write 'Neither blue nor red nor yellow'. This is ridiculous. The famous passage

. . . neither death, nor life, nor angels, nor principalities, nor powers, nor things present, nor things to come, nor height, nor depth, nor any other creature, shall be able to separate us from the love of God . . .

is as good English today as it was three hundred years ago.

(iii) *Nor* and *Or.* When should *nor* be used and when *or?* If a *neither* or an *either* comes first there is no difficulty; *neither* is always followed by *nor* and *either* by *or.* There can be no doubt that it is wrong to write 'The existing position satisfies neither the psychologist, the judge, or the public'. It should have been 'neither the psychologist, nor the judge, nor the public'. But when the initial negative is a simple *not* or *no*, it is often a puzzling question whether *nor* or *or* should follow. Logically it depends on whether the sentence is so framed that the initial negative runs on into the second part of it or is exhausted in the first; practically it may be of little importance which answer you give, for the meaning will be clear.

He did not think that the Bill would be introduced this month, nor indeed before the recess.

'He did not think' affects everything that follows *that.* Logically therefore *nor* produces a double negative, as though one were to say 'he didn't think it wouldn't be introduced before the recess'.

The blame for this disorder does not rest with Parliament, or with the bishops, or with the parish priests. Our real weakness is the failure of the ordinary man.

The Complete Plain Words

Here the negative phrase 'does not rest' is carried right through the sentence, and applies to the bishops and the parish priests as much as to Parliament. There is no need to repeat the negative, and *or* is logically right. But *nor* is so often used in such a construction that it would be pedantic to condemn it: if logical defence is needed one might say that 'did he think it would be introduced' in the first example, and 'does it rest' in the second were understood as repeated after *nor*. But if the framework of the sentence is changed to:

The blame for this disorder rests not with Parliament, nor with the bishops, nor with the parish priests, but with the ordinary man,

it is a positive verb (*rests*) that runs through the sentence; the original negative (*not*) is attached not to the verb but to *Parliament*, and exhausts itself in exonerating Parliament. The negative must be repeated, and *nor* is rightly used.

(iv) *Not*.
(*a*) 'Not all'.
It is idiomatic English, to which no exception can be taken, to write 'all officials are not good draftsmen' when you mean that only some of them are. Compare 'All that glisters is not gold'. But it is clearer, and therefore better, to write 'Not all officials are good draftsmen'.
(*b*) 'Not . . . but.'
It is also idiomatic English to write 'I did not go to speak but to listen'. It is pedantry to insist that, because logic demands it, this ought to be 'I went not to speak but to listen'. But if the latter way of arranging a 'not . . . but' sentence runs as easily and makes your meaning clearer, as it often may, it should be preferred.
(*c*) 'Not . . . because.'
Not followed by *because* sometimes leads to ambiguity. 'I did not write that letter because of what you told me' may mean either 'I refrained from writing that letter because of what you told me' or 'It was not because of what you told me that I wrote that letter'. Avoid this ambiguity by rewriting the sentence.

178

TROUBLES WITH NUMBER

The rule that a singular subject requires a singular verb, and a plural subject a plural verb, is an easy one to remember and generally to observe. But it is extraordinary how often this simple rule is transgressed, even by educated writers with some pretensions to a high standard of writing. One would not expect to find two examples in successive paragraphs of an important White Paper (*The Reorganisation of Central Government*, 1970, Cmnd. 4506):

> Public administration and management in central government has stood up to these strains.
> The systematic formulation of policy and the presentation to Ministers of defined options for decision provides them with the opportunity for . . .

And when Mr Anthony Grey was nominated for a National Press Award as 'Journalist of the Year' one would not expect the formal citation to say that

> his refusal to submit to sustained pressures on mind and spirit were worthy of the highest traditions of journalism.

Other examples will be found on p. 289. But the rule has its difficulties.

(i) Collective words.

In using collective words or nouns of multitude (*Department, Parliament, Government, Committee* and the like), ought we to say 'the Government have decided' or 'the Government has decided'; 'the Committee are meeting' or 'the Committee is meeting'? There is no rule; either a singular or a plural verb may be used. The plural is more suitable when the emphasis is on the individual members, and the singular when it is on the body as a whole. 'A committee *was* appointed to consider this subject'; 'the committee *were* unable to agree'. Sometimes the need to use a pronoun settles the question. We cannot say 'The committee leaves its hats in the hall', nor, without risk of misunderstanding, 'The committee were smaller when I sat on them'.

But the number ought not to be varied in the same document without good cause. Accidentally changing it is a common form of carelessness:

> The firm *has* given an undertaking that in the event of *their* having to restrict production . . .
> The industry *is* capable of supplying all home requirements and *have* in fact been exporting.
> Any representative body must retain the right to represent *their* fellows as *it* thinks right.
> The Corporation *has* not asked for any advice . . . and I do not doubt *its* ability to deal with the immediate situation *themselves*.

Conversely a subject plural in form may be given a singular verb if it signifies a single entity such as a country (the United States has agreed) or an organisation (the United Nations has resolved) or a measure (six miles is not too far; twelve months is a long time to wait).

(ii) Words linked by *and*.

To the elementary rule that two singular nouns linked by *and* should be given a plural verb justifiable exceptions can be found where the linked words form a single idea. The stock example is Kipling's 'The tumult and the shouting dies'; 'the tumult and the shouting', it is explained, are equivalent to 'the tumultuous shouting'. But *die* would not have rhymed with *sacrifice*. Rhyming poets must be allowed some licence.

It is safer to observe the rule, and not to use the singular verb except where the linked words are so closely associated that they might almost be hyphened. 'Cut and thrust is the essence of good debating' is unobjectionable. Sometimes the singular verb is needed for clarity. 'Bread and butter is good for you' does not mean quite the same as 'Bread and butter are good for you'.

Other instances of singular verbs with subjects linked by *and* cannot be so easily explained away. They are frequent when the verb comes first. Shakespeare has them ('Is Bushy, Green and the Earl of Wiltshire dead?') and so have the translators of the Bible ('Thine is the kingdom, the power and the glory'). If we may never attribute mere carelessness to great writers, we must explain these by saying that the singular verb is more vivid, and should be understood as repeated with each noun – 'Is Bushy, (is) Green and (is) the Earl of Wiltshire dead?' Those who like to have everything tidy may get some satisfaction from this, but the writer of official English should forget about these refinements. He should stick to the simple rule. Examples of its unjustified breach will be found on pp. 179 and 207.

(iii) Words linked by *with*.

If the subject is singular the verb should be singular. 'The Secretary of State together with the Under-Secretary is coming'.

(iv) Alternative subjects.

Either and *neither* must always have a singular verb unless one of the alternative subjects is a plural word. It is a very common error to write such sentences as:

I am unable to trace that either of the items have been paid.
Neither knowledge nor skill are needed.

(v) When *each* is the subject of a sentence the verb is singular and so is any pronoun:

Each has a room to himself.

When a plural noun or pronoun is the subject, with *each* in apposition, the verb is plural:

They have a room each.

(vi) Attraction.

The verb must agree with the subject, and not allow itself to be attracted into the number of the complement. Modern grammarians will not pass 'the wages of sin is death'. The safe rule for the ordinary writer in sentences such as this is to regard what precedes the verb as the subject and what follows it as the complement, and so to write 'the wages of sin are death' and 'death is the wages of sin'.

A verb some way from its subject is sometimes lured away from its proper number by a noun closer to it, as in:

We regret that assurances given us twelve months ago that a sufficient supply of suitable local labour would be available to meet our requirements *has* not been fulfilled.

So far as the heating of buildings in permanent Government occupation *are* concerned ...

Comprehensive information about the work of the Ministry examiners and the results *are* already published by HMSO in the annual reports of the licensing authorities.

Sometimes the weight of a plural pushes the verb into the wrong number, even though they are not next to one another:

Thousands of pounds' worth of damage *have* been done to the apple crop.

In these sentences the italicised words are blunders. So is the common attraction of the verb into the plural when the subject is *either* or *neither* in such sentences as 'Neither of the questions have been answered' or 'Either of the questions were embarrassing'. But in one or two exceptional instances the force of this attraction has conquered the grammarians. With the phrase *more than one* the pull of *one* is so strong that the singular is always used (e.g. 'more than one question was asked'), and owing to the pull of the plural in such a sentence as 'none of the questions were answered' *none* has come to be used indifferently with a singular or a plural verb. Conversely, owing to the pull of the singular *a* in the expression *many a*, it always takes a singular verb. 'There's many a slip twixt cup and lip' is idiomatic English. In *a great many* and *a few*, on the other hand, the *a* has not prevailed; both require a plural verb ('a few win, a great many lose'). There is also the idiomatic 'a happy five years', 'a surprising 253 votes', where some such collective noun as *total* or *number* is to be understood ('a total of five happy years', 'the surprising number of 253 votes'). See *Number* on p. 184.

(vii) It is a common slip to write *there is* or *there was* where a plural subject requires *there are* or *there were*.

There was available one large room and three small ones.

Was should be *were*.

It is true that Ophelia said 'there is pansies'. But she was not herself at the time.

(viii) Phrases like *either or both* cause difficulty. *Either* needs a singular verb and *both* a plural one. But it would be absurd to write 'unless either or both of his parents is or are dead'; and still more so to write 'When either or both of his parents is or are away, he writes daily to him or her or them, as the case may be'. Unless the difficulty can be conveniently avoided by rearranging the sentence, it is best to let the matter be settled by whichever word is nearer to the verb, and write 'If either or both are dead' and 'Is either or both dead?'

(ix) Certain nouns are sometimes puzzling.

Agenda, though in form plural, has been admitted to the language as a singular word. Nobody would say 'the agenda for Monday's meeting *have* not yet reached me'. If a word is needed for one of the components of the agenda, say 'item No. so-and-so of the agenda', not 'agendum No. so-and-so', which would be the extreme of pedantry. If one is wanted for the plural of the word itself it must be *agendas* or *agenda papers*.

Data, unlike *agenda*, remains the plural word that it is in Latin.

Unless firm data is available at an early date . . .
Data that is four to twelve years old is of limited use.

These are wrong. *Is* should be *are*.

If a singular is wanted, it is usually *one of the data*, not *datum*. The ordinary meaning of *datum* is:

Any position or element in relation to which others are determined: chiefly in the phrases: *datum point*, a point assumed or used as a basis of reckoning, adjustment or the like – *datum line*, a horizontal line from which heights and depths of points are reckoned, as in a railroad plan . . . (Webster.)

The press is a medium of mass communication; so is radio; so is television. They are sometimes collectively called 'the mass media', or just 'the media'. But I have recently both seen and heard *the mass media* treated as singular ('the mass media is responsible for . . .'). This is, and will surely continue to be, inexcusable. The singular *medium*, unlike *agendum*, is in constant and unpedantic use; its plural can only be *media* and *media* can only be plural.

Means in the sense of 'means to an end' is a curious word; it may be treated either as singular or as plural. Supposing, for instance, that you wanted to say that means had been sought to do something, you may if you choose treat the word as singular and say 'a means was sought' or 'every means was sought'. Or you may treat it as plural and say 'all means were sought'. Or again, if you use just the word *means* without any word such as *a* or *every* or *all* to show its number, you may give it a singular or plural verb as you wish: you may say either 'means was sought' or 'means were sought'; both are idiomatic. Perhaps on the whole it is best to say 'a method (or way) was sought' if there was only one, and 'means were sought' if there was more than one.

Means in the sense of monetary resources is always plural.

Number. Like other collective nouns *number* may take either a singular or a plural verb. Unlike most of them, it admits of a simple and logical rule. When all that it is doing is forming part of a composite plural subject, it should have a plural verb, as in:

A large number of people are coming today.

But when it is standing on its own legs as the subject it should have a singular verb, as in:

The number of people coming today is large.

The following are accordingly unidiomatic:

There is a number of applications, some of which were made before yours.
There is a large number of outstanding orders.

The true subjects are not 'a number' and 'a large number' but 'a-number-of-applications' and 'a-large-number-of-out-standing-orders', and both these subjects require the plural verb *are*. Those who find these distinctions difficult to observe have an obvious way out of their difficulty – they should write *many* instead of *a large number of*. And even those to whom all is crystal-clear would often be well advised to do the same.

Of the following examples the first has a singular verb that should be plural and the second a plural verb that should be singular.

There was also a number of conferences calling themselves peace conferences which had no real interest in peace.

The number of casualties in HMS *Amethyst* are thought to be fifteen.

Those kind of things. The use of the plural *these* or *those* with the singular *kind* or *sort* is common in conversation, and instances of it could be found in good authors. But it has not yet quite established itself as a permissible idiom in good writing, and until it does so it is as well to humour the purists by writing *things of that kind.*

TROUBLES WITH PREPOSITIONS

(i) Ending sentences with prepositions.

Do not hesitate to end a sentence with a preposition if your ear tells you that that is where the preposition goes best. There used to be a rather half-hearted grammarians' rule against doing this, but no good writer ever heeded it, except Dryden, who seems to have invented it. The translators of the Authorised Version did not know it ('but I have a baptism to be baptised with'). The very rule itself, if phrased 'do not use a preposition to end a sentence with', has a smoother flow and a more idiomatic ring than 'do not use a preposition with which to end a sentence'. Sometimes, when the final word is really a verbal particle, and the verb's meaning depends on it, they form together a phrasal verb (see pp. 96–7) – *put up with* for instance – and to separate them makes nonsense. It is said that Sir Winston Churchill once made this marginal comment against a sentence that clumsily avoided a prepositional ending: 'This is the sort of English up with which I will not put'. The ear is a pretty safe guide. Over a hundred years ago Dean Alford protested against this so-called rule. 'I know', he said, 'that I am at variance with the rules taught at very respectable institutions for enabling

young ladies to talk unlike their elders. But that I cannot help.'
The story is well known of the nurse who performed the remarkable feat of getting four* prepositions at the end of a
sentence by asking her charge: 'What did you choose that book
to be read to out of for?' She said what she wanted to say
perfectly clearly, in words of one syllable, and what more can
one ask?

(ii) Cannibalism by prepositions.

Cannibalism is the name given by Fowler to a vice that prepositions are specially prone to, though it may infect any part
of speech. One of a pair of words swallows the other:

> Any articles for which export licences are held or for which
> licences have been applied.

The writer meant 'or for which export licences have been
applied for', but the first *for* has swallowed the second.

For circumlocutory prepositions (*in regard to* and the like)
see pp. 87–9.

(iii) Some particular prepositions.

(*a*) *Between* and *among*. The *OED* tells us – and no one needs
to be told twice – to ignore those who say that *between* must
only be used of two things and that when there are more the
preposition must be *among*. It goes on to say (and again we shall
all agree):

> *Between* is still the only word available to express the relation of
> a thing to many surrounding things severally and individually,
> *among* expressing a relationship to them collectively and vaguely:
> we should not say 'the space lying among the three points', or 'a
> treaty among three powers' or 'the choice lies among the three
> candidates in the select list' or 'to insert a needle among the closed
> petals of a flower'.

---

*There are really only three. *Out* is an adverb, forming, with *of*, a
composite preposition. Even the improved variant 'What did you bring
that book I don't like to be read aloud to out of from up for?' cannot
fairly be credited with more than the same three – *to*, *out of* and *for*.
From is a mere repetition of *out of* and *up* is an adverb going with *bring.*
I have never yet seen a genuine example of more than three. B.D.F.

The Handling of Words

(*b*) *Between each.* Grammarians generally condemn the common use of *between* with *each* or *every*, as in 'there will be a week's interval between each sitting'. It is arguable that this can be justified as a convenient way of saying 'between each sitting and the next', and that, considering how common it is, only pedantry can object. But those who want to be on the safe side can say either 'weekly intervals between the sittings' or 'a week's interval after each sitting'.

(*c*) *Between ... or* and *between ... and between.* If *between* is followed by a conjunction, this must always be a simple *and.* It is wrong to say 'the choice lies between Smith or Jones', or to say 'we had to choose between taking these offices and making the best of them and between perhaps finding ourselves with no offices at all'. If a sentence has become so involved that *and* is not felt to be enough it should be recast. This mistake is not unknown in high places:

It is thought that the choice lies between Mr Trygve Lie continuing for another year or the election of Mr Lester Pearson.

And in the following, more exotic, example we find *as opposed to* being used instead of *and*:

There is a distinction between giving local authorities a share in the proceeds of a local tax as opposed to making them free to fix their own tax rates for their own areas.

(*d*) For *between you and I* see *I and me* (pp. 194–5).

(*e*) *Due to.* *Owing to* long ago established itself as a prepositional phrase. But the orthodox still keep up the fight against the attempt of *due to* to do the same: they maintain that *due* is an adjective and should not be used otherwise. That means that it must always have a noun to agree with. You may say: 'Floods due to a breach in the river bank covered a thousand acres of land'. But you must not say: 'Due to a breach in the river bank a thousand acres of land were flooded'. In the first *due to* agrees properly with floods, which were in fact due to the breach. In the second it can only agree with a thousand acres of land which were not due to the breach, or to anything else except the Creation.

Due to is rightly used in:

The closing of the telephone exchange was due to lack of equipment. (*Due to* agrees with *closing*.)

The delay in replying has been due to the fact that it was hoped to call upon you. (*Due to* agrees with *delay*.)

Due to is wrongly used in:

We must apologise to listeners who missed the introduction to the talk due to a technical fault.

There was no play at Trent Bridge today due to the rain.

Not all students receive such instruction due to the lack of specialised staff.

Many readers feel very strongly against the 'incorrect' use of *due to*, common though it is. The sensible writer should therefore try to form a habit of using it correctly, though he may well feel that there are many points more worth his attention. However the battle finally goes, it will still be wrong to say that the reason for A is due to B (a form of 'overlapping' – see pp. 233–4): we must say either that A is due to B or that the reason for A is B. The writer of the following has got into a muddle:

Recent correspondence regarding the increased weight of coins carried in our pockets appears to be very much to the point. The main reason I feel however is not so much due to the 50p coin as due to the fact that there is no intermediate coin between 10p and 50p.

The second sentence of this reads more or less correctly if both its *due to*'s are omitted; but there are of course better ways of casting it, such as 'But I think the increased weight is mainly due, not to the 50p coin, but to the absence of any intermediate coin . . .' or 'But I think the main cause is not the 50p coin but the absence of . . .'

Perhaps the writer of the following was afraid of using *due to* and *owing to* wrongly; by avoiding both he fell into a different sort of error.

The developments which are described below have arisen more as a consequence of a creation of climate by X rather than by positive action on his part.

If he had formed the habit of using *due to* correctly he might have written '. . . are due more to the climate that X has created than to anything positive that he has done'.

(*f*) *Following*. Grammarians do not admit *following* as a preposition, though its use as one is becoming so common that they may soon have to give it *de facto* recognition. The ortho- dox view is that it is the participle of the verb *follow*, and must have a noun to agree with, as it has in:

Such rapid promotion, following his exceptional services, was not unexpected.

But as a preposition it is unnecessary when it usurps the place of *in consequence of*, *in accordance with*, *because of*, or *as a result of*, as in:

Following judgments of the High Court, Ministers of Religion are not regarded as employed under a contract of service.
It has been brought to my notice following a recent visit of an Inspector of this Ministry to the premises of . . . that you are an insured person under the Act.
Following heavy rain last night the wicket is very wet.

Still less can there be any justification for it with a merely temporal significance. It might perhaps put in a plea for a useful function as meaning something between the two – between the *propter hoc* of those prepositional phrases and the *post hoc* of *after*. This announcement might claim that justification:

A man will appear at Bow Street this morning following the destruction of Mr Reg Butler's statue of the Political Prisoner.

But the word shows little sign of being content with that rather subtle duty. More and more, under the strong lead of BBC announcers, it is becoming merely a pretentious substitute for *after*.

Following the orchestral concert, we come to a talk by Mr X.
Following that old English tune, we go to Latin America for the next one.

(g) *Prior to.* There is no good reason to use *prior to* as a preposition instead of *before*. *Before* is simpler, better known and more natural, and therefore preferable. It is moreover at least questionable whether *prior to* has established itself as a preposition. By all means use the phrase a *prior engagement*, where *prior* is doing its proper job as an adjective. But do not say that you made an engagement *prior to* receiving the second invitation.

Mr X has requested that you should submit to him, immediately prior to placing orders, lists of components. . . .

Sir Adrian Boult is resting prior to the forthcoming tour of the BBC Symphony Orchestra.

In sentences such as these *prior to* cannot have any advantage over the straightforward *before*.

Previous to as a preposition is perhaps less common than *prior to*. It is equally objectionable, and everything said above about the one applies to the other.

TROUBLES WITH PRONOUNS

'The use of pronouns', said Cobbett, 'is to prevent the repetition of nouns, and to make speaking and writing more rapid and less encumbered with words.' In more than one respect they are difficult parts of speech to handle.

(i) It is an easy slip to use a pronoun without a true antecedent.

He offered to resign but it was refused.

Here *it* has no true antecedent, as it would have had if the sentence had begun 'he offered his resignation'. This is a purely grammatical point, but unless care is taken over it a verbal absurdity may result. Cobbett gives this example from Addison:

There are indeed but very few who know how to be idle and innocent, or have a relish of any pleasures that are not criminal; every diversion they take is at the expense of some one virtue or other, and their very first step out of business is into vice or folly.

As Cobbett points out, the only possible antecedent to *they* and *their* is the 'very few who know how to be idle and innocent', and that is the opposite of what Addison means.

(ii) Be sure that there is no real ambiguity about the antecedent. This is more than a grammatical point; it affects the intelligibility of what you write. Special care is needed when the pronouns are *he* and *him*, and more than one male person has been mentioned. We must not make our readers guess, even though it may not be difficult to guess right. As Jespersen points out, a sentence like 'John told Robert's son that he must help him' is theoretically capable of six different meanings. It is true that Jespersen would not have us trouble overmuch when there can be no real doubt about the antecedent, and he points out that there is little danger of misunderstanding the theoretically ambiguous sentence:

If the baby does not thrive on raw milk, boil it.

Nevertheless, he adds, it is well to be very careful about one's pronouns.

Here are one or two examples, to show how difficult it is to avoid ambiguity:

Mr S told Mr H he was prepared to transfer part of his allocation to his purposes provided that he received £10,000.

The *his* before *purpose*s refers, it would seem, to Mr H and the other three pronouns to Mr S.

Mr H F saw a man throw something from his pockets to the hens on his farm, and then twist the neck of one of them when they ran to him.

Here the change of antecedent from the man to Mr H F and back again to the man is puzzling at first.

There are several possible ways of removing ambiguities such as these. Let us take by way of illustration the sentence, 'Sir Henry Ponsonby informed Mr Gladstone that the Queen had been much upset by what he had told her' and let us assume that the ambiguous *he* refers to Mr Gladstone. We can make the antecedent plain by

1. Not using a pronoun at all, and writing 'by what Mr Gladstone had told her'.
2. Parenthetic explanation – 'by what he (Mr Gladstone) had told her'.
3. The *former-latter* device – 'by what the latter had told her'.
4. By rewriting the sentence – 'The Queen was much upset by what Mr Gladstone told her, and Sir Henry Ponsonby so informed him'.
5. The device that Henry Sidgwick called 'the polite alias' and Fowler 'elegant variation', and writing (say) 'by what the Prime Minister had told her', or 'the G.O.M.' or 'the veteran statesman'.

It may safely be said that the fifth device should seldom if ever be adopted, and the third only when the antecedent is very close. For a particularly disreputable example of a pronoun with doubtful antecedents see the word *They* in line 17 of p. 304.

(iii) Do not be shy of pronouns.

So far we have been concerned in this section with the dangers that beset the user of pronouns. But we should be concerned also with the danger of not using them when we ought. Legal language, which must aim above all things at removing every possible ambiguity, is more sparing of pronouns than ordinary prose, because of an ever-present fear that the antecedent may be uncertain. For instance, opening at random an Act of Parliament, I read:

The Secretary of State may by any such regulations allow the required notice of any occurrence to which the regulations relate, instead of being sent forthwith, to be sent within the time limited by the regulations.

Anyone not writing legal language would have avoided repeating *regulations* twice; he would have put *they* in the first place and *them* in the second.

Ordinary writers should not allow themselves to become infected with pronoun-avoidance. If they do, the result is that what they write is often, in Cobbett's phrase, more 'encumbered with words' than it need be.

The examiner's search would in all cases be carried up to the date of the filing of the complete specification, and the examiner (he) need not trouble his head with the subject of disconformity.

The Ministry of Agriculture and Fisheries are anxious that the Rural Land Utilisation Officer should not in any way hinder the acquisition or earmarking of land for educational purposes, but it is the duty of the Rural Land Utilisation Officer (his duty) to ensure . . .

Arrangements are being made to continue the production of these houses for a further period, and increased numbers of these houses (them) will, therefore, be available.

Often the repeated word is embroidered by *such*:

. . . the admission of specially selected Public Assistance cases, provided that no suitable accommodation is available for such cases (them) in a home . . .

This also is no doubt due to infection by legal English, where this use of *such* is an indispensable device for securing economy of words. The draftsman, whose concern is to make his meaning certain beyond the possibility of error, avoids pronouns lest there should be an ambiguity about their antecedents, but escapes the need for repeating words of limitation by the use of *such* or *such . . . as aforesaid*. The rest of us need not usually be so punctilious.

But using *such* in the way the lawyers use it is not always out of place in ordinary writing. Sometimes it is proper and useful.

One month's notice in writing must be given to terminate this agreement. As no such notice has been received from you . . .

Here it is important for the writer to show that in the second sentence he is referring to the same sort of notice as in the first and the *such* device is the neatest way of doing it.

(iv) It is usually better not to allow a pronoun to precede its principal. If the pronoun comes first the reader may not know what it refers to until he arrives at the principal.

I regret that it is not practicable, in view of its size, to provide a list of the agents.

Here, it is true, the reader is only momentarily left guessing what *its* refers to. But he would have been spared even that if the sentence had been written:

I regret that it is not practicable to provide a list of the agents; there are too many of them.

(v) *Each other*. Grammarians used to say that *each other* is the right expression when only two persons or things are referred to and *one another* when there are more than two. But Fowler, quoted with approval by Jespersen, says of this so-called rule, 'This differentiation is neither of present utility nor based on historical usage'.

(vi) *Former* and *latter*. Do not hesitate to repeat words rather than use *former* or *latter* to avoid doing so. The reader probably has to look back to see which is which, and so you annoy him and waste his time. And there is no excuse at all for using *latter* merely to serve as a pronoun, as in:

In these employments we would rest our case for the exclusion of young persons directly on the grounds of the latter's moral welfare. (Their moral welfare.)

Remember that *former* and *latter* can refer to only two things and if you use them of more than two you may puzzle your reader. If you want to refer otherwise than specifically to the last of more than two things, say *last* or *last-mentioned*, not *latter*.

(vii) *I* and *me*. About the age-long conflict between *it is I* and *it is me*, no more need be said than that, in the present stage of the battle, most people would think 'it is I' pedantic in talk and 'it is me' improper in writing.

What calls more for examination is the practice of using *I* for *me* in combination with some noun or other pronoun, e.g. 'between you and I', 'let you and I go'. Why this has become so prevalent is not easy to say. Perhaps it comes partly from an excess of zeal in correcting the opposite error. When Mrs Elton said 'Neither Mr Suckling nor me had ever any patience with them', and Lydia Bennet 'Mrs Forster and me are such

194

friends', they were guilty of a vulgarism that was, no doubt, common in Jane Austen's day, and is not unknown today. (Jane Austen never allows her heroes or heroines to use it.) One might suppose that this mistake was corrected by teachers of English in our schools with such ferocity that their pupils are left with the conviction that such combinations as *you and me* are in all circumstances ungrammatical.

It is the combination of oneself with someone else that proves fatal. The official who wrote: 'I trust that it will be convenient to you for my colleague and I to call upon you next Tuesday' would never, if he had been proposing to come alone, have written 'I trust that it will be convenient to you for I to call upon you . . .'. A sure and easy way of avoiding this blunder is to ask oneself what case the personal pronoun would have been in – would it have been *I* or *me*? – if it had stood alone. It should remain the same in partnership as it would have been by itself.

The association of someone else with oneself sometimes prompts the use of *myself* where a simple *I* or *me* is all that is needed, e.g. 'The inspection will be made by Mr Jones and myself'. *Myself* should be used only for emphasis ('I saw it myself') or as the reflexive form of the personal pronoun ('I have hurt myself').

(viii) *It.* This pronoun is specially troublesome because the convenient English idiom of using *it* to anticipate the subject of a sentence tends to produce a plethora of *its*. A correspondent sends me this example:

It is to be expected that it will be difficult to apply A unless it is accompanied by B, for which reason it is generally preferable to use C in spite of its other disadvantages.

This, he justly says, could be put more effectively and tersely by writing:

C is generally preferable, in spite of its disadvantages, because application of A without B is difficult.

See pp. 293 and 294 for further examples of *it*-trouble.

(ix) *One*.

(*a*) *One* has a way of intruding in such a sentence as 'The problem is not an easy one'. 'The problem is not easy' may be a neater way of saying what you mean.

(*b*) What pronoun should be used with *one*? *His* or *one's*, for example? That depends on what sort of a *one* it is, whether 'numeral' or 'impersonal', to use Fowler's labels. Fowler illustrates the difference thus:

One hates *his* enemies and another forgives them (numeral).
One hates *one's* enemies and loves *one's* friends (impersonal).

But any sentence that needs to repeat the impersonal *one* is bound to be inelegant, and you will do better to rewrite it.

(*c*) 'One of those who . . .'. A common error in sentences of this sort is to use a singular verb instead of a plural, as though the antecedent of *who* were *one* and not *those* – to write, for instance, 'It is one of the exceptional cases that *calls for* (instead of *call for*) exceptional treatment'.

(x) *Same*. Four hundred years ago, when the Thirty-nine Articles were drawn up, it was good English idiom to use *the same* as a pronoun where we should now say *he* or *she*, *him* or *her*, *they* or *them*, or *it*.

The riches and goods of Christians are not common, as touching the right title and possession of the same, as certain Anabaptists do falsely boast.

This is no good reason for the present pronominal use of *the same* and *same*, which survives robustly in commercialese and still occasionally appears in official writing. This use of *same* is now by general consent reprehensible because it gives an air of artificiality and pretentiousness.

EXAMPLE	ALTERNATIVE VERSION
As you have omitted to insert your full Christian names, I shall be glad if you will advise me of same.	As you have omitted to insert your full Christian names, I shall be glad if you will let me know what they are.

With reference to the above matter, and my representative's interview of the 12th October, relative to same . . .

I enclose the necessary form for agreement and shall be glad if you will kindly complete and return same at your early convenience.

With reference to this matter and my representative's interview of the 12th October about it . . .

(For *same* substitute *it*.)

In the following sentence,

I am informed that it may be decided by X Section that this extra will not be required. I await therefore their decision before taking further action in an attempt to provide.

I like to think that the writer stopped abruptly after *provide*, leaving it objectless, in order to check himself on the brink of writing *same*. But he might harmlessly have written *it*.

(xi) *They* for *he or she*. It is common in speech, and not unknown in serious writing, to use *they* or *them* as the equivalent of a singular pronoun of a common sex, as in: 'Each insisted on their own point of view, and hence the marriage came to an end'. This is stigmatised by grammarians as a usage grammatically indefensible. The Judge ought, they would say, to have said 'He insisted on his own point of view and she on hers'. Jespersen says about this:

In the third person it would have been very convenient to have a common-sex pronoun, but as a matter of fact English has none and must therefore use one of the three makeshift expedients shown in the following sentences:
The reader's heart – if he or she have any. (Fielding)
He that hath ears to hear let him hear. (AV)
Nobody prevents you, do they? (Thackeray)

The official writer will be wise for the present to use the first or second, and not to be tempted by the greater convenience of the third, though necessity may eventually force it into the category of accepted idiom.

Whatever justification there may be for using *themselves* as

197

a singular common-sex pronoun, there can be no excuse for it when only one sex is referred to, as in:

The female manipulative jobs are of a type to which by no means everyone can adapt themselves with ease.

There is no reason why *herself* should not have been written instead of *themselves*.

(xii) *What*. *What*, in the sense of *that which*, or *those which*, is an antecedent and relative combined. Because it may be either singular or plural in number, and either subjective or objective in case, it needs careful handling.

Fowler says that its difficulties of number can be solved by asking the question 'what does it stand for?'

What is needed is more rooms.

Here Fowler would say that *what* means *the thing that*, and the singular verbs are right. On the other hand, in the sentence 'He no doubt acted with what are in his opinion excellent reasons', *are* is right because *what* is equivalent to *reasons that*. But this is perhaps over-subtle, and there is no great harm in treating *what* as plural in such a construction whenever the complement is plural. It sounds more natural.

Because *what* may be subjective or objective, writers may find themselves making the same word do duty in both cases, a practice condemned by grammarians. For instance:

This was what came into his head and he said without thinking.

What is here being made to do duty both as the subject of *came* and as the object of *said*. If we want to be punctiliously grammatical we must write either:

This is what (subjective) came into his head and what (objective) he said without thinking.

or, preferably:

This is what came into his head, and he said it without thinking.

(xiii) *Which*. The *New Yorker* of the 4th December 1948

quoted a question asked of the *Philadelphia Bulletin* by a correspondent:

> My class would appreciate a discussion of the wrong use of *which* in sentences like 'He wrecked the car which was due to his carelessness'.

and the answer given by that newspaper:

> The fault lies in using *which* to refer to the statement '*He wrecked the car*'. When *which* follows a noun it refers to that noun as its antecedent. Therefore in the foregoing sentence it is stated that the car was due to his carelessness, which is nonsense.

What is? Carelessness? is the *New Yorker*'s query.

Which shows how dangerous it is to dogmatise about the use of *which* with an antecedent consisting not of a single word but of a phrase. *Punch* has also provided an illustration of the same danger ('from a novel'):

> Mrs Brandon took the heavy piece of silk from the table, unfolded it, and displayed an altar cloth of her own exquisite embroidery . . . upon which everyone began to blow their nose. . . .

In the following example (which finds its place here because *whereupon* might as easily have been *upon which*) the antecedent is a phrase rather than a single word, but it is not the phrase that has actually been used: it is a phrase vaguely implied by what has gone before.

> The number of permissible absences by a member of the governing body [should] be only two per annum, whereupon the member shall be deemed to have vacated his office as Governor.

If this writer had thought out what he was trying to say he would have written:

> A Governor shall be deemed to have vacated his office if he is absent from more than two meetings in a year.

The fact is that this is a common and convenient usage, but needs to be handled discreetly to avoid ambiguity or awkwardness.

The required statement is in course of preparation and will be forwarded as soon as official records are complete; which will be in about a week's time.

Here it is unnecessary; the sentence can be improved by omitting the words 'which will be', and so getting rid of the relative altogether.

The long delay may make it inevitable for the authorities to consider placing the order elsewhere which can only be in the United States which is a step we should be anxious to avoid.

Here the writer has used *which* in this way twice in a single sentence, and shown how awkward its effect can be. He might have put a full stop after *elsewhere* and continued, 'That can only be in the United States and is a step we should be anxious to avoid'.

(xiv) *Which* and *that*. On the whole it makes for smoothness of writing not to use the relative *which* where *that* would do as well, and not to use either if a sentence makes sense and runs pleasantly without. But that is a very broad general statement, subject to many exceptions.

That cannot be used in a 'commenting'* clause; the relative must be *which*. With a 'defining'* clause either *which* or *that* is permissible.† When in a 'defining' clause the relative is in the objective case, it can often be left out altogether. Thus we have the three variants:

This case ought to go to the Home Office, *which* deals with police establishments. (Commenting relative clause.)

---

* These terms are explained on p. 244.

† At this point Gowers added 'but *that* is to be preferred'. His own practice complied with his precept. He did not use *that* in all his defining clauses by any means, but he did so more often than not. For my part, I find that I use *which* (or *who*) in defining clauses more freely than he did. I have omitted his statement that *that* is to be preferred, not because I think either his precept or his practice wrong, but because so firm a statement seems to me unnecessarily worrying to writers who are trying to be good, and the practice of good writers in this matter is, I think, changing. My amendments to Gowers' text give it a slightly different emphasis but I do not think he would seriously disagree with them. B.D.F.

The Department *that* deals with police establishments is the Home Office. (Defining relative clause.)

This is the case you said we ought to send to the Home Office. (Defining relative clause in which the relative pronoun, if it were expressed, would be in the objective case.)

There are still some people who try to insist that to use *which* or *who* in a defining clause is wrong, and that every such clause must have *that* (except of course where a preposition precedes the relative). There is no justification for this, and there never has been. *Which* and *who* in defining relative clauses have always been as good English as *that*. ('He that hath ears to hear', but also 'He who would valiant be'.) It is certain that insistence on *that* in all defining clauses gives an arid and affected impression. There are some sentences in which *that* comes more naturally, others in which it does not.

It is possible that *that* is becoming less common in good writing, particularly where the antecedent is personal. At the beginning of the preceding paragraph 'There are still some people *that* try to insist . . .' would not be wrong, but surely *who* is nowadays more natural. Yet it would be quite wrong to say that in modern usage *who* is always preferred to *that* if the antecedent is personal.

The matter has further ramifications. There is for instance the question of punctuation, which is dealt with on pp. 244–6. Again, it is not always easy to say whether the relative clause is defining or commenting; some partake of the nature of both. (In the last sentence but one I intended 'which is dealt with on pp. 244–6' as a commenting clause; but it would not be impossible to omit the comma and read it as a defining one.) And it is possible to identify a type which is best described neither as defining nor as commenting but as predicative ('the dog it was that died'); in such clauses *that* nearly always seems the more natural. See also pp. 291–2.

The truth is that for nearly all writers, whatever their level of excellence, the ear is a reliable guide. It will usually produce a sensible choice between *that* and *which* (or *who*) in a defining clause and it will never allow *that* in a commenting one. (I have found one or two commenting *thats* but they are so rare as to be classed as freaks.) The best advice that can be given on the whole subject of relatives in defining and commenting clauses is 'Don't fuss'.*

That is an awkward word because it may be one of three parts of speech – a conjunction, a relative or demonstrative pronoun and an adjective. 'I think that the paper that he wants is in that box' illustrates the three in the order given. More than one modern writer has tried the experiment of spelling the word differently (*that* and *thatt*) according to its function; but not all readers are likely to find this expedient helpful, and any official who used it would be likely to get into trouble.

It is a sound rule that *that* should be dispensed with whenever this can be done without loss of clarity or dignity. For instance, the sentence just given might be written with only one *that* instead of three: 'I think the paper he wants is in that box'. Some verbs seem to need a conjunctive *that* after them more than others do. *Say* and *think* can generally do without. The more formal words like *state* and *assert* cannot.

The conjunctive *that* often leads writers into error, especially in long sentences. This is a matter not so much of rule as of being careful.

It was agreed that, since suitable accommodation was now available in a convenient position, and that a move to larger offices was therefore feasible, Treasury sanction should be sought for acquiring them.

Here a superfluous *that* has slipped into the middle of the sentence.

All removing residential subscribers are required to sign the special condition, that if called upon to share your line that you will do so.

*Here is a sentence with four defining relative clauses: 'The quality that charms all women who know him is the effrontery that enables him to pay outrageous compliments which really ring true'. The possible permutations of *that* and *which* (or *who*) number sixteen. Of these you will probably agree that at least half seem perfectly natural, and this may convince you that 'Don't fuss' is sound advice. B.D.F.

The second *that* is another case of careless duplication.

As stated by the Minister of Fuel and Power on the 8th April, a standard ration will be available for use from 1st June, 1948, in every private car and motor cycle currently licensed and that an amount equivalent to the standard ration will be deducted. . . .

The draftsman of this forgot how he had begun his sentence. He continued it as though he had begun 'The Minister of Fuel and Power stated . . .' instead of 'As stated by the Minister of Fuel and Power'. The consequence was that he put in a *that* which defies both sense and grammar.

The Ministry allow such demonstrations only if the materials used are provided by the staff and that no food is sold to the public.

In this sentence the use of *that* for *if* is less excusable because the writer had less time to forget how he had begun.

Their intention was probably to remove from the mind of the native that he was in any way bound to work and that the Government would protect him from bad employers.

This example shows the need of care in sentences in which *that* has to be repeated. If you do not remember what words introduced the first *that*, you may easily find yourself, as here, saying the opposite of what you mean. What this writer meant to say was that the intention was to remove the first idea from the native's mind and to put the second into it, not, as he has accidentally said, to remove both.

(xv) *Who* and *whom. Who* is the subjective case and *whom* the objective. The proper use of the two words should present no difficulty. But we are so unaccustomed to different case-formations in English that when we are confronted with them we are liable to lose our heads. In the matter of *who* and *whom* good writers have for centuries been perverse in refusing to do what the grammarians tell them. They will insist on writing sentences like 'Who should I see there?' (Addison), 'Ferdinand whom they suppose is drowned' (Shakespeare), 'Whom say men that I am?' (translators of the Bible). Now any schoolboy can

see that, by the rules, *who* in the first quotation, being the object
of *see*, ought to be *whom*, and that *whom* in the second and
third quotations, being in the one the subject of *is*, and in the
other the complement of *am*, ought to be *who*. What then is the
ordinary man to believe? There are some who would have us
do away with *whom* altogether, as nothing but a mischief-
maker. That might be a useful way out, but *whom* will take
some killing. Shakespeare and the translators of the Bible have
their followers today, not only among journalists ('. . . a number of Members or candidates whom we believe can contribute
to the character of Parliament', 'He was not the man whom the
police think may be able to help them'), but also among distinguished writers such as Sir Winston Churchill ('moves made by
Republican malcontents to displace their leader by someone
whom they imagined would be a more vigorous President'), E.
M. Forster ('A creature whom we pretend is here already'),
Lord David Cecil ('West, whom he knew would never be seduced away from him') and Somerset Maugham ('Bateman
could not imagine whom it was that he passed off as his
nephew'). This usage is moreover defended by Jespersen.

Sometimes, though more rarely, the opposite mistake is
made :

A Chancellor who, grudging as was the acknowledgment he received for it, everyone knew to have saved his party.

And not even the most liberal grammarian would defend:

They find . . . younger children who have had their mother's care
since birth and whom, it seems to them, are preferred.

It has not yet become pedantic – at any rate in writing – to
use *who* and *whom* in what grammarians would call the correct
way, and the ordinary writer should so use them, ignoring the
vagaries of the great. He should be specially careful about such
sentences as:

The manager should select those officers *who* he desires should
sign on his behalf.
The manager should select those officers *whom* he authorises to
sign on his behalf.

The Handling of Words

There has been some argument about *who* should be authorised to sign on the manager's behalf.

Whoever baits a slightly different trap:

If the front door swings open for Mr Wilson it opens too for whomever else can hang on to those charismatic coat-tails.

There is no doubt that *whomever else* is wrong here. It is equivalent to *anyone else who*, and *whoever* is necessary.

(xvi) *Whose.* There used to be a grammarians' rule that *whose* must not be used of inanimate objects: we may say 'authors whose books are famous', but we must not say 'books whose authors are famous'; we must fall back on an ugly roundabout way of putting it, and say 'books the authors of which are famous'. This rule, even more than that which forbids the split infinitive, is a cramping one, productive of ugly sentences and a temptation to misplaced commas.

There are now a large number of direct controls, the purpose of which is to allocate scarce resources of all kinds between the various applicants for their use.

Here the writer, having duly respected the prejudice against the inanimate *whose*, finds that *controls the purpose* is an awkward juxtaposition, with its momentary flicker of a suggestion that *controls* is a verb governing *purpose*.* So he separates them by a comma, although the relative clause is a 'defining' one (see pp. 244–6), and the comma therefore misleading. In his effort to avoid one ambiguity he has created another. But sensible writers have always ignored the rule, and sensible grammarians have now abandoned it. You may use '*whose* inanimate' without any feeling of guilt, as in:

*Care should be taken to avoid the 'false scent' that comes from grouping words in a way that suggests a different construction from the one intended, however fleeting the suggestion may be. In the sentence:

'Behind each part of the story I shall tell lies an untold and often unsuspected story of hard work . . .'

the words 'I shall tell lies' irresistibly group themselves together until the eye has passed on. Never try to correct this sort of thing with a comma; always reconstruct. Consider also the mask of the bizarre behind on p. 306.

The hospital whose characteristics and associations link it with a particular religious denomination.

That revolution the full force of whose effects we are beginning to feel.

There has been built up a single centrally organised blood-transfusion service whose object is . . .

TROUBLES WITH VERBS

(i) *ing endings.*

Words ending in *ing* are mostly verbal participles or gerunds, and, as we shall see, it is not always easy to say which is which. By way of introduction it will be enough to observe that when they are of the nature of participles they may be true verbs (*I was working*) or adjectives (*a working agreement*) or in rare cases prepositions (*concerning this question*) or conjunctions (*supposing this happened*); if they are of the nature of gerunds they are always nouns (*I am pleased at his coming*) – or rather a hybrid between a noun and a verb, for you may use the gerund with the construction either of a noun (*after the careful reading of these papers*) or of a mixture between a verb and a noun (*after carefully reading these papers*). It is most confusing, but fortunately we are seldom called on to put a label on these words, and so I have preferred to give this section an indeterminate title.

Numerous pitfalls beset the use of *ing*-words. Here are some of them.

(*a*) Absolute construction.

This is, in itself, straightforward enough. The absolute construction, in the words of the *OED*, is a name given to a phrase 'standing out of grammatical relation or syntactical construction with other words'. In the sentence 'The chairman having restored order, the committee resumed', the phrase 'the chairman having restored order' forms an absolute construction.

But there is no absolute construction in the sentence 'The chairman, having restored order, called on the last speaker to continue'. Here *the chairman* is the subject of the sentence.

Because of a confusion with that type of sentence, it is a

curiously common error to put a comma in the absolute construction. See COMMA (iv) p. 246.

(*b*) Unattached (or unrelated) participle.

This blunder is rather like the last. A writer begins a sentence with a participle (which, since it is a sort of adjective,
must be given a noun to support it) and then forgets to give it
its noun, thus leaving it 'unattached'.

Arising out of a collision between a removal van and a fully
loaded bus in a fog, E.C.F., removal van driver, appeared on a
charge of manslaughter.

Grammatically in this sentence it was the van-driver, not the
charge against him, that arose out of the collision. He probably
did; but that is not what the writer meant.

Whilst requesting you to furnish the return now outstanding you
are advised that in future it would greatly facilitate . . .

Requesting is unattached. If the structure of this rather
clumsy sentence is to be retained it must run 'Whilst requesting
you . . . I advise you that . . .'

Many letters to the Press start with an unattached participle,
like *disagreeing* in the following example:

Sir,
Whilst not disagreeing with the authors of the *London and Cambridge Economic Bulletin*, present conditions require that emphasis
be given for the need for direct Government action to restore
profitability.

What the writer means is, 'I do not disagree with . . ., but
what really needs emphasising in present conditions is the need
for . . .' He may be a good economist, but he is not a good
writer. Note *given for* instead of *given to* (cf. p. 295). And later
in the same letter he writes 'Investment and production is bound
to stagnate . . . if . . .'

As I have said, some *ing*-words have won the right to be
treated as prepositions. Among them are *regarding*, *considering*,
owing to, *concerning* and *failing*. When any of these is used as

a preposition, there can be no question of its being an un-attached participle. There is nothing wrong with:

Considering the attack that had been made on him, his speech was moderate in tone.

If, however, *considering* were used not as a preposition-participle but as an adjective-participle, it could be unattached. It is so in:

Considering the attack on him beneath his notice, his speech was moderate in tone.

Past participles, as well as present, may become unattached:

Administered at first by the National Gallery, it was not until 1917 that the appointment of a separate board and director enabled a fully independent policy to be pursued.

The writer must have started with the intention of making the Tate Gallery (about which he was writing) the subject of the sentence but changed his mind, and so *administered* is left unattached.

Formal application is now being made for the necessary wayleave consent, and as soon as received the work will proceed.

Grammatically *received* can only be attached to work; and that is nonsense. The writer should have said 'as soon as this is received'.

(c) Unattached gerund.

A gerund can become unattached in much the same way as a participle:

Indeed we know little of Stalin's personality at all: a few works of Bolshevik theory, arid and heavy, and speeches still more im-personal, without literary grace, repeating a few simple formulas with crushing weight – after reading these Stalin appears more a myth than a man.

Grammatically 'after reading these' means after Stalin has read them, not after we have.

The use of unattached participles and gerunds is becoming so

common that grammarians may soon have to throw in their
hand and recognise it as idiomatic. But they have not done so
yet; so it should be avoided.

(*d*) Gerund versus infinitive.

In what seems to be a completely arbitrary way, some nouns,
adjectives and verbs like to take an infinitive, and some a
gerund with a preposition. For instance:

Aim at doing	Try to do
Dislike of doing	Reluctance to do
Capable of doing	Able to do
Demur to doing	Hesitate to do
Prohibit from doing	Forbid to do

Instances could be multiplied indefinitely. There is no rule; it
can only be a matter of observation and consulting a dictionary
when in doubt.

(*e*) The 'fused participle'.

All authorities agree that it is idiomatic English to write 'the
Bill's getting a second reading surprised everyone': that is to
say it is correct to treat *getting* as a gerund requiring *Bill's* to be
in the possessive. What they are not agreed about is whether it is
also correct to treat *getting* as a participle, and write 'the *Bill*
getting a second reading surprised everyone'. If that is a legitimate grammatical construction, the subject of the sentence,
which cannot be *Bill* by itself, or *getting* by itself, must be a
fusion of the two. Hence the name 'fused participle'.

This is not in itself a matter of any great interest or importance, though it has led to much strife among grammarians.
What is certain is that sometimes we feel one construction to
be the more idiomatic, and sometimes the other, and, in particular, that proper names and personal pronouns seem to demand the gerund. Nobody would prefer 'He coming (or Smith
coming) surprised me' to 'His coming (or Smith's coming) surprised me'. That is sure ground.

For the rest, it is always possible, and generally wise, to be on
the safe side by turning the sentence round, and writing neither
'the Bill getting, etc.' (which offends some purists) nor 'the

Bill's getting, etc.' (which sounds odd to some ears) but 'everyone was surprised that the Bill got a second reading'.

(ii) *Subjunctive.*

The subjunctive is the mood of imagination or command. Apart from the verb *to be*, it has no form separate from the indicative, except in the third person singular of the present tense, where the subjunctive form is the same as the indicative plural (*he have*, not *he has*; *he go*, not *he goes*). Generally therefore, in sentences in which the subjunctive might be fitting, neither the writer nor the reader need know or care whether the subjunctive is being used or not.

But the verb *to be* spoils this simple picture. The whole of the present tense is different, for the subjunctive mood is *be* throughout – *I be, he be, we be, you be* and *they be*. The singular (but not the plural) of the past tense is also different – *I were* and *he were* instead of *I was* and *he was*. In the subjunctive mood what looks like the past tense does not denote pastness; it denotes a greater call on the imagination. Thus:

'If he is here' implies that it is as likely as not that he is.
'If he be here' is an archaic way of saying 'if he is here'.
'If he were here' implies that he is not.

Twenty years ago one would have said that the subjunctive was dying, being superseded more and more by the indicative, and that its only remaining regular uses were:

(*a*) In certain stock phrases: 'Be it so', 'God bless you', 'come what may', 'if need be' and others.

(*b*) In legal or formal language: 'I move that Mr Smith be appointed Secretary'.

(*c*) In conditional sentences where the hypothesis is not a fact:

Were this true, it would be a serious matter.
If he were here I would tell him what I think of him.

(*d*) With *as if* and *as though*, if the hypothesis is not accepted as true, thus:

He spoke of his proposal as if it were a complete solution of the difficulty.

But in America usage (*b*) has never been confined to formal language; it is usual in such sentences as 'I ask that he be sent for', 'It is important that he be there', and even in the negative form 'he insisted that the statement not be placed on record'; in all these the custom in this country is to insert a *should*.

It is remarkable – for it seems contrary to the whole history of the development of the language – that under the influence of American English the use of the subjunctive is creeping back into British English, perhaps helped by the influence of German-American. The following examples from British writing are twenty years old:

No one would suggest that a unique, and in the main supremely valuable, work be halted.
Public opinion demands that an inquiry be held.
He is anxious that the truth be known.

Things have gone much further in the last twenty years, and it is now very common indeed to prefer *be* to *should be* in sentences like these.

But the American usage is by no means confined to the verb *to be*. One of my diplomatic correspondents has supplied me with the following, on which I cannot improve:

It was in 1954, I think, that President Eisenhower declared: 'It is important that we have an adequate supply of hydrogen bombs'. I pointed out to my American colleague that in English English this meant 'We have got an adequate supply and this is important'. He replied that no American could possibly interpret it in that way; to him it meant 'we have not got an adequate supply and it is important that we should acquire one'. (Of course he did not say 'we have not got', or even 'gotten', but 'we do not have'; but I have translated him into English for simplicity of comparison.) By now any verb can be found in the subjunctive: 'it was decided that the committee invite Professor X to give evidence' or, if the decision had been otherwise, 'it was decided that the committee not grant audience to Professor X'. Nor is the usage confined to such formal occasions: I have just seen, in a popular book on dieting, 'I recommended that he come down to 125–130 lbs'; and it is also verbal and colloquial, 'I suggested to Tony yesterday that he drop in for a drink this evening'.

As seems always to happen, a usage like this extends its triumphs from America to Britain. Here are two examples that caught my eye in the space of a week: from *The Times*, 'The Government should insist that the Northern Ireland Government implement reforms' and from a draft put up for my signature, 'In my view it is not necessary that he speak English'. I am convinced that before the century is out we shall all be using the subjunctive quite regularly as if (to quote G. M. Young) we had all been 'born in Marburg and cradled in Michigan'.

Such being the facts, what should be the recommendation to the official? Here I feel a little diffident by reason of my age: the First Secretary Commercial in my office who uses the subjunctive so fluently is 39 years old; to a man of 25 it is no doubt a matter of course. You can point out that it is always easy to avoid using the subjunctive: I altered 'necessary that he speak' to the more natural 'necessary for him to speak' almost automatically. In my opinion we should yield only gradually to the invasion and your recommendation should be to avoid using the subjunctive for three reasons:

(*a*) it still gives an air of stiffness and pomposity;

(*b*) it encourages the use of verbs in the passive rather than the active mood, with impersonal rather than personal subjects (contrast 'the committee decided to adjourn' with 'it was decided that the committee adjourn'), and this is generally undesirable on stylistic grounds;

and finally, and weakest of all,

(*c*) there are still some older people, perhaps senior officials in your own or other departments, who find this usage novel and disagreeable.

(iii) *Misuse of the passive.*

Grammarians condemn such constructions as the following, which indeed condemn themselves by their contorted ugliness:

The report that is proposed to be made.
Several amendments were endeavoured to be inserted.
A question was threatened to be put on the paper.
A sensational atmosphere is attempted to be created.

Anyone who finds that he has written a sentence like this should recast it, e.g. 'the proposed report', 'attempts were made to insert several amendments', 'a threat was made to put a question on the paper', 'an attempt is being made to create a sensational atmosphere'. 'Motion made: that the words proposed to be left out stand part of the question' is an ancient and respectable Parliamentary formula, but should not be allowed to infect ordinary writing. Even the House of Commons has now abandoned it in favour of 'that the amendment be made' – though on grounds of convenience rather than grammar.

Hope should not be used in the passive except in the impersonal phrase *it is hoped*. We may say 'It is hoped that payment will be made next week', or 'payment is expected to be made next week', but not 'payment is hoped to be made next week'. The phrasal verb *hope for*, being transitive, can of course be used in the passive.

(iv) *Omission of verb.*

Where a verb is used with more than one auxiliary (e.g. 'he must and shall go') make sure that the main verb is repeated unless, as in this example, its form is the same. It is easy to slip into such a sentence as:

The steps which those responsible can and are at present taking to remedy this state of affairs.

Can taking makes no sense. The proper construction is shown in:

The board must take, and are in fact taking, all possible steps to maintain production.

(v) *Shall* and *will.**

Twenty pages devoted to this subject in *The King's English* begin with the following introduction:

*With unusual diffidence I have assumed that since I am a Scot nothing I may say about *shall* and *will*, or about *would* and *should,* is likely to command any respect south of the Cheviots. I have therefore left these passages exactly as Gowers wrote them, except that I have cut out one of his examples of pedantry on the part of discredited grammarians; it seemed to me too silly to merit even condemnatory mention. B.D.F.

It is unfortunate that the idiomatic use, while it comes by nature to southern Englishmen (who will find most of this section superfluous), is so complicated that those who are not to the manner born can hardly acquire it; and for them the section is in danger of being useless. In apology for the length of these remarks it must be said that the short and simple directions often given are worse than useless. The observant reader soon loses faith in them from their constant failure to take him right; and the unobservant is the victim of false security.

The Fowlers' view in short amounts to this: that if anyone has been brought up among those who use the right idiom, he has no need of instruction; if he has not, he is incapable of being instructed, because any guidance that is short and clear will mislead him and any that is full and accurate will be incomprehensible to him.

Every English text-book will be found to begin by stating the rule that to express the 'plain' future *shall* is used in the first person and *will* in the second and third:

I shall go
You will go
He will go

and that if it is a matter not of plain future but of volition, permission or obligation it is the other way round:

I will go (I am determined to go, or I intend to go)
You shall go (You must go, or you are permitted to go)
He shall go (He must go, or he is permitted to go)

But the idiom of the Celts is different. They have never recognised 'I shall go'. For them 'I will go' is the plain future. The story is a very old one of the drowning Scot who was misunderstood by English onlookers and left to his fate because he cried, 'I will drown and nobody shall save me'.

American practice follows the Celtic, and in this matter, as in so many others, the English have taken to imitating the American. If we go by practice rather than by precept, we can no longer say dogmatically that 'I will go' for the plain future is wrong, or smugly with Dean Alford:

I never knew an Englishman who misplaced *shall* and *will*; I hardly ever have known an Irishman or Scotsman who did not misplace them sometimes.

The Irish and the Scots are having their revenge for our bland assumption that English usage must be 'right' and theirs 'wrong'.

Nevertheless the rule for the official must be to be orthodox on doubtful points of doctrine, and text-book orthodoxy in England still prescribes *shall* with the first person to express the plain future.

(vi) *Would* and *should*.

The various shades of meaning of *would* and *should* derive in the main from the primary ideas of resolve in *will* and of obligation in *shall*: ideas illustrated in their simplest form by 'he would go' (he was determined to go, or he made a habit of going) and 'he should go' (he ought to go).

As colourless auxiliaries, merely indicating the subjunctive mood, the text-book rule is that *should* is used in the first person and *would* in the second and third. *Should*, which is colourless in the first person, resumes its tinge of *ought* in the others: in 'If you tried you should succeed' it has a nuance not present in 'If I tried I should succeed'. But the rule requiring *should* in the first person is now largely ignored (compare *shall* and *will*); *would* and *should* are used indifferently. Even a Professor of Poetry can now use them for what seems to be merely elegant variation:

If we could plot each individual poet's development, we would get a different pattern with each and we would see the pattern changing. . . . We should notice Mr Auden, for example, breaking suddenly away from the influence of Thomas Hardy . . .

In such a phrase as 'In reply to your letter of . . . I would inform you . . .' *would* is not a mere auxiliary expressing the conditional mood; it retains the now archaic meaning of 'I should like to'. In general, however, I would deprecate the use of this expression on the ground that, since it is archaic, it cannot help being stiff.

'It would appear' and 'I should think' are less dogmatic, and therefore more polite, ways of saying 'it appears' and 'I think'.

(vii) *Split infinitive.*

The grammarians' well-known rule against splitting an infinitive means that nothing must come between *to* and the verb. Broadminded grammarians have described it as a bad name and a bad rule; and many people (including so good a writer as Bernard Shaw) have regarded it as a mere fetish, which it is not only permissible but laudable to flout. Yet it has so strong a hold on the popular mind that even those who advocate rebellion usually betray some prickings of conscience, by adopting either too apologetic or too defiant a tone.

The first edition of *Plain Words* recorded this conclusion:

Still, there is no doubt that the rule at present holds sway, and on my principle the official has no choice but to conform; for his readers will almost certainly attribute departures from it to ignorance of it, and so, being moved to disdain of the writer, will not be 'affected precisely as he wishes'.

The first edition of *The Complete Plain Words* did not quite recant, but gave qualified approval to a less austere view suggested by a correspondent:

. . . it is judicious for an official to avoid splitting whenever he can do so without sacrificing clarity, ease and naturalness of expression. But rather than make that sacrifice he should resolutely split.

I* see no great difference between these two precepts, for I believe that to split an infinitive is never necessary – well, hardly ever – in order to achieve clarity, ease and naturalness; and if that is so it is much better not to split, because of the offence which a split may cause to those readers who, rightly or wrongly, think that a split infinitive is a sure sign of illiteracy.

*Fraser speaking. I have no reason to think that Gowers would have disagreed with the view expressed in this paragraph. But it is not quite what he said; and because I think it is what needs to be said I have recast the rest of this section on the split infinitive so as to bring it out more clearly. B.D.F.

The words *I want to fully understand you* may well spring to
one's lips in conversation. *I want fully to understand you* is
clear but unnatural. *I want to understand you fully* is both clear
and natural; it may indeed spring as readily to one's lips in conversation as the split infinitive. It will offend neither conformist
nor rebel, and it is only sensible to conclude that it is the best
version of the three. In a longer sentence, such as *I want to fully
understand why grammarians talk such nonsense*, to put *fully* at
the end of the sentence is admittedly not the answer; but here it
would sit perfectly naturally after *understand*.

If a man thinks that he needs to occasionally split an infinitive
and therefore will not promise to never split one, he is entitled
to think so. But I would prefer him to say that he needs to split
an infinitive occasionally (or occasionally needs to split an infinitive) and therefore will not promise never to split one. Putting
it this way may even lead him to question what he has hitherto
thought.

I could support my thesis by many examples. I will select only
one. It comes from a very long sentence in a very long letter to
The Times from four distinguished Welshmen (two knights and
two bishops) who disliked certain proposals for changes in the
structure of local government:

. . . Cardiff . . . is only just emerging as a capital city in every sense
of the word and it is ludicrous to drastically reduce its powers at a
time when so many efforts are being made to unify . . .

Clearly there are several easy and natural ways of avoiding
this split infinitive, such as:

. . . it is ludicrous to reduce its powers drastically . . .
. . . to reduce its powers drastically is ludicrous . . .
. . . a drastic reduction in its powers is ludicrous . . .

But when you start trying over in your mind which is best you
can see that the split is unnecessary, not only because *drastically*
need not be where it is, but because it need not be there at all.
The sentence is stronger without it; for what the writers are
objecting to as ludicrous is not a drastic reduction in Cardiff's

powers but any reduction at all. (This is even clearer from the whole letter than it is from the extract.) Their words imply that though a drastic reduction is ludicrous a small reduction may be quite acceptable. Their split infinitive jerks the reader into noticing this implication; and if it is really what they meant I suspect that they will have split their supporters as well as their infinitive. If they had thought out more clearly what they meant they could have found a dozen better ways of saying it.

This example therefore illustrates not only the dictum that most split infinitives are unnecessary, but also the far more important dictum that where you find bad writing you are likely to find unclear thinking too.

Gowers wrote that the rule against splitting an infinitive is a bad rule because it increases the difficulty of writing clearly and makes for ambiguity by inducing writers to place adverbs in unnatural and even misleading positions. I agree that it certainly does have this effect, but nearly always, I think, unnecessarily. All too often a writer will avoid a split infinitive, with obvious effort, by adopting an unnatural order of words where a perfectly natural order is available to him.

In the first edition Gowers used an example about hailstones:

Some of the stones . . . must have been of such a size that they failed completely to melt before they reached the ground.

This is indeed ambiguous. Did the hailstones reach the ground completely frozen or incompletely melted? The second is probably what the writer meant, and he probably committed the ambiguity because he was scared of the split infinitive (*failed to completely melt*). But though I agree that this is a bad sentence I would not agree that the second meaning requires the split infinitive. It seems to me that the second meaning is clearly expressed, and most naturally expressed, by *failed to melt completely*, and the first by *completely failed to melt*. The writer was scared into unnaturalness and ambiguity when a much better escape-route was open. He would of course have done better still to recast the sentence so as to avoid any of these troubles, for instance by writing:

Some of the stones must have been too big to melt completely before reaching the ground.

or (if the other meaning is intended):

Some of the stones must have been too big to melt at all before reaching the ground.

Note, incidentally, that in both these versions the vague and faintly pompous phrase *of such a size that they failed to melt* has become *too big to melt* – a change for the better, surely.

The split infinitive taboo, leading as it does to the putting of adverbs in awkward places, is so potent that it produces an impulse to put them there even though there is not really any question of avoiding a split infinitive. The infinitive can be split only by inserting something between *to* and the word which, with *to*, forms the infinitive of the verb. Thus, *to fully understand* is a split infinitive. So is *to fully have understood*. But *to have fully understood* is not. The writer of the sentence 'They appeared completely to have adjusted themselves to it' almost certainly put the adverb in that uncomfortable position because he thought that to write 'to have completely adjusted' would be to split an infinitive. (But even if he did think that, why did he not put the adverb at the end of the sentence? This would have been far more natural and would have exposed him to no hurtful suspicions.) Many other examples can be found which suggest that the split infinitive taboo leads some people to think it wrong to put an adverb between any auxiliary and any part of a verb, or between any preposition and any part of a verb, even where there is no infinitive in the sentence at all.

A sensible writer should try to write correctly, but he should pay no attention to a mere grammarians' taboo which militates against simple, clear and natural writing. I therefore do not say that a split infinitive is never justifiable; but I do say that it is hardly ever the only natural way, or even the most natural way, of expressing what you mean. My advice therefore is that you should always try to avoid splitting your infinitives, not because you care about the taboo, but because you care about your reputation with your readers. There is nearly always an easy

and natural way of doing so. Before long you will be regularly
succeeding without even trying, and you will be writing much
more easily and acceptably as a result.

Gowers suggested that even the most vigorous rebel against
the taboo could hardly condone such a resolute crescendo of
splitting as the following:

> The tenant hereby agrees:
>   (i) to pay the said rent;
>   (ii) to properly clean all the windows;
>   (iii) to at all times properly empty all closets;
>   (iv) to immediately any litter or disorder shall have been made
> by him or for his purpose on the staircase or landings or
> any other part of the said building or garden remove the
> same.

Gowers was doubtless right. But surely this is a museum piece.
To improve it (which is easy) would be to spoil it. Like some
appallingly bad poem it acquires a weird beauty of its own, and
every successive reading increases our awe for its creator.

SOME POINTS OF IDIOM

AGREE

Following the example set by *approve*, *agree* is showing a
disposition to shake off its attendant prepositions *to*, *on* and
with, and to pose as a transitive verb. 'I agree your figures', 'We
must agree the arrangements for this', 'I agree your draft'.
Some correspondents would have me castigate this, but I do not
think there is any great harm in it. After all, the Chairman of
the meeting says 'Is that agreed?' not 'Is that agreed to?' and
his dutiful hearers murmur 'Agreed, agreed' rather than 'Agreed
with, agreed with'. It is true that established idiom requires 'I
agree with your figures', 'We must agree on the arrangements'
and 'I agree with' or (if from a superior) 'I agree to your draft'.
But the change has probably come to stay, and will be absorbed
into English idiom.

AVAIL

The proper construction is to avail oneself of something. Avoid the ugly passive construction such as 'this opportunity should be availed of'. 'Taken' or 'seized' or 'made use of' will do instead.

AVERSE and ADVERSE

It is usual to say *averse from*, though there is good authority for *averse to*. (What cat's averse to fish?) But *adverse* is always *to*.

CIRCUMSTANCES

It used to be widely held by purists that to say 'under the circumstances' must be wrong because what is around us cannot be over us. 'In the circumstances' was the only correct expression. But these purists have not prevailed. There is good authority for *under the circumstances*, and if some of us prefer *in the circumstances* (as I do), that is a matter of taste, not of rule.

COMPARE

There is a difference between *compare to* and *compare with*; the first is to liken one thing to another; the second is to note the resemblances and differences between two things. Thus:

Shall I compare thee to a summer's day?
If we compare the speaker's notes with the report of his speech in *The Times* . . .

CONSIST

There is a difference between *consist of* and *consist in*. *Consist of* denotes the substance of which the subject is made; *consist in* defines the subject.

The writing desks consist of planks on trestles.
The work of the branch consists in interviewing the public.

DEPEND

It is wrong in writing, though common in speech, to omit the *on* or *upon* after depends, as in:

It depends whether we have received another consignment by then.

DIFFER

In the sense of to be different, the idiom is to differ *from*.
In the sense of to disagree, it is either to differ *from* or to differ *with*, which you please.

DIFFERENT

There is good authority for *different to*, but *different from* is today the established usage. *Different than* is not unknown even in *The Times*:

The air of the suburb has quite a different smell and feel at eleven o'clock in the morning or three o'clock in the afternoon than it has at the hours when the daily toiler is accustomed to take a few hurried sniffs of it.

But this is condemned by the grammarians, who would say that *than* in this example should have been *from what*. *Different than* is, however, common in America.

DIRECT and DIRECTLY

Direct, although an adjective, is also no less an adverb than *directly*. To avoid ambiguity, it is well to confine *directly* to its meaning of *immediately* in time, and so avoid the possibility of confusion between 'he is going to Edinburgh direct' and 'he is going to Edinburgh directly'. Here are two examples, the first of the right use of *direct* and the second of the wrong use of *directly*:

Committees should notify departments direct of the names and addresses of the banks.

He will arrange directly with the authority concerned for the recruitment and training of technicians.

DOUBT

British idiom requires *whether* or *if* after a positive statement and *that* or *but that* after a negative.

I doubt whether he will come today.
I have no doubt that he will come today.

But in America *I doubt that* is common form.

EITHER

Either means one or other of two or more. Its use in the sense of each of two, as in:

> On either side the river lie
> Long fields of barley and of rye,

or in:

The concert will be broadcast on either side of the nine o'clock news,

is accepted idiom.

EQUALLY

Do not let *as* intrude between *equally* and the word it qualifies. Not *equally as good*, but *equally good*. Do not write 'This applies equally to A as to B'. *As* should be *and*.

FIRST and FIRSTLY

There used to be a grammarians' rule that you must not write *firstly*; your enumeration must be: *first, secondly, thirdly*. It was one of those arbitrary rules whose observance was supposed by a certain class of purist to be a hallmark of correct writing. This rule, unlike many of the sort, had not even logic on its side. Of late years there has been a rebellion against these rules, and I do not think that any contemporary grammarian will mind much whether you say *first* or *firstly*. Moreover, if you have chosen *first* it is perfectly permissible to do without the *-ly* words altogether and write *first*, *second*, *third*.

FIRST TWO

For more than a hundred years petty arguments have been carried on from time to time round the question whether one should say *the first two* or *the two first*. Some famous grammarians, notably Dean Alford and Jespersen, have supported *the two first*, but the majority of expert opinion is overwhelmingly against them. So *the first two* holds the field. But the point is not important. Everyone knows what you mean, whichever you say.

FOLLOWS (AS FOLLOWS)

Do not write *as follow* for *as follows*, however numerous may be the things that follow. 'The construction in *as follows* is impersonal, and the verb should always be used in the singular' (*OED*).

GOT

Have got, for *possess* or *have*, says Fowler, is good colloquial but not good literary English. Others have been more lenient. Dr Johnson said:

'He has got a good estate' does not always mean that he has acquired, but barely that he possesses it. So we say 'the lady has got black eyes', merely meaning that she has them.

And Dr Ballard has written: *

* *Teaching and Testing English*. The same writer's *Thought and Language* contains an even longer and more spirited defence of *got*.

What is wrong with the word? Its pedigree is beyond reproach. If the reader will consult the Oxford English Dictionary he will find that Shakespeare uses the word. So does Swift; Ruskin uses it frequently, and Augustine Birrell in *Obiter Dicta* asks 'What has the general public got to do with literature?' Johnson in his Dictionary gives possession as a legitimate meaning of the verb to get, and quotes George Herbert. Indeed he uses it himself in a letter to Boswell. The only inference we can draw is that it is not a real error but a counterfeit invented by schoolmasters.

When such high authorities differ, what is the plain man to think? If it is true, as I hold it to be, that superfluous words are an evil, we ought to condemn 'the lady has got black eyes', but not 'the lady has got a black eye'. Still, writing for those whose prose inclines more often to primness than to colloquialisms, and who are not likely to overdo the use of *got*, I advise them not to be afraid of it. The Americans have the handy practice of saying 'I have gotten' for 'I have obtained' and reserving 'I have got', if they use this word at all, for 'I possess'. But the usual way for an American to express an Englishman's 'I haven't got' is 'I don't have'.

HARD and HARDLY

Hard, not *hardly*, is the adverb of the adjective *hard*. *Hardly* must not be used except in the sense of *scarcely*. *Hardly earned* and *hard-earned* have quite different meanings.

Hardly, like *scarcely*, is followed by *when*, not by *than*, in such a sentence as 'I had hardly begun when I was interrupted'. *Than* sometimes intrudes from a false analogy with 'I had no sooner begun than I was interrupted'.

HELP

The expression 'more than one can help' is a literal absurdity. It means exactly the opposite of what it says. 'I won't be longer than I can help' means 'I won't be longer than is unavoidable', that is to say, longer than I *can't* help. But it is good English idiom.

They will not respect more than they can help treaties exacted from them under duress. (Winston Churchill, *The Gathering Storm*.)

Writers who find the absurdity of the phrase more than they can stomach can always write 'more than they must' instead.

HOPEFULLY, THANKFULLY, REGRETFULLY

A new use for *hopefully* has recently been introduced in America and is rapidly spreading in Britain. It can be illustrated by the following three sentences, referring to a cricket match:

The spectators waited hopefully for the rain to stop.
Hopefully our opponents will be dismissed before the tea interval.
Our team will start their innings hopefully immediately after tea.

In the first sentence *hopefully* is doing the ordinary job of an adverb in qualifying the verb: it tells us how the spectators waited. In the second it is used in the new way: it does not tell us how the opponents will be dismissed but how the speaker feels about it now. 'Our opponents will (we hope) be dismissed before the tea interval.' In the third we cannot tell which way it is being used: it could be equivalent to a parenthetical *we hope*, or it could be telling us that our side will certainly start their innings immediately after tea and will do so in a state of hope (that they will make the runs or that it will not rain again). But if the new use is intended the ambiguity could be avoided by putting a comma after *innings* or by putting *hopefully* at the beginning of the sentence.

This new use of *hopefully* has been lambasted on both sides of the Atlantic, but it continues to spread. It is of course quite illogical, but that is not fatal to its survival. Idioms are apt to be obstinately illogical (see pp. 160–61), and it seems to me that the new use of *hopefully* has now established itself as a new idiom. The careful writer is now faced with a new duty – to make sure that whenever he uses *hopefully* for either purpose he avoids any ambiguity about which use he intends.

More recently still, *thankfully* has adopted a similar course, taking the meaning *I am thankful to say* rather than *gratefully*.

Thus: *I accepted a drink thankfully* (normal use); *Thankfully some beer was still left* (new use); *Thankfully I at once quenched my thirst* (may be either).

Other adverbs may follow these examples before long. *Regretfully* is already sometimes used to mean *I regret to say*. But this is rather perverse, because *regrettably* is already available for this meaning. *Hopefully* and *thankfully* can at least claim to be filling a gap left by the absence of *hopeably* and *thankably*.

INCULCATE

One *inculcates* ideas into people, not people with ideas; *imbue* would be the right word for that. A vague association with *inoculate* may have something to do with the mistaken use of *inculcate with*.

INFORM

Inform cannot be used with a verb in the infinitive, and the writer of this sentence has gone wrong:

I am informing the branch to grant this application.

He should have said *telling*, *asking* or *instructing*. For the American use of *inform* without an object, see p. 270.

LESS and FEWER

The following is taken from *Good and Bad English* by Whitten and Whitaker:

Less appertains to degree, quantity or extent; *fewer* to number. Thus, *less* outlay, *fewer* expenses; *less* help, *fewer* helpers; *less* milk, *fewer* eggs.

But although *fewer* applies to number do not join it to the word itself: a *fewer* number is incorrect; say a *smaller* number.

Less takes a singular noun, *fewer* a plural noun; thus, *less* opportunity, *fewer* opportunities.

Here is a good example of the wrong use:

. . . including only a handful of West Indians and even less Asians.

Not only should *less* be *fewer*, but the metaphor of a handful is ill chosen in this context; *a few* or *very few* would have been better.

ORDER (IN ORDER THAT)

May or *might* are the words to follow 'in order that'. It is incorrect to write 'in order that no further delay will occur' or 'in order that we can have a talk on the subject'. And it is stilted to write *in order to* where *to* will serve equally well. Jack and Jill did not go up the hill in order to fetch a pail of water. English idiom recognises *so as to* and *so that they might* as alternative ways of expressing purpose. The American *so* without *that* ('so they could fetch a pail of water') is heard in conversation but is not yet established in written English.

OTHERWISE

This word, though an adverb, has had the odd experience of being used more and more as an adjective, a noun or a verb.

The adjective that *otherwise* dispossesses is *other*. This is exemplified in such a sentence as 'There are many difficulties, legal and otherwise, about doing what you ask'.

The noun or verb that *otherwise* displaces is whatever noun or verb has the contrary meaning to the one just mentioned. In:

I will say nothing about the reasonableness or otherwise of what you ask.

I have had one case which turned on the validity or otherwise of a Nigerian customary marriage.

We shall be glad if you will now confirm or otherwise your desire to avail yourself of our offer.

the words replaced are *unreasonableness*, *invalidity* and *deny*.

All these uses can be condemned as ungrammatical, and since it is just as easy in the first case to write *other* and in the others either to omit *or otherwise* or to substitute the appropriate noun or verb, there is no reason why one should not be on the safe side and do the grammatical thing.

Sometimes *other* gets its revenge, and supplants *otherwise*.

It is news to me that a sheep improves the land other than by the food fed through it.

. . . decisions . . . taken other than in the context of a coherent development/conservation strategy for the whole region.

PREFER

You may say 'He prefers writing to dictating' or 'he prefers to write rather than to dictate', but not 'he prefers to write than to dictate'.

PREVENT

You may choose any one of three constructions with *prevent*: *prevent him from coming*, *prevent him coming* and *prevent his coming*. The first usually sounds the most natural.

PURPORT (verb)

The ordinary meaning of this verb is 'to profess or claim by its tenor', e.g. 'this letter purports to be written by you'. The use of the verb in the passive is an objectionable and unnecessary innovation. 'Statements which were purported to have been official confirmed the rumours' should be 'statements which purported to be official confirmed the rumours'.

REGARD

Unlike *consider*, *count* and *deem*, *regard* requires an *as* in such a sentence as 'I regard it as an honour'.

REQUIRE

Require should not be used as an intransitive verb in the sense of *need* as it is in:

You do not require to do any stamping unless you wish (you need not).

Special arrangements require to be worked out in the light of local circumstances (special arrangements will have to be . . .).

SUBSTITUTE

To *substitute* means to put a person or thing in the place of another; it does not mean to take the place of another. When *A* is removed and *B* is put in its place, *B* is substituted for *A* and *A* is replaced by *B*. *Substitute* is wrongly used in:

The Minister said he hoped to substitute coarse grain with home-grown barley.

The Minister ought either to have used the verb *replace*, or, if he insisted on the verb *substitute*, to have said 'to substitute home-grown barley for coarse grain'.

SUCH and SO

It will take some time to unravel such a complicated case.
So complicated a case will take some unravelling.

Both these constructions are good English. There are those who say that the first is ungrammatical, and that we ought always to use the second. But if we choose to regard them as pedants we shall have Fowler on our side, and so cannot be far wrong. Sometimes one construction flows more easily, sometimes the other. Thus, it would not be wrong, but most people would find it less natural, to use 'so complicated a case' in the first of these sentences and 'such a complicated case' in the second.

TRY

Try and is well established in conversational use. *Try to* is to be preferred in serious writing.

UNEQUAL

The idiom is unequal *to*, not *for*, a task.

VERY

One of the most popular objects of the chase among amateur hunters of so-called grammatical mistakes used to be *very* with a past participle – 'very pleased', for instance. It is true that *very* cannot be used grammatically with a past participle – that one cannot, for instance, say 'The effect was very enhanced'; we must say *much* or *greatly*. But when the participle is no longer serving as a verb, and has become in effect an adjective, it is legitimate to use *very* with it as with any other adjective. There can be no objection to 'very pleased', which means no more than 'very glad', or to 'very annoyed', which means no more than 'very angry'. But it will not do to say 'very inconvenienced' or 'very removed', and in between are doubtful cases where it will be as well to be on the safe side and refrain from *very*.

WORTH

Worth has a prepositional force, and needs an object. This object may be either *while* (i.e. the spending of time) or something else. It is therefore correct to say 'this job is worth while'; it is also correct to say 'this job is worth doing'. But one object is enough, and so it is wrong to say 'this job is worth while doing'.

Worth-while as an adjective ('a worth-while job') needs its hyphen. (See p. 256.)

SOME COMMON CAUSES OF
CONFUSED EXPRESSION

Confusion between more and less

It is curiously easy to say the opposite of what one means when making comparisons of quantity, time or distance, especially if they are negative. A common type of this confusion is to be found in such statements as 'Meetings will be held at not less than monthly intervals', when what is meant is that the meetings will be not less frequent than once a month, that is to say, at not more than monthly intervals. A similar confusion led during the war to the issue of a Control of Maps Order prohibiting the sale of maps drawn to a scale greater than one mile to the inch, instead of greater than one inch to the mile, as was intended.

Much more and *much less* sometimes get transposed, as do *most of all* and *least of all*. Short sentences present little difficulty.

He cannot walk, much less run.
I dislike cats, most of all Siamese.

But in longer sentences the writer sometimes goes astray, as in:

He finds it difficult to walk slowly on level ground, much less run up a hill with a pack on his back.

I do not approve of cats treating me as an intruder in my own house, most of all those horrible Siamese.

Maximum and *minimum* sometimes cause a similar confusion, leading to the use of one for the other. An example is the following sentence, which is taken from a passage deprecating the wounding of wild animals by taking too long shots at them:

It would be impossible to attempt to regulate shooting by laying down minimum ranges and other details of that sort.

It would indeed.

Another correspondent sends, as an instance of ambiguity of a similar kind,

On the mainland of Ross the population has been more than halved in the past twenty years.

Though not actually ambiguous, this is certainly not the clearest way of saying that the population has fallen to less than half.

Expression of multiples

We learn at an early age that if we want to declare one figure to be a multiple of another the proper way of doing so is to say that the first is so many times the second, 'Nine is three times three'. But in later life some of us seem to forget this and to say 'Nine is three times greater (or three times more) than three'. Not only is this an unnecessary distortion of a simple idiom, but a stickler for accuracy might say even that it was misleading: the figure that is three times greater (or more) than three is not nine but twelve. I was moved to these reflections by the following passage:

The figure set for the production of iron ore in 1955 is 3,500,000 tons, more than twelve times greater than in 1936; for pig-iron it is

2,000,000 tons, ten times greater than in 1936; for cement 4,000,000 tons, twice as much as in 1936.

The writer of this seems to have forgotten the formula of his multiplication tables until reminded of it by finding himself up against the awkwardness of having to say 'twice greater'. Confusion is even more likely to be caused if percentages are used. 'Production was 250 per cent greater than in 1928' leaves the reader guessing whether it was $2\frac{1}{2}$ times or $3\frac{1}{2}$ times as great.

Overlapping

By this I mean a particular form of what the grammarians call *tautology*, *pleonasm* or *redundancy*. Possible varieties are infinite, but the commonest example is writing 'the reason for this is because . . .' instead of either 'this is because' or 'the reason for this is that . . .', as in the first of these examples.

The Ministry of Food say that the reason for the higher price of the biscuits is because the cost of chocolate has increased.

The subject of the talk tonight will be about. . . . (A confusion between 'the subject will be . . .' and 'the talk will be about . . .')

The reason for the long delay appears to be due to the fact that the medical certificates went astray. (A confusion between 'the reason is that the certificates went astray' and 'the delay is due to the fact that the certificates went astray'.)

The cause of the delay is due to the shortage of materials. (A confusion between 'the cause of the delay is the shortage' and 'the delay is due to the shortage'.)

By far the greater majority . . . (A confusion between 'the great majority' and 'by far the greater part'.)

He did not say that all actions for libel or slander were never properly brought. (A confusion between 'that all actions . . . were improperly brought' and 'that actions . . . were never properly brought'.)

An attempt will be made this morning to try to avert the threatened strike. (Those who were going to do this might have attempted to do it or tried to do it. But merely to attempt to try seems rather half-hearted.)

Save only in exceptional circumstances will any further development be contemplated. (A confusion between 'only in exceptional circumstances will any further development be contemplated' and 'save in exceptional circumstances no further development will be contemplated'.)

The common fault of duplicating either the future or the past is a form of this error.

The most probable thing will be that they will be sold in a Government auction.

This should be 'The most probable thing is that they will be'.

The Minister said he would have liked the Government of Eire to have offered us butter instead of cream.

This should be 'he would have liked the Government of Eire to offer . . ;'

Qualification of absolutes

Certain adjectives and adverbs cannot properly be qualified by such words as *more, less, very, rather*, because they do not admit of degrees. *Unique* is the outstanding example. When we say a thing is *unique* we mean that there is nothing else of its kind in existence; *rather unique* is meaningless. But we can of course say *almost unique*.

It is easy to slip into pedantry here, and to condemn the qualification of words which are perhaps strictly absolutes but are no longer so treated – *true*, for instance, and *empty* and *full*. We ought not to shrink from saying 'very true', or 'the hall was even emptier today than yesterday' or 'this cupboard is fuller than that'. But this latitude must not be abused. It is strained when an official circular defines 'draining a bulk tank' as 'removing the liquid contents that remain after emptying'; it is certainly carried too far in this quotation:

It may safely be said that the design of sanitary fittings has now reached a high degree of perfection.

Nor should we condone the expression *more or less wholly*, even though I found it in a book on style by an eminent contemporary man of letters. Nor does the comparative seem happily chosen in *more virgin*, which a correspondent tells me he has seen in an advertisement.

Repetition

Pronouns were invented to avoid the necessity of repeating nouns. The section on PRONOUNS (pp. 190–206) deals with this subject, and also with the device known as 'the polite alias' or 'elegant variation'.

Unnecessary repetition of a word is irritating to a reader. If it can be avoided in a natural way it should. For instance, in the sentence 'The Minister has considered this application, and considers that there should be a market in Canada', the repetition of 'consider' gives the sentence a clumsy and careless air. The second one might just as well have been 'thinks'. It would have been easy also to avoid the ugly repetition of *essential* in the sentence 'It is essential that the Minister should have before him outline programmes of essential works'; or of *further* in the sentence 'Meanwhile I do not think there is anything further we can do to further the project at this stage'. But where the same thing or act is repeatedly mentioned, it is better to repeat a word than to avoid it in a laboured and obvious way.

Irritating repetition of a sound (assonance) is usually mere carelessness.

The controversy as to which agency should perform the actual contractual work of erection of houses.

Reverting to the subject of the letter the latter wrote. . . (This is indefensible because it could so easily be avoided by calling 'the latter' by name.)

Since a certain amount of uncertainty still appears to exist. (This is not even true, for I feel sure that what really existed was an uncertain amount of uncertainty.)

A FEW POINTS OF SPELLING

AUTARCHY

Autarchy means absolute sovereignty. *Autarky* (sometimes mis-spelt *autarchy*) means self-sufficiency. The difference in spelling reflects the different Greek words from which they are derived.

CONNECTION, CONNEXION

Both spellings are permissible.

CONSENSUS

The spelling *concensus* is wrong. A consensus is the result of common consent; it has nothing to do with censuses.

DEPENDANT

In the ordinary usage of today *dependant* is a noun meaning 'a person who depends on another for support, position, etc.' (*OED*). *Dependent* is an adjective meaning relying on or subject to something else. Dependants are dependent on the person whose dependants they are.

ENQUIRY

Enquiry and *inquiry* have long existed together as alternative spellings of the same word. In America *inquiry* is dislodging *enquiry* for all purposes. In England a useful distinction is developing: *enquiry* is used for asking a question and *inquiry* for making an investigation. Thus you might enquire what time the inquiry begins.

FOREGO

To *forego* is to go before (the foregoing provisions of this Act.) To *forgo* is to go without, to waive (he will forgo his right).

ISE OR IZE

On the question whether verbs like *organise* and nouns like *organisation* should be spelt with an *s* or a *z* the authorities differ. There are some verbs (e.g. *advertise*, *comprise*, *despise*, *advise*, *exercise* and *surmise*) which are never spelt with a *z* in this country. There are others (such as *organize*) for which many people, particularly if they have had a classical education, prefer a *z*; but the latest authorities incline to the view that in these cases *s* is permissible. This being so, the simplest course is to use an *s* in all cases, for that will never be wrong, whereas *z* sometimes will be. But do not condemn those who use a *z* in its right place.*

LOTH, LOATH

This adjective means *unwilling* and the dictionaries allow both spellings for it. But it is better to stick to *loth*, just to show that you are clear about the difference between the adjective *loth* and the verb *to loathe* (meaning *to detest*).

---

*Fowler's more austere view was that *ize* should always be used where the verb has been formed by using the suffix equivalent to the Greek suffix *-izein* (which retained its *z* when Latinised), but that *ise* should continue to be always used for words such as those quoted above which have been formed in a different way. Gowers specifically rejected this view in *The Complete Plain Words* but allowed it to stand in his revised edition of Fowler's *Modern English Usage*. His first, more permissive view is, I think, clearly preferable. I cannot regard *realise* or *Latinise* as wrong. B.D.F.

10

PUNCTUATION

> That learned men are well known to disagree on this subject
> of punctuation is in itself a proof, that the knowledge of it, in
> theory and practice, is of some importance. I myself have
> learned by experience, that, if ideas that are difficult to under-
> stand are properly separated, they become clearer; and that,
> on the other hand, through defective punctuation, many pas-
> sages are confused and distorted to such a degree, that some-
> times they can with difficulty be understood, or even cannot be
> understood at all.

> ALDUS MANUTIUS. *Interpungendi ratio*, 1466. From the
> translation in *Punctuation, its Principles and Practice* by T. F.
> and M. F. A. Husband (Routledge, 1905).

THIS is a large subject. Whole books have been written about
it, and it is still true, as it apparently was 500 years ago, that no
two authorities completely agree. Taste and common sense are
more important than any rules; you put in stops to help your
reader to understand you, not to please grammarians. And you
should try so to write that he will understand you with a minimum of help of that sort. Fowler said:

> It is a sound principle that as few stops should be used as will do
> the work. . . Everyone should make up his mind not to depend on
> his stops. They are to be regarded as devices, not for saving him
> the trouble of putting his words in the order that naturally gives the
> required meaning, but for saving his reader the moment or two
> that would sometimes, without them, be necessarily spent on reading
> the sentence twice over, once to catch the general arrangement, and
> again for the details. It may almost be said that what reads wrongly
> if the stops are removed is radically bad; stops are not to alter the
> meaning, but merely to show it up. Those who are learning to write
> should make a practice of putting down all they want to say without
> stops first. What then, on reading over, naturally arranges itself
> contrary to the intention should not be punctuated, but altered; and
> the stops should be as few as possible consistently with the recog-
> nised rules.

Punctuation

The symbols we shall have to consider in this chapter are the apostrophe, colon, comma, dash, full stop, hyphen, inverted commas, question mark, semicolon. It will also be a suitable place to say something about capital letters, paragraphs, parentheses and sentences.*

APOSTROPHE

The only uses of the apostrophe that call for notice are (*a*) its use to denote the possessive of names ending in *s* and of pronouns, (*b*) its use before a final *s* to show that the *s* is forming the plural of a word or symbol not ordinarily admitting of a plural and (*c*) its use with a defining plural (e.g. *Ten years' imprisonment*).

(*a*) There is no universally accepted code of rules governing

---

*Fashion in punctuation changes much more slowly than fashion in the use of language, and this chapter seemed to me to need less revision than any of the preceding ones. I have brought a few passages up to date; for instance, in the section on hyphens Gowers referred his readers to Fowler's elaborate article in the original *Modern English Usage*, and I refer mine to the much shorter and much more sensible article which replaces it in Gowers' revision of that work. Otherwise I have left the chapter virtually as Gowers wrote it; for he seems to me consistently right, whether he is giving a ruling or stating a preference or leaving the matter completely open.

But it is impossible to revise a book thoroughly without noticing the author's own punctuation habits; and I have noticed that Gowers' practice differs in some respects from mine. For instance, I am more sparing of commas between co-ordinate clauses; I share his affection for the semicolon but I am sure I use the colon more freely than he did; and I sometimes find myself using a pair of dashes or a pair of brackets where he would (I think) have used a pair of commas. I do not think these differences would have incurred his disapproval, and I have not attempted, in writing new material for this book, to adapt my usual practice to his; nor of course have I presumed to adapt his to mine. I hope the differences will not be obvious to the reader, for I believe that a mark of sound punctuation is that the reader does not notice it; and I trust that my punctuation, though slightly different from Gowers', is no more obtrusive and no less 'correct'. B.D.F.

the formation of the possessive case of names ending in *s*. Logic would insist on adding another *s* as well as an apostrophe; and this is certainly the commonest practice with monosyllables – Mr Jones's room, St James's Street, not Mr Jones' room, St James' Street. But with longer names some people sometimes let an apostrophe do the job alone. For an example see the footnote on the previous page. It matters little.

As to pronouns, all these except the pronoun *one* dispense with an apostrophe in their possessive cases – *hers*, *yours*, *theirs*, *ours* and *its*, but *one's*, not *ones*. *It's* is not the possessive of *it* but a contraction of *it is*: the apostrophe is performing its normal duty of showing that a letter has been omitted.

(*b*) Whether an apostrophe should be used to denote the plural of a word or symbol that does not ordinarily make a plural depends on whether the plural is readily recognisable as such. Unless the reader really needs help it should not be thrust upon him. It is clearly justified with single letters: 'there are two o's in woolly'; 'mind your p's and q's'. Otherwise it is rarely called for. It should not be used with contractions (e.g. MPs) or merely because what is put into the plural is not a noun. Editors of Shakespeare do without it in 'Tellest thou me of ifs', and Rudyard Kipling did not think it necessary in:

> One million Hows, two million Wheres,
> And seven million Whys.

(*c*) Whether one should use an apostrophe in such expressions as 'Ten years imprisonment' is a disputed and not very important point. The answer seems to be that if *ten years* is regarded as a descriptive genitive (like *busman's* in *busman's holiday*) we must write *years'*; if as an adjectival phrase there must be no apostrophe but the words must be hyphened (see HYPHEN). In the singular (*a year's imprisonment*) *year's* can only be a descriptive genitive.

In such phrases as *games master* and *customs examination*, *games* and *customs* are clearly adjectival, and need no apostrophe.

Punctuation

CAPITALS

Several correspondents have asked me to say something about the use of capital letters. The difficulty is to know what to say. No one needs telling that capitals are used for the first letter in every sentence, for proper names, for the names of the months and days and for the titles of books and newspapers. The only difficulty is with words that are sometimes written with capitals and sometimes not. Here there can be no general rule; everyone must do what he thinks most fitting. But two pieces of advice may perhaps be given:

(i) Use a capital for the particular and a small letter for the general. Thus:

It is a street leading out of Oxford Street.
I have said something about this in Chapter 1; I shall have more to say in later chapters.
In this case the Judge went beyond a judge's proper functions.
Many parliaments have been modelled on our Parliament.

(ii) Whatever practice you adopt, be consistent throughout any document you are writing.

COLON

About the use of the colon there is even less agreement among the authorities than about the use of other stops. All agree that its systematic use as one of a series of different pause-values has almost died out with the decay of formal periods. But some hold that it is still useful as something less than a full stop and more than a semicolon; others deny it. Into this we need not enter; it will be enough to note that the following uses are generally recognised as legitimate:

(*a*) To mark more sharply than a semicolon would the anti-thesis between two sentences.

In peace-time the Civil Service is a target of frequent criticism: in war-time criticism is very greatly increased.

In some cases the executive carries out most of the functions: in others the delegation is much less extensive.

(*b*) To precede an explanation or particularisation or to introduce a list or series: in the words of Fowler 'to deliver the goods that have been invoiced in the preceding words'.

The design of the school was an important part of the scheme: Post Office counters with all the necessary stores were available and maps and framed specimens of the various documents in use were exhibited on the walls of light and cheerful classrooms.

News reaches a national paper from two sources: the news agencies and its own correspondents.

For the second purpose the dash is the colon's weaker relative.

COMMA

The use of commas cannot be learned by rule. Not only does conventional practice vary from period to period, but good writers of the same period differ among themselves. Moreover stops have two kinds of duty. One is to show the construction of sentences – the 'grammatical' duty. The other is to introduce nuances into the meaning – the 'rhetorical' duty. 'I went to his house and I found him there' is a colourless statement. 'I went to his house, and I found him there' hints that it was not quite a matter of course that he should have been found there. 'I went to his house. And I found him there.' This indicates that to find him there was surprising. Similarly you can give a different nuance to what you write by encasing adverbs or adverbial phrases in commas. 'He was, apparently, willing to support you' throws a shade of doubt on his bona fides that is not present in 'He was apparently willing to support you'.

The correct use of the comma – if there is such a thing as 'correct' use – can only be acquired by common sense, observation and taste. Present practice is markedly different from that of the past in using commas much less freely. The fifteenth-century passage that heads this chapter is peppered with them with a liberality not approved by modern practice. I am not sure whether fifteenth-century practice would have produced:

The unassisted steering is so tiring, and slow in response, as to be dangerous, particularly on winding hilly roads, and cross-country.

But to us now this profusion of commas suggests a very slow thinker. Most of us would do without any of them except the one after *dangerous*, though we might possibly add one (after *winding*) which the writer surprisingly omitted.

I shall attempt no more than to point out some traps that commas set for the unwary, and those who want to know more about the subject I would refer to Carey's *Mind the Stop*,* a little book which has the rare merit of explaining the principles of punctuation without getting lost in its no-man's-land. I shall deal first with some uses of the comma that are generally regarded as incorrect, and then with uses which, though they may not be incorrect, need special care in handling, or are questionable.

A. *Incorrect Uses*

(i) The use of a comma between two independent sentences not linked by a conjunction. The usual practice is to use a heavier stop in this position, usually a semicolon. 'Tom is handsome; Dick is clever.' (See also under SEMICOLON, pp. 261–2.)

We wrote on the 12th May asking for an urgent report regarding the above contractor's complaint, this was followed up on the 24th May by a telephone call.

You may not be aware that a Youth Employment Service is operating throughout the country, in some areas it is under the control of the Ministry of Labour and National Service and in others of the Education Authorities.

There should be a semicolon after *complaint* in the first quotation and *country* in the second.

The Department cannot guarantee that a licence will be issued, you should not therefore arrange for any shipment.

I regret the delay in replying to your letter but Mr X who was dealing with it is on leave, however, I have gone into the matter . . ;

* Cambridge University Press, 1939; Pelican Books, 1971.

There should be a semicolon or a full stop after *issued* in the first quotation and a full stop after *leave* in the second.

But where the independent sentences number more than two and the last two are linked by a conjunction, a comma will do to link the others. 'Tom is handsome, Dick is clever and Harry is neither.'

(ii) The use of one comma instead of either a pair or none.

This very common blunder is more easily illustrated than explained. It is almost like using one only of a pair of brackets. Words that are parenthetical may be able to do without any commas, but if there is a comma at one end of them there must be one at the other end too.

Against all this must be set considerations which, in our submission are overwhelming. (Omit the comma.)

We should be glad if you would inform us for our record purposes, of any agency agreement finally reached. (Either omit the comma or insert one after *us*.)

It will be noted that for the development areas, Treasury-financed projects are to be grouped together. (Either omit the comma or insert one after *that*.)

The first is the acute shortage that so frequently exists, of suitable premises where people can come together. (Omit the comma.)

The principal purpose is to provide for the division between the minister and the governing body concerned, of premises and property held partly for hospital purposes and partly for other purposes. (Omit the comma.)

(iii) The use of commas with 'defining' relative clauses.

Relative clauses fall into two main classes. Grammarians give them different labels, but *defining* and *commenting* are the most convenient and descriptive. If you say 'The man who was here this morning told me that', the relative clause is a defining one; it completes the subject 'the man', which conveys no definite meaning without it. But if you say, 'Jones, who was here this morning, told me that', the relative clause is commenting; the subject 'Jones' is already complete and the relative clause merely adds a bit of information about him which may or may not be important but is not essential to the definition of the subject. A commenting clause should be within commas; a defining one should not. This is not an arbitrary rule; it is a utilitarian one. If you do not observe it, you may fail to make your meaning clear, or you may even say something different from what you intend. For instance:

A particular need is provision for young women, who owing to war conditions have been deprived of normal opportunities of learning homecraft. . . .

Here the comma announces that the relative clause is 'commenting'; it is added by way of explanation why young women in general had this need after the war. Without the comma the relative clause would be read as a 'defining' one, limiting the need for this provision to those particular young women who had in fact been deprived of those opportunities. Conversely:

Any expenditure incurred on major awards to students, who are not recognized for assistance from the Ministry, will rank for grant. . . .

Here the comma is wrong. The relative clause must be 'defining'. The commas suggest that it is 'commenting' and imply that no students are recognised for assistance.

I have made enquiries, and find that the clerk, who dealt with your enquiry, recorded the name of the firm correctly.

The relative clause here is a defining one. The comma turns it into a commenting one and implies that the writer has only one clerk. The truth is that one of several is being singled out; and this is made clear if the commas after *clerk* and *enquiry* are omitted.

The same mistake is made in:

The Ministry issues permits to employing authorities to enable foreigners to land in this country for the purpose of taking up employment, for which British subjects are not available.

The grammatical implication of this is that employment in general is not a thing for which British subjects are available.

An instruction book called 'Pre-aircrew English', supplied during the war to airmen in training in a Commonwealth country, contained an encouragement to its readers to 'smarten up their English'. This ended:

> Pilots, whose minds are dull, do not usually live long.

The commas convert a truism into an insult.

(iv) The insertion of a meaningless comma into an 'absolute phrase'.

An absolute phrase (e.g. 'then, the work being finished, we went home') always has parenthetic commas round it. But there is no sense in the comma that so often carelessly appears inside it.

> The House of Commons, having passed the third reading by a large majority after an animated debate, the bill was sent to the Lords.

The insertion of the first comma leaves the House of Commons in the air waiting for a verb that never comes. (See pp. 206–7.)

(v) The use of commas in an endeavour to clarify faultily constructed sentences. (See also p. 163.)

It is instructive to compare the following extracts from two documents issued by the same Department:

> It should be noted that an officer who ceased to pay insurance contributions before the date of the commencement of his emergency service, remained uninsured for a period, varying between eighteen months and two-and-a-half years, from the date of his last contribution and would, therefore, be compulsorily insured if his emergency service commenced during that period.

> Officers appointed to emergency commissions direct from civil life who were not insured for health or pensions purposes at the commencement of emergency services are not compulsorily insured during service.

Why should the first of these extracts be full of commas and the second have none? The answer can only be that, whereas the second sentence is short and clear, the first is long and obscure. The writer tried to help the reader by putting in five commas, but all he did was to give him five jolts. The only place where there might have been a comma is after *last contribution*, and there the writer has omitted to put one.

Another example of the same abuse of a comma is:

Moreover, directions and consents at the national level are essential prerequisites in a planned economy, whereas they were only necessary for the establishment of standards or for grant-aid and borrowing purposes, in the comparatively free system of yesterday.

The proper place for 'in the comparatively free system of yesterday' is after *whereas*, and it is a poor second-best to try to throw it back there by putting a comma in front of it. (Note also the superfluous adjective in *essential prerequisites*; see p. 82.)

The most barefaced attempt I have come across to correct a slovenly sentence by a comma was perpetrated by a Colonial bishop, who wrote to *The Times* a letter containing the sentence:

I should like to plead with some of those men who now feel ashamed to join the Colonial Service.

After the publication of the letter the bishop wrote again to *The Times*, saying:

The omission of a comma in my letter makes me seem to suggest that men might feel ashamed of joining the Colonial Service. My typescript reads, 'I should like to plead with some of those men who now feel ashamed, to join the Colonial Service'.*

(vi) The use of a comma to mark the end of the subject of a verb, or the beginning of the object.

It cannot be said to be always wrong to use a comma to mark the end of a composite subject, because good writers sometimes do it deliberately. For instance, one might write:

The question whether it is legitimate to use a comma to mark the end of the subject, is an arguable one.

But the comma is unnecessary; the reader does not need its help. To use commas in this way is a dangerous habit; it encourages a writer to shirk the trouble of so arranging his sentences as to make their meaning plain without punctuation.

* Quoted in Gowans Whyte, *An Anthology of Errors* (Chaterson, 1947).

I am however to draw your attention to the fact that goods subject to import licensing which are despatched to this country without the necessary licence having first been obtained, are on arrival liable to seizure . . .

If the subject is so long that it seems to need a boundary post at the end, it would be better not to use the slovenly device of a comma but to rewrite the sentence in conditional form.

. . . if goods subject to import licensing are despatched . . . they are on arrival . . .

In the following sentence the comma merely interrupts the flow:

I am now in a position to say that all the numerous delegates who have replied, heartily endorse the recommendation.

Postponement of the object may get a writer into the same trouble.

In the case of both whole-time and part-time officers, the general duties undertaken by them include the duty of treating without any additional remuneration and without any right to recover private fees, patients in their charge who are occupying Section 5 accommodation under the proviso to Section 5 (1) of the Act.

This unlovely sentence obviously needs recasting. One way of doing this would be:

The general duties undertaken by both whole-time and part-time officers include the treating of patients in their charge who are occupying Section 5 accommodation under the proviso to Section 5 (1) of the Act, and they are not entitled to receive additional remuneration for it or to recover private fees.

(vii) The use of commas before a clause beginning with *that*. A comma was at one time always used in this position:

It is a just though trite observation, that victorious Rome was itself subdued by the arts of Greece. (Gibbon.)
The true meaning is so uncertain and remote, that it is never sought. (Johnson.)
The author well knew, that two gentlemen . . . had differed with him. (Burke.)

We are more sparing of commas nowadays, and this practice has gone out of fashion. 'Indeed it is safe to say that immediately before the conjunction *that* a comma will be admissible more rarely than before any other conjunction.'*

B. *Correct uses*

If we turn from uses of the comma generally regarded as incorrect to those generally regarded as legitimate, we find one or two that need special care.

(i) The use of commas with adverbs and adverbial phrases.
(*a*) At the beginning of sentences.

> In their absence, it will be desirable ...
> Nevertheless, there is need for special care ...
> In practice, it has been found advisable ...

Some writers put a comma here as a matter of course. But others do it only if a comma is needed to emphasise a contrast or to prevent the reader from going off on a wrong scent, as in:

> A few days after, the Minister of Labour promised that a dossier of the strike would be published.
> Two miles on, the road is worse.

On the principle that stops should not be used unless they are needed, this discrimination is in general to be commended. But on the principle that the meaning should wherever possible be clear without stops, these particular sentences are blameworthy. It would have been better to dispense with the commas by writing 'A few days afterwards' and 'The road is worse two miles on'.

(*b*) Within sentences.

To enclose an adverb in commas is, as we have seen, a legitimate and useful way of emphasising it. 'All these things may, eventually, come to pass' is another way of saying 'All these things may come to pass – eventually'. Or it may serve to emphasise the subject of the sentence: 'He, however, thought differently'. The commas underline *he*. But certain common adverbs

*Carey, *Mind the Stop.*

such as *therefore*, *however*, *perhaps*, *of course*, present difficulties because of a convention that they should always be enclosed in commas, whether emphasised or not. This is dangerous; the only safe course is to treat the question as one not of rule but of common sense, and to judge each case on its merits. Lord Dunsany blames printers for this convention:

The writer puts down 'I am going to Dublin perhaps, with Murphy.' Or he writes 'I am going to Dublin, perhaps with Murphy.' But in either case these pestilent commas swoop down, not from his pen, but from the darker parts of the cornices where they were bred in the printer's office, and will alight on either side of the word *perhaps*, making it impossible for the reader to know the writer's meaning, making it impossible to see whether the doubt implied by the word *perhaps* affected Dublin or Murphy. I will quote an actual case I saw in a newspaper. A naval officer was giving evidence before a Court, and said, 'I decided on an alteration of course.' But since the words 'of course' must always be surrounded by commas, the printer's commas came down on them . . . and the sentence read, 'I decided upon an alteration, of course'!

The adverb *however* is specially likely to stand in need of clarifying commas. For instance, Burke wrote:

The author is compelled, however reluctantly, to receive the sentence pronounced on him in the House of Commons as that of the Party.

The meaning of this sentence would be different if the comma after *reluctantly* were omitted, and one inserted after *however*.

The author is compelled, however, reluctantly to receive, etc.

(ii) The 'throw-back' comma.

A common use of the comma as a clarifier is to show that what follows it refers not to what immediately precedes it but to something further back. William Cobbett, in the grammar that he wrote for his young son, pointed out that 'You will be rich if you be industrious, in a few years' did not mean the same as 'you will be rich, if you be industrious in a few years'. The comma that precedes the adverbial phrase *in a few years* indicates that that phrase refers not to 'if you be industrious' but to the whole clause 'you will be rich if you be industrious'. As usual, the device is clumsy. The proper way of writing the sentence is 'You will be rich in a few years if you be industrious'. If words are arranged in the right order these artificial aids will rarely be necessary. Examples of the dangers of the 'throw-back' comma will be found on pp. 198–200 under the heading *which*.

(iii) Years in commas.

Printers and typists used to be taught that, in dates, the year must be encased in commas. ('On the 2nd August, 1950, a committee was appointed; on the 6th December, 1951, it reported.') No usefulness can be claimed for this practice to offset its niggling and irritating appearance, and in the practice of Government Departments it has now been abandoned. But I expect that House Rules and Secretarial Colleges will put up a successful resistance to so revolutionary an idea.

(iv) Commas in series.
(*a*) Nouns and phrases.
In such a sentence as:

The company included Ambassadors, Ministers, Bishops and Judges.

commas are always put after each item in the series up to the last but one, but practice varies about putting a comma between the last but one and the *and* introducing the last. Neither practice is wrong. Those who favour a comma (a minority, but gaining ground) argue that, since a comma may sometimes be necessary to prevent ambiguity, there had better be one there always. Supposing the sentence were:

The company included the Bishops of Winchester, Salisbury, Bristol, and Bath and Wells.

the reader unversed in the English ecclesiastical hierarchy needs the comma after *Bristol* in order to sort out the last two bishops. Without it they might be, grammatically and geographically, either (*a*) Bristol and Bath and (*b*) Wells, or (*a*) Bristol and (*b*) Bath and Wells. Ambiguity cannot be justified by saying that those who are interested will know what is meant and those who are not will not care.

(b) Adjectives.

Where the series is of adjectives preceding a noun, it is a matter of taste whether there are commas between them or not:

A silly verbose pompous letter, and
A silly, verbose, pompous official letter.

are equally correct. The commas merely give a little emphasis to the adjectives. Where the final adjective is one that describes the species of the noun, it must of course be regarded as part of the noun, and not be preceded by a comma. Thus:

A silly, verbose, pompous official letter.

DASH

The dash is seductive; it tempts the writer to use it as a punctuation maid-of-all-work that saves him the trouble of choosing the right stop. We all know letter-writers who carry this habit to the length of relying on one punctuation mark only – a nondescript symbol that might be a dash or might be something else. Moreover the dash lends itself easily to rhetorical uses that may be out of place in humdrum prose. Perhaps that is why I have been tempted to go to Sir Winston Churchill's war speeches for examples of its recognised uses.

(a) In pairs for a parenthesis.

No future generation of English-speaking folks – for that is the tribunal to which we will appeal – will doubt that we were guiltless.

(b) To introduce an explanation, amplification, paraphrase, particularisation or correction of what immediately precedes it.

They were surely among the most noble and benevolent instincts of the human heart – the love of peace, the toil for peace, the strife for peace, the pursuit of peace, even at great peril.

Overhead the far-ranging Catalina air-boats soared – vigilant protecting eagles in the sky.

The end of our financial resources was in sight – nay, had actually been reached.

(*c*) To indicate that the construction of the sentence, as begun, will be left unfinished (what the grammarians call *anacoluthon*).

But when you come to other countries – oddly enough I saw a message from the authorities which are most concerned with our Arab problem at present, urging that we should be careful not to indulge in too gloomy forecasts.

(*d*) To gather up the subject of a sentence when it is a very long one; after the long loose canter of the subject you need to collect your horse for the jump to the verb.

The formidable power of Nazi Germany, the vast mass of destructive munitions that they have made or captured, the courage, skill and audacity of their striking forces, the ruthlessness of their central war direction, the prostrate condition of so many people under their yoke, the resources of so many lands which may to some extent become available to them – all these restrain rejoicing and forbid the slightest relaxation.

Similarly with the jump from the verb.

I would say generally that we must regard all those victims of the Nazi executioners in so many lands, who are labelled Communists and Jews – we must regard them just as if they were brave soldiers who die for their country on the field of battle.

(*e*) To introduce a paradoxical, humorous or whimsical ending to a sentence.

He makes mistakes, as I do, though not so many or so serious – he has not the same opportunities.

(*f*) With a colon to introduce a substantial quotation or a list (e.g. *as follows*: –). This, though common, is unnecessary since either the colon or the dash can do all that is needed by itself.

FULL STOP

The full stop is an exception to the rule that stops should be few. I have no advice to give about it except that it should be plentifully used: in other words to repeat the advice I have already given that sentences should be short. I am not, of course, suggesting that good prose never contains long ones. On the contrary, the best prose is a judicious admixture of the long with the short. Mark Twain, after advising young authors to write short sentences as a rule, added:

At times he may indulge himself with a long one, but he will make sure that there are no folds in it, no vaguenesses, no parenthetical interruptions of its view as a whole; when he has done with it, it won't be a sea-serpent with half of its arches under the water; it will be a torch-light procession.*

If you can write long sentences that you are satisfied really merit that description, by all means surprise and delight your readers with one occasionally. But the short ones are safer. I have said more about this on pp. 31 and 262–4.

Always use a full stop to separate statements between which there is no true continuity of thought. For example, *and* is too close a link in these sentences:

There are 630 boys in the school and the term will end on April 1st.
As regards Mr Smith's case a report was made on papers A B 340 and I understand he is now dead.

HYPHEN

The author of the style-book of the Oxford University Press of New York (quoted in Perrin's *Writer's Guide*) says 'If you take hyphens seriously you will surely go mad'. I have no intention of taking hyphens seriously.

It seems natural to use a hyphen in 'hair-remover', but Fowler pointed out that 'superfluous hair-remover' can only mean a hair-remover that nobody wants. Neither 'superfluous-hair remover' nor 'superfluous-hair-remover' is quite satisfactory, and some of us might settle for 'superfluous hair remover'. But it seems odd that the addition of the adjective should lead us to abandon the hyphen that is natural in the compound noun standing by itself. The truth is that there is no satisfactory

*Quoted in Earle's *English Prose, its Elements, History and Usage*, 1890.

answer. The same sort of difficulty presents itself in 'fried fish merchant'.

If I attempted to lay down any rules I should certainly go astray, and give advice not seemly to be followed. For instance, the general practice of hyphening *co* when it is attached as a prefix to a word beginning with a vowel has always seemed to me absurd, especially as it leads to such possibilities of misunderstanding as *unco-ordinated* must present to a Scotsman. If it is objected that ambiguity may result, and readers may be puzzled whether *coop* is something to put a hen in or a profit-sharing association, this should be removed by a diaeresis (*coöp*) not a hyphen (*co-op*). That is what a diaeresis is for. But to Englishmen the diaeresis has a slightly foreign air; so it is probably vain to urge its freer use.

I will attempt no more than to give a few elementary warnings. Those who would like more may refer to the six columns of advice given in the revised edition of Fowler's *Modern English Usage*.

(i) Do not use hyphens unnecessarily. If, for instance, you must use *overall* as an adjective (though this is not recommended) write it like that, and not *over-all*.

But if you do split a word with a hyphen, make sure you split it at the main break. Though you may write *self-conscious*, if you wish to have a hyphen in the word, you must not write *unself-conscious* but *un-selfconscious*.

(ii) To prevent ambiguity a hyphen should be used in a compound adjective (e.g. *first-class*, *six-inch*, *copper-coloured*, *water-cooled*). The omission of a hyphen between *government* and *financed* in the following sentence throws the reader on to a false scent:

When Government financed projects in the development areas have been grouped . . .

But remember that words which form parts of compound adjectives when they precede a noun may stand on their own feet when they are doing a different duty, and then they must not be hyphened. 'A first-class compartment' needs a hyphen, but 'to travel first class' does not. There must be hyphens in 'the balance-of-payment difficulties' but not in 'the difficulties are over the balance of payments'. A worth-while job is one that is worth while.

(iii) Avoid as far as possible the practice of separating a pair of hyphenated words, leaving a hyphen in mid-air. To do this is to misuse the hyphen (whose proper function is to link a word with its immediate neighbour) and it has a slovenly look. The saving of one word cannot justify writing

Where chaplains (whole- or part-time) have been appointed

instead of 'where chaplains have been appointed, whole-time or part-time'.

In a passage already quoted on p. 64,

. . . the Committee will meet at three or four monthly intervals . . .

the meaning would have been clearer with hyphens after *three* and *four*, and the writer could have avoided leaving the first in the air (*three- or four-monthly*) by writing *three-monthly or four-monthly*. But, as suggested on p. 64, it would be better still to recast the sentence.

INVERTED COMMAS

I have read nothing more sensible about inverted commas than this from the *ABC of English Usage*:

It is remarkable in an age peculiarly contemptuous of punctuation marks that we have not yet had the courage to abolish inverted commas . . . After all, they are a modern invention. The Bible is plain enough without them; and so is the literature of the eighteenth century. Bernard Shaw scorns them. However, since they are with us, we must do our best with them, trying always to reduce them to a minimum.

I have only two other things to say on this vexatious topic.

One is to give a warning against over-indulgence in the trick of encasing words or phrases in inverted commas to indicate that they are being used in a slang or technical or facetious or some other unusual sense. This is a useful occasional device;

instances may be found in this book. But it is a dangerous habit, as I have pointed out on p. 18.

The second question is whether punctuation marks (including question and exclamation marks) should come before or after the inverted commas that close a quotation. This has been much argued, with no conclusive result. It does not seem to me of great practical importance, but I feel bound to refer to it, if only because a correspondent criticised me for giving no guidance in *Plain Words* and accused me of being manifestly shaky about it myself. The truth is that there is no settled practice governing this most complicated subject. Pages were written about it by the Fowlers in *The King's English*, but their conclusions are by no means universally accepted.

There are two schools of thought. Most books on English advise that stops should be put in their logical positions. If the stops are part of the sentence quoted, put them within the inverted commas. If they are part of a longer sentence within which the quotation stands, put them outside the inverted commas. If the quotation and the sentence embracing it end together, so that each needs a stop at the same time, do not carry logic to the lengths of putting one inside and one out, but be content with the one outside. To give three simple examples of the application of this advice to question marks:

I said to him 'Why worry?'
Why did you say to him 'Don't worry'?
Why did you say to him 'Why worry'? (Strictly 'Why worry?'?)

Some publishers will not have this. They dislike the look of stops outside inverted commas if they can possibly be put inside. Here is an extract from a publisher's House Rules:

Commas, full stops, etc., closing matter in quotation marks may be placed before the final quotation marks, whether they form part of the original extract or not, provided that no ambiguity is likely to arise as to exactly what is quoted and what is not; this rule may not be as logical as that which insists on placing the punctuation marks strictly *according to the sense*, but the printed result looks more pleasing and justifies the convention.

But we need not concern ourselves here with questions of taste in printing. The drafter of official letters and memoranda is advised to stick to the principle of placing the punctuation marks according to the sense. He will find that many good publishers do likewise – including the publishers of this book.

PARAGRAPHS

Letters, reports, memoranda and other documents would be unreadable if they were not divided into paragraphs, and much has been written on the art of paragraphing. But little of it helps the ordinary writer; the subject does not admit of precise guidance. The chief thing to remember is that, although paragraphing loses all point if the paragraphs are excessively long, the paragraph is essentially a unit of thought, not of length. Every paragraph must be homogeneous in subject matter, and sequential in treatment of it. If a single sequence of treatment of a single subject goes on so long as to make an unreasonably long paragraph, it may be divided into more than one. But you must not do the opposite, and combine into a single paragraph passages that have not this unity, even though each by itself may be below the average length of a paragraph.

PARENTHESIS

The purpose of a parenthesis is ordinarily to insert an illustration, explanation, definition, or additional piece of information of any sort into a sentence that is logically and grammatically complete without it. A parenthesis may be marked off by commas, dashes or brackets. The degree of interruption of the main sentence may vary from the almost imperceptible one of explanatory words in apposition,

Mr Smith, the secretary, read the minutes.

to the violent one of a separate sentence complete in itself:

A memorandum (six copies of this memorandum are enclosed for the information of the Board) has been issued to management committees.

Parentheses should be used sparingly. Their very convenience is a reason for fighting shy of them. They enable the writer to dodge the trouble of arranging his thought properly; but he does so at the expense of the reader, especially if the thought that he has spatch-cocked into the sentence is an abrupt break in it, or a long one, or both. The second of the two examples just given shows an illegitimate use of the parenthesis. The writer had no business to keep the reader waiting for the verb by throwing in a parenthesis that would have been put better as a separate sentence. The following examples are even worse:

. . . to regard day nurseries and daily guardians as supplements to meet the special needs (where these exist and cannot be met within the hours, age, range and organisation of nursery schools and nursery classes) of children whose mothers are constrained by individual circumstances to go out to work . . .

If duties are however declined in this way, it will be necessary for the Board to consider whether it should agree to a modified contract in the particular case, or whether – because the required service can be provided only by the acceptance of the rejected obligations (e.g. by a whole-time radiologist to perform radiological examinations of paying patients in Section 5 beds in a hospital where the radiologists are all whole-time officers) – the Board should seek the services of another practitioner . . .

These are intolerable abuses of the parenthesis, the first with its interposition of 21 words in the middle of the phrase 'needs of children', and the second with its double parenthesis, more than 40 words long, like two snakes eating each other. There was no need for either of these monstrosities. In both examples the main sentence should be allowed to finish without interruption, and what is now in the parenthesis, so far as it is worth saying, should be added at the end:

. . . to regard day nurseries and daily guardians as supplements to meet the special needs of children whose mothers are constrained . . . and whose needs cannot be met . . .
. . . or whether the Board should seek the services of another practitioner, as they will have to do if the required service can be provided only . . .

Here is a parenthesis that keeps the reader waiting so long for the verb that he has probably forgotten what the subject is:

Close affiliation with University research in haematology – and it may be desirable that ultimately each Regional Transfusion Officer should have an honorary appointment in the department of pathology in the medical school – will help to attract into the service medical men of good professional standing.

In former days, when long and involved periods were fashionable, it was customary after a long parenthesis to put the reader on the road again by repeating the subject with the words 'I say'. Thus the writer of the last example would have continued after 'medical school' with the words 'close affiliation with University research in haematology, I say, will help to attract, etc.'. Now that this handy device has fallen into disuse, there is all the more need not to keep the reader waiting. There was no necessity to do so here. What is said as a parenthesis might just as well have been said as an independent sentence following the main one.

It is not only the reader who may forget where he was when the parenthesis started. Sometimes even the writer does, as in the letter quoted on p. 32.

... Owing to a shortage of a spare pair of wires to the underground cable (a pair of wires leading from the point near your house back to the local exchange, and thus a pair of wires essential to the provision of a telephone service for you) is lacking ...

The writer thought he had entered the parenthesis with the words 'Owing to the fact that a spare pair of wires to the underground cable' and he continued conformably when he emerged.

QUESTION MARK

Only direct questions need questions marks; indirect ones do not. There must be one at the end of 'Have you made a return of your income?' but not at the end of 'I am writing to ask whether you have made a return of your income'.

It is usual but not necessary to put question marks at the end of requests cast into question form for the sake of politeness. 'Will you please let me know whether you have made a return of your income?'

For the position of question marks in relation to inverted commas see p. 257.

SEMICOLON

Do not be afraid of the semicolon; it can be most useful. It marks a longer pause, a more definite break in the sense, than the comma; at the same time it says 'Here is a clause or sentence too closely related to what has gone before to be cut off by a full stop'. The semicolon is a stronger version of the comma.

The scheme of work should be as comprehensive as possible and should include gymnastics, games, boxing, wrestling and athletics; every endeavour should be made to provide facilities for swimming.

If these arrangements are made in your factory you should take any difficulty which you may have to these officers when they call; you need not write to the Tax Office or call there.

These two sentences illustrate the common use of the semicolon. Each consists of two clauses. If these had been linked by the conjunction *and*, a comma might have been enough after *athletics* and *call*. But where there is no conjunction a comma is not enough; the stop must be either a semicolon or a full stop. (See pp. 243–4.) The writers of these sentences felt that the clauses were not closely enough linked to justify a conjunction but too closely linked to admit of a full stop. They therefore rightly chose the middle course of a semicolon.

Each of the following sentences needs a semicolon in place of the comma:

The Company is doing some work on this, it may need supplementing.

If it is your own pension please say what type it is, if it is your mother's then it need not be included in your income.

Even where the break in the sense is not too strong to be

marked by a comma, a semicolon may nevertheless be a kindness to the reader. In 'This is a good car, but it is too expensive' we need no more than a comma, if that, after *car*. But if either or both parts of the sentence are longer than this, and still more if they contain commas of their own, a semicolon may be expedient to direct the reader's attention aright or to enable him to catch his breath. In 'This is, in most people's opinion, a good car; but it is too expensive', or in 'The 4-door saloon, which has a more powerful engine, is a good car; but the fact that it still sells badly, despite intensive advertising, shows that it is too expensive', the semicolon is only good manners.

The semicolon is also useful for avoiding the rather dreary trailing participles with which writers often end their sentences:

The postgraduate teaching hospitals are essentially national in their outlook, their geographical situation being merely incidental.

An attempt to devise permanent machinery for consultation was unsuccessful, the initial lukewarm response having soon disappeared.

There is nothing faulty in the grammar or syntax of these sentences, and the meaning of each is unambiguous. But they have a tired look. They can be wonderfully freshened by using the semicolon, and rewriting them:

The postgraduate teaching hospitals are essentially national in their outlook; their geographical situation is merely incidental.

An attempt to devise permanent machinery for consultation was unsuccessful; the initial lukewarm response soon disappeared.

SENTENCES

A sentence is not easy to define. Many learned grammarians have tried, and their definitions have been torn in pieces by other learned grammarians. But what most of us understand by a sentence is what the *OED* calls the 'popular definition': 'such a portion of composition or utterance as extends from one full stop to another'. That definition is good enough for our present purposes, and the question we have to consider is what general guidance can be given to a writer about what he should put between one full stop and the next.

The two main things to be remembered about sentences by those who want to make their meaning plain is that they should be short and should have unity of thought. Here is a series of 84 words between one full stop and another, which violates all the canons of a good sentence. In fact it might be said to explode the definition, for it would be flattering to call it a 'sentence'. It is better described as gibberish.

Forms are only sent to applicants whose requirements exceed one ton, and in future, as from tomorrow, forms will only be sent to firms whose requirements exceed five tons, and as you have not indicated what your requirements are, I am not sending you forms at the moment because it is just possible that your requirements may be well within these quantities quoted, in which case you may apply direct to the usual suppliers, of which there are several, with a view to obtaining your requirements.

If we prune this of its verbiage, and split it into three short sentences, a meaning will begin to emerge.

Only firms whose requirements exceed five tons now need forms. Others can apply direct to the suppliers. As you do not say what your requirements are I will not send you a form unless I hear that you need one.

The following is an even worse example of a meandering stream of words masquerading as a sentence:

Further to your letter of the above date and reference in connection with an allocation of . . . , as already pointed out to you all the allocations for this period have been closed, and I therefore regret that it is not possible to add to the existing allocation which has been made to you and which covers *in toto* your requirements for this period when originally received, by virtue of the work on which you are engaged, a rather higher percentage has been given to you, namely 100 per cent of the original requirements and at this stage I am afraid it is not practicable for you to increase the requirement for the reasons already given.

The fault here is excessive verbiage rather than of combining into one sentence thoughts that ought to have been given several. The thought is simple, and can be conveyed in two sentences, if not in one:

Your original application was granted in full because of the importance of your work. I regret that the amount cannot now be increased, as allocation for this period has been closed.

11

SOME RECENT TRENDS

> It is quite impossible to stop the progress of language – it is like the course of the Mississippi, the motion of which is at times scarcely perceptible yet even then it possesses a momentum quite irresistible. Words and expressions will be forced into use in spite of all the exertions of all the writers in the world.
>
> WEBSTER

THE language has not stood still during the last twenty years. In revising the earlier chapters of this book I have sought to bring up to date the judgments made in them on particular points of usage. In this chapter I attempt a more general look at the main changes which have come about in normal English usage, particularly in official and academic writing, and what has mainly caused them. I add a section on vogue words and modish writing by way of illustrating both the inevitability of change and the unfortunate results if novel words and expressions are overused, misused or used affectedly instead of being allowed to make their way into normal usage, if they can, on their merits.

THE TREND TOWARDS INFORMALITY

Since the last war there has been a steady trend away from what is sometimes called 'them-language' or 'mandarin prose' and towards much greater informality of expression. The growth of literacy, the lowering of social barriers, the increased spate of words put out for popular consumption by the press, broadcasting and television, the more or less conscious sense of growing egalitarianism, have all contributed to this.

The trend has affected nearly all sorts of writing. 'Commercialese' is still surprisingly widespread in commercial correspondence ('your favour to hand', 'of even date', and so on), but in official correspondence 'officialese' is now comparatively rare. Conversational forms like *don't, can't, he's* are now quite commonly used in articles in the press (including leading articles) which would certainly have eschewed them twenty years ago. Twenty years hence they may be equally common in many other types of serious writing where they are still eschewed. A good example of the abandonment of 'them-language' is the notice in Red Arrow buses in London 'Please do not speak to the driver while he is driving'. A few years ago this would have been 'Passengers are requested not to communicate with the driver while the vehicle is in motion'. (On the other hand, there is a Government office where doors still bear the notice 'This door must not be left in an open position'.)

Most people will agree that the trend towards greater informality in the use of the written word is to be welcomed rather than deplored. But it sets some problems for the official, whether he is writing a letter or drafting a document for publication. Remembering the advice 'Be human', he does not want his letter to seem stuffy or condescending by modern standards, but if he uses too informal a style he is at risk of being thought impertinent or facetious; his reader does not want a pompous reply, but he does expect a serious one. Similarly, in a formal statement of important Government policy a certain degree of dignity is necessary if the desired impact is to be made. A modern official will almost certainly avoid 'Her Majesty's Government have been driven to the conclusion, after long and earnest consideration, that this proposition cannot be brought within the realms of practicability in the foreseeable future'. But 'Her Majesty's Government don't think this is on' will not quite do either.

Another, and more subtle, difficulty is that without the ready-made, pompous phrases which were once characteristic of official writing, saying to the reader in effect 'Pay attention: this is an important official communication', the writer is too often at a loss to know how to make any impact at all.

One of my Civil Service correspondents puts these difficulties very well:

Some Recent Trends

My impression is that the more extreme kind of civil service 'mandarin prose', having been consistently pilloried over the past two or three decades, is now rarely encountered. The main trouble now seems to be simply a general level of dullness and feebleness; the kind of writing which although not palpably 'bad' has absolutely no positive virtues; which lies completely dead on the page and fails to 'come across' to the reader; fails, that is, in its essential job of effective communication.

A general malaise of this kind is difficult to diagnose and cure. I offer a few suggestions of my own about the basic reasons *why* one so often comes across people whose high mental qualities and alert intelligence seem to desert them utterly as soon as they put pen to paper.

(*a*) Too much writing in the civil service is done on the assumption that people will be more or less compelled to read the stuff because it is their job to do so. It is here that the professional writer's disciplines are most obviously lacking and badly needed. Anyone who writes for money is in precisely the opposite position. He knows that he *must* always strive to keep his readers' attention, and that he will not do so if he is wordy, abstract and dull.

(*b*) It is very difficult to write well. . . . This fact seems to be insufficiently known and appreciated; and I suspect that very often the reason for poor writing is simply that not enough trouble has been taken over it.

(*c*) Although, as I have said, the extremes of pomposity are now rare, quite a few people still seem to feel that there is, or ought to be, a special kind of dignified and elevated language for the use of Government servants; just as European diplomacy used to be conducted in French and Catholic church services in Latin. This feeling seems to be both deeply ingrained and widely spread, and I don't think it should simply be mocked; one ought to try and get at the underlying causes.

And of course the other extreme is equally bad. We do not want official writing to be loose, slangy, chatty or jocular.

I agree with all this, and it does not apply to official writing only; but a gloss needs to be added to the first paragraph. It must not be thought that the abandonment of old-fashioned pomposities has left *nothing* but dullness and feebleness. Very often, unfortunately, the place of one bad habit has been taken by another, under the compulsion of other influences to which I now turn.

THE INFLUENCE OF AMERICA

American English (by which I mean, for the most part, United States English) differs from British English not only in pronunciation but in many points of spelling, vocabulary and syntax. This is not a matter of 'right' or 'wrong'; what is right or usual on one side of the Atlantic is wrong or unusual on the other. It would be absurd for us to assume that an American word, expression or construction is necessarily better than its British equivalent just because it seems novel; and equally absurd to say that a novelty imported from America can never become respectable over here. The Americans' talent for apt and racy language is brilliantly manifested in much of their slang; but it is not confined to slang, and British English has been greatly enriched by adopting some of its products. Sometimes, again, what seems an American innovation is in fact an old English usage (such as the verb *to loan*) which has survived across the Atlantic but been abandoned in the land of its origin.

When we consider that American English has been assaulting these islands with ever-increasing weight and persistence for many years, through films, magazines, radio and television, to say nothing of American service-men and American tourists, we may well marvel at the sturdy resistance put up by British popular usage. *Petrol*, *autumn*, *lift* and *pavement* have not surrendered to *gasolene* (or *gas*), *fall*, *elevator* and *sidewalk*. There is nothing logical about this. Logically, we ought to admit that *sidewalk* is a better word for its purpose than *pavement* and utterly forbid the ambiguous *gas* to oust the unambiguous *petrol*. Yet of these four American words *gas* has probably made the most progress in Britain, and *sidewalk* the least. Other examples have been given in earlier chapters of common American usages which are not, or at least not yet, accepted as British English.

All this is fruitful ground for students of comparative linguistics and I shall not venture on their preserves. What we are concerned with here is the extent to which those who write British English and who 'use words as tools of their trade in administration or business' should allow themselves to be influenced by the assaults of American English. They should not, I suggest, put up any resistance to words which aptly fill a real need – as did *teenager*, *doodle* and *commuter*, now well established in British English. For example, unlike some of my correspondents, I see no objection to allowing *update* to do the work of *bring up to date*, and though *meaningful* is at present a much over-used vogue word it seems to me a useful and respectable recruit to the language. So does the verb *to host*, meaning *to be host at*. Nor do I see any harm in the newly coined *guesstimate*, meaning an estimate so rough that it is little better than a guess.

But they should not lightly allow a newcomer to supplant a perfectly good British word, particularly if the newcomer has no pretensions to greater aptness or beauty. Thus, there is no sense in preferring *transportation* to *transport* or *envision* to *envisage*. Nor should they be seduced by such ungainly temptresses as *in the event that* (if), *at this time* (now) or *as of now* (now). The Americanisms *check up on* and *face up to* have secured a fairly firm foothold on these shores. It can perhaps be urged in their favour that they slightly intensify the meaning of the simple verbs *check* and *face*. But as suggested on p. 97 we must view with suspicion the tendency to add to simple verbs strings of adverbs and prepositions which make little or no difference to the meaning; the danger is that the simple verb will eventually be robbed of its right to mean anything by itself. In Britain boy meets girl and should continue to do so, even though in America he meets with her, or even meets up with her. (*Meet with*, in British English, is used only where what is met is abstract – a man can meet with opposition and an expedition can meet with disaster – and even there *meet* is often used alone. Of course one can meet force with sweet reason or disaster with courage but those are different constructions.) *Consult with* and *visit with* are other Americanisms which should be made unwelcome; *consult* and *visit* should not be rendered impotent.

The American secretary of an international committee wrote to members in advance:

> Dr A has informed of his desire to attend but is not able to make firm plans at this time. In the event that he will be unable to attend the Session he plans to send a representative.

Has informed of his desire is not admissible in Britain. In British English *inform* needs an object (e.g. 'has informed me of his desire'). Alternatively some such word as 'expressed' or 'indicated' must be substituted for *informed of*. A well-trained British secretary would have written:

> Dr A has said that he would like to attend the Session but cannot yet make firm plans. If he cannot come he will send a representative.

Different than and *preferable than* are not uncommon in America but are not correct in British English, which requires *different from* and *preferable to*.

But these differences in usage do not present nearly so serious a menace as the tortured, polysyllabic style of much American official and academic writing – what President Roosevelt stigmatised as 'gobbledygook'. Here the British resistance has been by no means as sturdy as one could wish.

The subjects that seem to be most seriously infected with this disease are defence, sociology and business management. In all these subjects American thinking and American practice have made a great impact on this side of the Atlantic in recent years. If, as a result, our defences are stronger, our social thinking more enlightened and our managers more efficient than they used to be, we must be duly grateful. But these pearls of wisdom reach us in a copious wrapping of cotton wool and corrugated cardboard, and it is no ingratitude to enjoy the pearls and discard the wrapping. Many British writers seem to think that unless they display the wrapping they will be suspected of not having received the pearls.

Here are a few examples of 'American-style' writing which anyone who cares for good English must roundly condemn.

They show, I think, that American influence is not only perni-
cious but pervasive, for some are by American writers and some
by British and the reader will not, I am sure, be able to tell
which are which (particularly as I have anglicised the spelling
of the American specimens).

Many developments are now occurring in the new technology in
education, particularly in employment of computers and new information systems . . . One application might be to provide tools for
collaboration between the students and teacher-advisers in the
scheduling of specific events arranged to meet learning needs.
Matching of expressed interests, capabilities and existing resources
(similar to computer dating) could eventually provide a process
whereby activity nodes could be generated interactionally, rather
than dictated by traditional estimates. Times and meeting places at
each local campus or field centre could well be co-ordinated through
a central scheduling, information and publicity service to minimise
conflicts, and to maximise the uses of special facilities.

This seems to mean that computers and other mechanical
aids could be used to work out time-tables more efficiently, with
less overlap.

Examination of specific instances indicated that in most cases
where retirement dissatisfaction existed advance activity programming by individuals had been insignificant or even lacking.

This probably means that most retired people who were
bored had given little or no thought before they retired to what
they were going to do.

A detailed knowledge of the problem areas and their solution has
been accumulated, and the necessity to commence production prior
to the completion of the development proving trials, would appear
to be an acceptable risk. The exception to this philosophy will be the
radio-sonde, since no previous development has taken place, and
hence this item will remain on the critical path for both development and production.

A risk is sometimes a necessity, but you will not often find a
necessity described as a risk. The example is, however, more
intelligible than the next two, which I cannot attempt to interpret.

Diffusibility of knowledge throughout the environment in which the families are to move is essential if the full expression of their potentiality is to become explicit in action. Facts pertaining to experience of every sort that the family is in course of digesting give the context and the full flavour of consciousness to their experience.

The establishment of minimum constraints for an optimization of free growth combining elements of user-design for both the individual and the community, forms the basis of this project. The basic order devised is intended to establish a democratic inter-change between human and technological factors. The order devised will stimulate multiplicity, multiformity, micro and macro relations; all expressed through logically derived dimensional and functional modules themselves articulated by a system of guiding lines.

The American assault is made not only directly through American English but also indirectly through 'United Nations English'. Many of the publications of the United Nations, of their specialised agencies and of other international bodies bear eloquent witness to the prominent and influential part played in their activities by the United States. Another reason why United Nations English differs from British English is that it often emanates from men and women on the staff of these bodies who use English rather than any of the other official languages but whose native tongue is not English at all. These publications are usually seen in draft by British officials or delegates, but however good their use of their own tongue may be they cannot insist that a draft should always be translated into good British English, and it is not always tactful for them to try.

Here are a few examples of United Nations English. They illustrate the influence of American English rather than that of English used as a second language.

At present many factors lead to a serious public health problem in the form of protein calorie malnutrition and other forms of malnutrition resulting from dietary deficiencies of vitamins and minerals which affect particularly infants, pre-school children and expectant and nursing mothers.

The emphasis should be placed both on methods and procedures to evolve a scientific approach, introduce quantitative criteria and also the development of built-in evaluation procedures.

The resources now available to the evaluation service do not permit any substantial intensification of the work to meet these goals.

The role of the public sector will, however, remain a subsidiary one and its efforts will be co-ordinated, to the extent possible, with the contributions of the private economy. With regard to the volume of public capital aid, due account will be taken of international standards within the limits of budgetary possibilities.

With respect to the question whether the financial communities in the donor and recipient countries should be widely alerted or not, the confidentiality of the warnings should be maintained.

Just as we cannot reasonably object to the use of American English by Americans, so we cannot reasonably object to the use of United Nations English by the United Nations. But that is not to say that we should allow either to influence British English for the worse.

THE INFLUENCE OF SCIENCE AND TECHNOLOGY

As science and technology develop they use new words to express new concepts and new techniques as well as new inventions; and they have developed more rapidly during the last twenty years than ever before. The effect on the language is threefold. First, the scientists and technologists must find ways of explaining themselves to each other. (This is 'expert to expert' language and as explained in Chapter 2 is outside the scope of this book.) Second, they must find ways of explaining themselves to the rest of us. Third, the rest of us will start using the new terms ourselves, both literally and metaphorically. Since America contributes powerfully to science and technology, and consequently to the language they use, there will be some overlap between this section and the last.

Some years ago Sir Lawrence Bragg (then Cavendish Professor of Experimental Physics at Cambridge) wrote as follows:

I will try to define what I believe to be lacking in our present courses for science undergraduates. They do not learn to write clearly and briefly, marshalling their points in due and aesthetically satisfying order, and eliminating inessentials. They are inept at those turns of phrase or happy analogy which throw a flying bridge across a chasm of misunderstanding and make contact between mind and mind. They do not know how to talk to people who have had a different training from them, and how to carry conviction when decisions on plans for action of vital importance to them are made . . . The gift of expression is important to them as scientists, the best research is wasted when it is extremely difficult to discover what it is all about . . . It is even more important when scientists are called upon to play their part in the world of affairs, as is happening to an increasing extent.

No doubt these strictures are still apt to much that is written on scientific or technical subjects. But there is enough good, clear writing to make it evident that if the writer knows his subject and takes trouble he can get his meaning across to the ordinary reader without torturing the language. Many scientific journalists do this extremely well, but I choose a few examples from non-professional writers.

Otoliths are not a new discovery, but few of us know what they are. This writer cures our ignorance very agreeably:

The rate of growth in our temperate waters varies seasonally; it is faster in the summer months, when the water is warmed and more food is available, than in winter. This difference of growth rate can be seen as growth zones or rings on the fish scales or in the ear-stones (otoliths). The scale or otolith shows a ringed pattern which, as in the cross-section of a tree-trunk, represents annual growth. In some fish the rings are easier to read in the scales, in others the otoliths are clearer, but the principle of age determination is the same. Because the growth of the scale or otolith is in direct proportion to the growth of the fish, the size of the fish at any previous stage of its life can also be estimated and years of good growth distinguished from years of poor growth.

Here is a routine announcement in the press of a new type of twistlock:

Twistlocks for securing ISO freight containers to trailers . . . are announced by Messrs X. They can be operated after the container has been loaded on to the vehicle if need be. Weighing only 16lbs, they are equally suitable for flat platform or skeletal trailers, and fit flush to the deck so as not to interfere with conventional loads. Being smaller than former types, they are particularly suitable for both rigid vehicles and 'swap body' systems. A selection of handles for different trailers are designed to be conspicuous when in the un-locked position, as a safety measure.

I am sure this twistlock is as serviceable and workmanlike as the style in which it is described. The *are* in the last sentence can indeed be faulted grammatically, but it can also be defended as a natural 'attraction' (see p. 181) in an un-selfconscious writer. Contrast the handles rightly described as 'in the unlocked position' with the doors on p. 266 left 'in an open position'.

Here is a good clear description of what caused an accident in a piece of hospital equipment:

The unit is fitted with an adjustable temperature control ('Thermostat' or 'Micromat') on the front panel of the steriliser which prevents the door from being opened until a pre-set temperature has been reached during the cooking cycle. The incident appears to have been caused by the control being wrongly set at 110°C. When the door was opened at this higher temperature a thermal shock acting on the bottles, which were still under high internal pressure, caused them to explode.

There is nothing, you may say, specially deserving of praise in these three examples. Quite so: anyone can write like this. But many do not. There is perhaps nothing specially deserving of blame in the following, but it is difficult to believe that it could not have been made easier for the general reader (for whom alone it was intended). Contrast it, for instance, with the passage about nuclear fuel elements quoted on the next page.

The immediate effects of the absorption of laser energy are mainly thermal, but depending on the intensity of the beam there may also be associated ultrasonic and mechanical effects. Ionisation may also be produced.

Nuclear energy, space travel and computers afford perhaps the most striking and the most familiar examples of the development of science and technology during the last twenty years.

Their exponents have not all been equally successful in their use of language, either in explaining themselves to the laity or in the new words and expressions that they have coined.

Nuclear energy has produced much excellent writing for popular consumption. Here is a good example.* It was written in 1956, when nuclear reactors were in their infancy and everything was utterly mysterious to the general reader.

The uranium rod in its can, the fuel element as it is called, is the key component in a nuclear reactor and is one of the most difficult to design. Consider the requirements. In order to transmit the heat generated in the uranium through the metal can to the cooling gas, the can must make good thermal contact with the uranium on the inside and transfer heat efficiently to the gas on the outside. At the same time it must not be corroded either by the gas or by the uranium and, as with everything inside a reactor core, it must absorb neutrons to the least possible extent. Finally it must be mechanically strong at the high temperature of operation, or the weight of the uranium inside would cause cracks and the can would cease to be effective in doing its job.

There is no difficulty in reading on. What of the uranium rod itself? How were the problems solved? It is all there, comprehensible and even exciting to the stupidest of us.

Space travel is more novel still and no doubt has many linguistic, as well as other, discoveries still to make. It is heartening to note its tendency, so far, to coin nice simple words and phrases like *weightlessness*, *space-suit*, *lift-off*, *heat-shield*, *splash-down* and *hard dock*. Some of these (like *fall-out* and *spin-off* from earlier technologies) will be acceptable additions to our store of metaphors. We shall know in a few years' time whether Britain, having abandoned her separate orbit, has really achieved a hard dock with the European Communities, or only a soft one.

Computers have produced a new vocabulary of their own, as they are entitled to do, but it is not a graceful one; and computer experts seem to take less trouble than most experts to express themselves grammatically or to make themselves plain to ordi-

*Kenneth Jay, *Calder Hall* (Methuen, 1956), p. 21.

nary readers. This is a pity, for as the years go by ordinary people are likely to have much more to do with computers than with nuclear energy or space travel.

An interesting feature of computer language is that the American spelling *program* has been adopted to denote a sequence of instructions fed into a computer and designed to solve a problem or attain a specific result. It would now be as contrary to British usage to use *programme* in this special sense as to use *program* in any other. Several other familiar words have been given special meanings. For instance, *hardware* means the electro-mechanical and electronic equipment which constitutes a computer and *software* the programs written for a computer and the supporting advisory, training etc. services. *Input* means 'data introduced into a computer from an external source' and *output* 'processed data or information transferred from the computer to an external device for storage or printing out or punching out'. There is no harm in any of this in its place, but *input*, in particular, has become an overworked vogue word in metaphorical uses, such as:

These lines of activity will be an essential input to the process of defining standards ...

Input and *output* are also used as verbs, to the annoyance of one correspondent, who writes that the verbs 'to input' and 'to output' make him want to upstand and outwalk.

Here are some examples of unhelpful writing about the use of computers. They all come from reports or booklets intended for non-experts.

Hardware faults had mainly affected the 1906 configuration. Multiplexing system faults had been contained by engineer intervention. A permanent solution was still being sought.

For such data to become part of an information flow for feedback its form must be standardised; therefore there must be a preferred vocabulary and an industrially acceptable library of operation descriptions. (*Data* as a singular, on which see p. 183, is particularly common in computer-land.)

The concept of major tasks (in the network) as factors whose parameters effectively separate the content of each task from the remainder of the project is a valid basis for future developments. (See p. 116 for more about the vogue word *parameter*.)

Using the indexed sequential method on an exchangeable disc, the time involved in accessing a record by searching several levels of index, and seeking index, data and overflow areas can amount to well over 200 msec. It is possible to improve upon these timings by systems optimisation.

And possible too, surely, to improve on this sort of language, which hinders rather than helps the spread of knowledge about computers. Just to show that it *can* be improved on, here is a passage from another booklet about computers:

Further, if the atmosphere is too dry, paper tape may become brittle and cards may shrink and curl; when the air is too damp cards may expand and jam the reading devices.

A novice in the world of computers is immediately reassured by these familiar words *brittle*, *shrink*, *curl* and *jam*; he may well have supposed that this is an alien and unfriendly world, in which a card will never 'curl' but always 'assume a helix-type configuration'.

Economics, the social and environmental sciences and business management are other branches of learning which have sprouted luxuriantly during the last twenty years. None of them has done the language much good.

Walter Salant has written* a witty and spirited appeal to his fellow economists in the United States to write more carefully and less obscurely; and several leading economists in this country write very acceptably. But we still find stuff like this:

Undue attachment to the thesis that inflation is the result solely of institutional factors might cause the contribution made to inflation by excess demand to be neglected and the existence of excess demand to be prolonged.

This may be good economics, but it is not good economy in the use of words. All these abstracts and passives are highly

* 'Writing and Reading in Economics' in the *Journal of Political Economy*.

inflationary. Even those of us who are not sure what 'institutional factors' are would have found it easier if the passage had read :

Inflation is caused not only by institutional factors but also by excess demand, and unless we recognise this and act on it excess demand is likely to continue.

But economists do not sin as badly on the whole as sociologists and environmental scientists. And the business schools and personnel management experts are the worst of all.

I suspect that one reason for obscure or pretentious writing by sociologists and environmental scientists is that their subjects have not yet gained as much academic esteem as they would like. Some of them strain after 'expert' language because they are afraid that if their manner is lucid their matter will be despised as elementary. But no sensible reader supposes that what is easy to understand must have been easy to think of; and where the matter really is elementary (as sometimes it is bound to be) obscurity of manner reduces, not increases, the reader's respect for the writer's intellectual power. 'Obscurely systematising the obvious' (a phrase stolen from one of my correspondents) is surely not the way to gain lasting academic renown.

The extraordinary language of the business schools and the personnel management experts is perhaps due partly to a similar feeling ('You *must* believe that this is a grand new science; just look at our grand new scientific language'). But it is undoubtedly due also to the influence of American gobbledygook.

My correspondents supplied me copiously with examples of bad writing by sociologists, environmental scientists and experts in business and personnel management. Some I have used elsewhere in this book, and I can afford space here for only a few others. All were written for ordinary people, not fellow experts, and some, I regret to say, were written by civil servants following bad academic example. Let us hope that both the drug-pushers and their victims will see the error of their ways before the whole literate population gets hooked.

The national significance of the distributive sector must be assessed also in the light of its high visibility and integration into the physical and social fabric of the community.

This means that shops are important in the life of the nation because they are easy to see and are part and parcel of our daily life.

The main quantitative thresholds (necessitating new works) should not be crossed in any of the towns with the exception of St Boswells, which is the only place where the substantial expenditure necessary for the implementation of new public utility networks is justified from the economic viewpoint.

This means that only at St Boswells can expenditure on new public utility systems be justified.

By selecting extrapolations of current or emerging tendencies that grow continuously out of today's world, and reflect the multifold trend and our current expectations, we create a 'surprise-free' projection – one that seems less surprising than any other specific possibility.

A mountain of 'expert' writing, a molehill of an idea.

Although certain broad zonational patterns are discernible in the geographical distribution of animals as well as in those of soils and vegetation, the mobility of animals and, in the case of some, seasonal altitudinal migrations mean that the zonation becomes indistinct.

This is from a published academic study. I have corrected both grammar and punctuation. It seems to tell us that animals move about more than plants do, and that when they have moved they are not in the same place as before.

The cognitive continuum is concerned with objectives related to knowledge and the intellectual abilities and skills, rising from comprehension to evaluation. The affective continuum covers the range of behavioural responses, from passive acceptance of stimuli to the organisation of taught values into a complex system which constitutes the whole characterisation of an individual.

This is what you may meet if you subject yourself to Management Training.

In the second place there are grounds for thinking that the availability of analytical assessments of jobs would facilitate the preparation of grade-descriptions for a new structure in a situation in which the allocation of jobs to grades at the stages of implementing and maintaining that structure would be undertaken by whole-job procedures.

This reads like a parody, but it is perfectly genuine.

My next example needs more space but is well worth it:

The need is often not that of utilizing resources efficiently, but of minimizing or restraining public expenditure *per se*. The tension which exists between this particular commonweal objective and the goal of adequately serving a clientele is probably one of the most pervasive determinants of the organizational environment within which social service personnel must work and clients' needs must be met. This tension is not inevitably a source of-administrative pathology, but the methods of managing this phenomenon which have evolved in different services (and their consequences) must be a central concern of an expanding body of welfare administration research. This fundamental restraint on resources is a key feature of the internal economy of all public social services.

The situation may be conveniently summarized. Statutory social services can be regarded as service organizations operating within the context of a commonweal organization – the parliamentary-governmental system. The commonweal goals pursued in the latter system may in different ways and to different degrees compete with and modify the enactment of service goals.

These two paragraphs seem to have everything – vogue words (like *resources* and *environment*), pomposities (like *utilize* for *use*), danger signs (like *situation*, *within the context of*), padding (*which exists* and plenty more), bad syntax (*the need of utilizing* instead of *the need to utilize*) and even, for good measure, a wrongly used Latin phrase (*per se*). You will see too that *ize* is preferred to *ise*, with unhappy results. The *z* is permissible in *organize*, but hardly in *utilize* or *summarize*. It would be much safer to prefer *ise*, as recommended on p. 237.

But I originally collected it for another reason – it illustrates the versatility of our modern *goals*. We learn, near the beginning, that a tension exists between objective A and goal B. By the end objective A is itself a goal, or rather goals; one sort of goal can be pursued and the other enacted; and the first can both compete with and modify the enactment of the second sort. No wonder we are told, a page or two further on, that the social services can be classified 'by reference to their major goal orientation'.

In the end I thought it best simply to proffer this passage as evidence in support of my theory that the indeterminate nature of sociology within the context of academic esteem is probably one of the most pervasive determinants of the linguistic environment within which sociologists must work and their readers' needs must be ignored.

I cannot resist adding two American examples, quoted by Dr Alexander Kohn in the *New Scientist*.

... the allocation of a very limited portion of a person's resources, abilities and energies to the ownership, maintenance and adornment of residential structures ...

... a set of arrangements for producing and rearing children the viability of which is not predicated on the consistent presence in the household of an adult male acting in the role of husband and father ...

Dr Kohn tells us that the first of these means 'They live in slums' and the second 'Dad is not home much of his time'.

One could multiply quotations. These perhaps suffice to suggest that if we could find in this country one economist, one sociologist and one teacher of business management who could each persuade his fellow professionals to write decently, the direct and indirect benefits to academic and official writing would be immense.

VOGUE WORDS

The written language is as subject to the whims of fashion as is speech or dress or art. Some words and turns of phrase become fashionable, are rapidly done to death and pass out of fashion in a few years. This is particularly true of the favourite words of politicians. It is quite possible, for instance, that *pragmatic, gritty, purposive* and *abrasive*, which led fairly quiet existences before the mid-1960s, have already had their day as vogue words and are now ready to resume their previous, less glamorous, duties. Some vogue words gain a permanent foothold and are often enrichments to the language. *Flamboyant, stalemate, analysis, dilemma*, which started as technical terms, were doubtless vogue words in their day; they have now lost their meretricious air and are doing an honest non-technical job (as, perhaps, is *meretricious*). Others linger on for many years without ever quite gaining either the respect of good writers or the guerdon of popular usage and eventually die unmourned. There is no saying how things will go. *Bottleneck* was all the rage in the 1940s; and it might well have won an honoured place, for its metaphorical use can be easily understood and is frequently apt. But it was so badly overused and mishandled when it was a new toy that few people now think it worth taking out of the cupboard. I have had to rewrite (pp. 111–12) what Gowers wrote about it twenty years ago. *Target, ceiling* and *blueprint*, nearcontemporaries of *bottleneck* as vogue words, have also been roughly handled in the toy-room but seem to have lasted better. The use of *image*, in such a sentence as 'This will improve my image', was unknown when Gowers first wrote, but it is now so prevalent that *image* can hardly be classed any longer as a vogue word at all. *Escalate*, no younger than *image*, is not yet nearly as respectable and its ultimate fate seems at present doubtful.

So anything written about particular vogue words is likely to be soon out of date. But there are perhaps some general points which will always remain valid. First, these words are often vivid and enlightening in their proper meaning, but where they are overworked their edge gets blunted and their force broken. Thus *traumatic* is now in danger of meaning little more than *unpleasant*, *breakthrough* of meaning merely some change for the better, *population explosion* of meaning a gradual rise in population. (By extension from this use of *explosion* the word *explode* now sometimes means merely *increase*, as in a statement to the press by a bank manager that 'the amount of cash handled has exploded by more than 100 per cent in the past decade'; he should have remembered the useful word 'doubled'.) In this way the currency is debased and the language impoverished. The process may be inevitable – there is no ultimate appeal from the verdict of popular usage – but it should not be accelerated by those who care about saying what they mean. The careful writer should therefore not use vogue words, merely because they are in vogue, for purposes which blunt their proper meaning.

But it would be foolish to say that he should not use vogue words at all. For some of them it is difficult to see any sensible use, but for many of them – perhaps most – there is a respectable job to do. Their services should be neither refused nor solicited merely because they are in fashion. It is the misuse and the overuse of vogue words that the good writer must guard against. Some examples of misuse are given in the following pages. Overuse is not so easily illustrated, but it is easily recognised when seen; and unless it is being done just for fun it is a sign of a bad writer. For what makes a writer reach repeatedly for a vogue word? A desire to show off? A reluctance to think? Neither of these is conducive to good writing. It is extraordinary how often you will find vogue words accompanied in the same sentence by pretentiousness or sloppiness or other signs of sickness. No motorist is to be blamed for sounding his horn. But if he sounds it repeatedly we are not only offended by the noise; we suspect him of being a bad driver in other respects too.

Here then is a list of words which at the present time, and in certain sorts of writing, can be classed as vogue words. Some of them are also mentioned in other chapters. If I had included every suggestion given me by my correspondents the list would have been far longer. I have tried to keep it within bounds by including only those words that seem to me to be particularly liable at the present time to overuse, misuse or use for pretentious effect only. It is most unlikely that everyone will agree with my choice. It is certain that such a choice would have been

very different ten years ago and will be very different ten years
hence.

abrasive
arguably
basically
breakthrough
capability (something between
    capacity and ability)
catalyst
charisma
complex (noun)
conceptual
confrontation
cost-benefits
cost-effectiveness
counter-productive
decision-making
dialogue
dichotomy
divisive
dynamic
escalate (and de-escalate)
euphoria
extrapolate
frame of reference
geared to
ground-rules
guide-lines
hindsight
interface
in terms of
involvement
low profile
macro- and micro-
marginal

maximise
meaningful
minimal
mix (noun)
motivation, motivated
ongoing (continual)
optimal
optimise
options
oriented, orientated
overall
parameters
participation
peripheral
permissive
pragmatic
predictable
purposive
resources
restructure
rethink
situation
spectrum (range)
stem from
structured ('the structured
    interview')
syndrome
traumatic
unstructured
variable (noun)
viable
-wise ('an impossible proposition
    resources-wise')

MODISH WRITING

By 'modish writing' I do not mean merely writing that uses
modern idiom and words in their newest meanings. No one can
achieve a fresh and lively style if he confines himself to uses that

were current twenty or thirty years ago; and to condemn modernity in the use of English is to insult the spirit of the language. I mean rather the sort of writing that forces its modernity on the reader by posture and display, like an incompetent model flaunting a new dress rather than a sensible woman wearing one. In 'modish writing' the writer goes out of his way to parade his knowledge of the latest vogue word or his ability to twist to new uses the vocabulary or the modes of expression that have lately become current in other contexts – in short, he is affected or pretentious rather than fresh or lively.

This sort of writing is usually the result not of an occasional lapse but rather of a wrong approach to the job of writing. It is therefore better illustrated by long passages than by short. But here are some short examples of what I would call 'modish writing'. In the first, for instance, it is hard to believe that the writer would have struck this ungainly posture if he had not wanted to display his familiarity with the vocabulary of computers.

The study has been designed to provide the essential link between land use planning and the programming of transport facility development, using as input a land use plan expressive of the nature and extent of desirable future development, and providing as output a definition of the transport system which will best serve the future needs of the area and permit its desirable development.

Without an educational system wherein inter-personal relationships are built up in the classroom the methodology of such objects as sex education for boys and girls is foredoomed to failure. The teacher in these reactions is ideally a catalyst in the furtherance of the ability of a child to express himself. In this day and age the child who fails in this respect whatever his endowment will be impoverished emotionally and will be deprived of the fullest health.

It must be noted that this analysis of benefits has concentrated on one formulation of economies of scale. There are of course different forms of the function which still reflect the nature of the postulated relationship between the variables; these alternative forms however would alter the numerical values of the indicators relating to each centre while probably still preserving the order.

These two aspects of programming and control in isolation from the context of monetary economy are only of marginal value. Cash is the incentive to action, and is the critical criterion when assessing options.

The complexity of value decisions that have to be made by personnel in contact with clients may be added (to technology and the nature of the primary tasks) as a potentially important variable in relation to the structure and style of management of social services.

12

SOME SELECTED PASSAGES

Words are meant to convey thought; if you take trouble in the use of words you are bound to clarify the thought which you wish to convey.

ANONYMOUS DIPLOMAT

IT may be useful to select a few pieces for detailed study – not so much of their literary merit as of their practical efficiency. This will enable us to pick up some of the points made in earlier chapters and note how easy it usually is to convert the bad into the acceptable.

I have chosen neither the best nor the worst that I could. I have a depressing selection of pieces, about equally divided between writing by officials and writing by others, which are bad almost beyond belief. To parade them for the ordinary reader's scorn would not meet my purpose. Nor would it be much use to present him with the brilliance of highly gifted writers and invite him to do likewise. I have therefore looked rather at some run-of-the-mill writing by sensible and educated people who neither possess nor need to possess high literary gifts, and I have chosen six specimens, neither outstandingly bad nor outstandingly good. I suggest that the first four fall below the standard that we could all successfully aim at and that the other two attain it.

But I could not resist adding to these six specimens one outstandingly good passage and one outstandingly bad, although they fall, for opposite reasons, outside the purpose of this chapter.

Specimen 1

My first specimen is a memorandum formally submitted to a House of Commons Select Committee. The writer is urging various improvements in the arrangements for training teachers, but the general effect of his advocacy is spoilt by carelessness, clichés and flaccidity.

It may seem a little unfair to take an eight-page memorandum and quote only its blemishes, or rather some of its blemishes. A much less unfavourable impression would have been given if I had quoted it in full, for the author can clearly write efficiently if he tries. But that is, of course, precisely my point: most sensible people can.

We find, in consecutive sentences, a *significantly higher level of expenditure* and *significant improvements are urgent*, meaning respectively *much more expenditure* and *big improvements are urgently needed*.

Within a few lines of each other are no fewer than three plural subjects with singular verbs:

The activities of the Pooling Committee, which does not include representation from those who are actually responsible for and/or engaged in the work of the colleges, *is* likely to restrict . . .

There can be no justification for the widely different standards applied to universities and non-university institutions in the provision made for students' leisure activities and which *applies* both to premises and recurrent expenditure.

. . . it is through active participation in such activities in their colleges that they build up the interests and the expertise which *allows* them to do so.

In the first of these sentences we also find *and/or*. This phrase is occasionally useful, particularly to a lazy writer, but is much better avoided (see p. 33). It is always ugly, usually unnecessary and sometimes downright wrong. It is also discourteous, because it nearly always forces the reader to read the sentence twice, which he would not have had to do if the writer had taken a little more trouble. Here it is easily avoided, for instance by writing 'which includes no college teachers or administrators'. All that *and/or* does is to note that some people both teach and administer and that the Committee has none of them either: we can do without that.

In the second sentence, not only should *applies* be *apply* but *and which* is wrong too (see pp. 168–9). The *and* should go. But the whole sentence clearly needs recasting. We need something like:

> The standard of provision, both capital and recurrent, for students' leisure activities is much lower in non-university institutions than in universities. There can be no justification for this.

We find fashionable but unsatisfactory phrases like:

> . . . all institutions concerned must do everything possible to maximise their cost effectiveness.
> . . . this is impossible in the context of a binary system of administration and control.

The words *do everything possible to* are quite unnecessary, for *maximise* by itself means to make as big as possible. I would rather say 'must do all they can to increase', for *maximise* is still a word to be avoided if possible. *Cost effectiveness* (which would be better with a hyphen) is a vogue word which must be allowed to run its course. In the second example, *in the context of* means *under* or *if there is*. (*Binary system* is a technical term in education and is not to be objected to.)

There are trailing, flaccid sentences like:

> It would be desirable for all universities to be involved in this kind of development to allow for smaller and more intimate groupings of colleges so improving communication within each group and promoting variety of course provision.
> This would be good management practice and would avoid the frustrating delays which occur under current procedures which in some cases also leave decisions over particular expenditures in the hands of those least competent to make them.

(Note incidentally the tendency to *make a decision over* something rather than to *take a decision about* it.)

We find also a good example of the evil influence exerted by vague abstract nouns like *measure*.

> Initially the university might expect to exercise a fairly tight measure of control over the colleges but as they gained in experience they could be given an increasing measure of independence.

These *measures*, whether tight or increasing, destroy the

virility of the writing. Let the university simply exercise 'fairly tight control', and later give 'more independence'. *Level, degree, character, nature* are other words of the same kind, useful on occasions but too often reached for by writers who shun direct and simple language (cf. pp. 141–2). For instance, this same writer has:

> It is right for those directly responsible to the taxpayer to determine the overall level of expenditure.

This simply means 'total expenditure'. I have already quoted his 'significantly higher level of expenditure'. Here are some other examples from other writers:

> The closely-meshed nature of the world network of air routes has led to . . .
> We came to the conclusion that this [guidance] would be of too general a nature to be helpful.
> . . . a scale of operations that will permit high levels of aircraft utilisation.
> The contact between client and organisation involves a high degree of face to face relationships.
> In many of the smaller workshops the work is of a comparatively simple nature.
> The forecasts were of so depressing a character that . . .

Finally, the following sentence will interest the student of 'commenting' and 'defining' relative clauses (see pp. 200–202):

> The thing to aim for is a flexible programme that allows for changes of mind as the course progresses but which also satisfies the vocational drive of those who already have a commitment to teaching on entry.

There are three relative clauses here, all 'defining'. So *that* and *which* (or *who*) are equally permissible. But the first two have the same antecedent, and it is careless and inconsistent to write 'a programme *that* allows . . . but *which* also satisfies'. Admittedly, the repetition of *that* would sound a bit awkward. The best answer here is to omit the second relative pronoun altogether ('a programme that allows . . . but also satisfies'). But the third relative clause defines quite a different antecedent, and whether *that* or *which* has been used for the first two the writer has a free choice between *that* and *who* for the third. He chose *who*, and so would I. (Incidentally, *aim for* is presumably a confusion between *go for* and *aim at*.)

These blunders and inelegances are surely plain enough. With the possible exception of the *that* and *which* in my last quotation, they must obtrude themselves on almost every reader and divert his attention from the merits of the arguments to the demerits of the writing. Yet this was the work of a highly educated man. He had handicapped himself as a controversialist by omitting to acquire elementary good habits as a writer.

Specimen 2

I have suggested elsewhere (pp. 279–82) that academic practitioners of social science are apt to use unnecessarily muddy English. The following two consecutive paragraphs from an Annual Report of the Social Science Research Council were probably drafted by a lay civil servant, but they show the same tendency. I have broken them up into numbered sections so as to provide a convenient basis for the commentary that follows. I have not troubled to point out faults of punctuation, of which there are at least three.

(1) The outcome of our conference deliberations was on the whole encouraging. (2) In matters of this kind the generalities, whether they are general statements of goodwill or of suspicion, are less significant than the points of view revealed in the detailed examination of specific problems which are of common concern to those engaged in research inside and outside government. (3) The working groups on particular research areas discovered that there were a number of important matters where the work of the academic social scientist, if it were informed more fully of the research activities and the results obtained by Government departments, could valuably complement the latter. (4) Indeed as Sir XY pointed out in his opening statement to the conference, much the most rapid growth point in Government social science research expenditure was in commissioned research done outside the Government machine. This was now considerably larger in value than the research on social science

undertaken by Government departments using their own resources. And the total volume of university research in these subjects sponsored by Government departments is larger than that sponsored by the SSRC. (5) Efficient communication on the content of research would, it is clear, greatly increase the cost-effectiveness of the total effort made by both sides. (6) A fuller report is given on page 20.

(7) The Council has felt from the beginning that in the sphere of the social sciences, information and publicity play a rather special role in the research process, different from that which it has in the natural sciences. The latter produce their visible concentrations of identifiable types of research effort much more readily than do the social sciences. It is much more difficult to discover in the social sciences where some particular problem is being tackled. (8) Since Government itself is responsible for prompting so large a part of the research that is done, there is a strong argument for a rule which would place an obligation on Government departments engaging in research to publicise the nature of their activity, except where it could positively be shown that this would be harmful to the national interest. There would of course be no compulsion about publishing all the results of an investigation – this must plainly remain a matter for discretion – the object would simply be to inform members of the social science community about work in progress which may impinge on their own research. (9) Unless the pre-conditions are established in this way for a continuing dialogue among social scientists with common research problems, the body of systematic knowledge about society will grow at a significantly slower pace than it is capable of achieving.

(1) We can pass this sentence, if we assume that the writer really means that it was the outcome of the deliberations that was encouraging, not the deliberations themselves.

(2) It is very difficult to attach any clear meaning to this sentence. The reader is left wondering who is making general statements, who is revealing whose points of view to whom, whether the generalisers, the revealers and the examiners are one, two or three sets of people, and whether the points of view are significant to any or all of them or to another set of people altogether (for instance, the readers of the sentence).

(3) The word *it* is troublesome. If it refers to *work* it makes no sense; if it refers to *the academic social scientist* it seems

disrespectful. And we must get rid of *the latter*. We may attempt a translation:

The working groups on particular areas of research found several important matters on which the academic social scientist could usefully complement the research work of Government departments if he knew more about what they were doing.

(4) Surely a *growth point* cannot be rapid, though the growth that springs from it may; and phrases like *considerably larger in value* are always suspect. Come to think of it, there seem to be only two 'growth points' in question – research commissioned by Government Departments and research done by them – and the whole thing can be put, just one third more shortly, like this:

Government expenditure on social science research commissioned from outside was now much greater, and was growing much more rapidly, than expenditure on research done by Government departments themselves. And Government departments now sponsor more university research in social science than the SSRC.

It is often important to distinguish between value and volume. But here the apparent distinction between the *value* of research in one sentence and its *volume* in the next is no distinction at all.

(5) Here is dear old *cost-effectiveness* again. But I doubt if it is what the writer means. I think he is only saying that overlapping can be avoided if everyone knows what everyone else is doing. 'Both sides'? Three have by now been mentioned – Government Departments, university researchers sponsored by Government Departments and university researchers sponsored by the SSRC. There may even be a fourth and a fifth – perhaps some research is sponsored by other authorities and perhaps some is not sponsored at all.

(6) Much the best sentence in the whole passage.

(7) The first sentence runs into more trouble with *it*. It clearly refers to *information and publicity*, which the word *play* rightly treats as plural; so we need 'they have' rather than 'it has'. And surely it is odd to speak of information and publicity playing

a role *in the research process. Visible concentrations of identifiable types of research effort* is a phrase no one can be proud of. These three sentences seem just a turgid way of saying something like:

The Council has always thought that there is a special need for information and publicity about the research being done in the social sciences. It is much more difficult to discover where a particular problem is being tackled than it is in the natural sciences.

(8) Here we have the same turgid style. For instance, *a rule which would place an obligation on* could be replaced by the single word *obliging* or *compelling*. *There would be no compulsion about publishing* means *They need not publish*. The word *positively* would be better placed before *harmful* and better still omitted.

(9) The mud has been creeping round our ankles. Here we are knee-deep. The sentence seems to mean:

Unless it is made possible in this way for social scientists to discuss their common research problems, systematic knowledge about society will not increase nearly as fast as it could.

These two long paragraphs conclude the opening section of the Report. Later sections, probably by different hands, are in general much more workmanlike. But on consecutive pages there are two short sentences which seem to deserve comment. The first is this:

In 1969/70 the Council gave some priority at the pool stage for new awards in management and planning.

Surely, in normal English, one gives a bun *to* a monkey, not *for* him; and surely *preference*, rather than *priority*, is meant. The second is this:

The value of a bursary is in general £50 per student less than that of a studentship, and in addition is liable to a parental contribution, as with undergraduate awards.

Most of us find it more natural to say 'A is worth less than B' than 'the value of A is less than that of B'; and it is perverse to choose *in addition*, rather than *moreover* or *also*, when you are talking about a deduction, not an addition. So, after rather testily crossing out *per student* as unnecessary to the sense, we translate as follows:

A bursary is generally worth £50 less than a studentship and, like an undergraduate award, it may be reduced by a parental contribution.

Or, if preferred (as the recipes say), we can put a semicolon after *studentship* and substitute *moreover* for *and*.

Specimen 3

My next specimen is not so bad. Thousands of pages of writing like this are produced every year, particularly in the annual reports of both public and private bodies. This paragraph comes from an Annual Report of the National Ports Council, an official body not staffed by civil servants. The Report as a whole is neither better nor worse than most.

The large development programme which is still continuing, the likely demands for progressive improvement of facilities, coupled with the very high interest rates now ruling, and the comprehensive reconstruction of manning structures, wages and terms of employment, confront the ports with a situation in which, giving all due weight to the benefits to be expected from increased management and operating efficiency, disposal of out-of-date assets and other measures within the control of management, it appears clear to the Council that it will be difficult to achieve a satisfactory and continuing financial net surplus.

There is nothing wrong here with the grammar or the syntax, and the vocabulary, though rather stilted, is by no means outrageous. A more sensitive writer would have avoided the reconstruction of structures; *situation* is, as so often, a bad sign; and *financial net surplus* seems to be just a grand way of saying *profit*. But what is chiefly wrong is that this is flat, tired, perfunctory, inconsiderate writing: inconsiderate, because the reader has to plough through a lot of words, perhaps more than once, before getting a clear idea of what this long and stodgy sentence is leading up to. The fault is not so much careless writing as skimped preliminary thinking.

Let us look more closely at what the writer is trying to say. It is not really very complicated. He is stating the Council's view that the ports are going to find it hard to make profits because the minuses outweigh the pluses. But the structure of his sentence does not follow the natural sequence of thought. He says that the minuses confront the ports with a situation in which, allowing for the pluses, the Council think profits will be hard to make. It would have been much easier if he had broken it up a bit, used fewer abstract words and chosen a more logical structure. He could have started with the Council's opinion and followed with their reasoning; or he could have described first the minuses and then the pluses (or the other way round) and then given us the Council's balanced conclusion. There is plenty of choice. Here is one possible redraft:

> The ports face heavy costs. A large development programme is not yet complete and still further improvements in facilities are likely to be demanded; interest rates are very high; and manning, wages and terms of employment are all being completely overhauled. The ports can take various steps to help their finances, for instance by disposing of out-of-date assets and improving their own efficiency. But, even so, they will clearly find it difficult to make and sustain satisfactory profits.

This does not seem to omit anything that the writer wanted to put in, but if it does the saving of fifteen words can be drawn on to repair the omission. I have not tried to make the redraft more lively or more interesting than the original; it is still a routine paragraph in a routine report, which few people are likely to read for pleasure. But those who have a duty to read it will perhaps find the duty less exhausting.

The lesson here is one which constantly recurs in this book. Think what you want to say before putting pen to paper; let your writing follow your thought; revise what you have written, with the reader's feelings in mind. The result may not be inspiring but it will be readable.

Specimen 4

Here is the first paragraph of a long, and presumably carefully prepared, Parliamentary statement about the modernisation of the Royal Naval Dockyards.

The following are the main features of the most far-reaching plans to modernise the dockyards at Devonport and Portsmouth in their history at a total estimated cost of £76 million which we hope to complete by the early 1980s, giving these two dockyards their first facelift of the century.

Here again the grammar and syntax are flawless (though the pernickety will object that it is surely not the plans that we hope to complete by the early 1980s but the execution of them). But the sentence is a sprawling monstrosity. The trouble is not that it is too long but that it contains too many different statements unskilfully cobbled together, and the final attempt to give it life with the word *facelift* fails miserably.

It would indeed be just possible to say all this in a single sentence, as follows:

Our plans to modernise the dockyards at Devonport and Portsmouth, which we hope to finish carrying out by the early 1980s at a total cost of £76 million, and the main features of which are set out below, are the most far-reaching in their history and will bring them up to date for the first time this century.

But it would be much better to make a bolder use of full stops. We ought to start with the grand news that the dockyards are going to be modernised (not with the less exciting news that the main features are in the following paragraphs) and then add the descriptive details. For instance:

We have decided to modernise the dockyards at Devonport and Portsmouth. The improvements will be the most radical in their history and will bring them up to date for the first time this century. We expect to spend about £76 million and to complete the work in the early 1980s. The main features are as follows.

If this is thought too plain it is possible to tack on some adjectival embroidery without tearing the material. For instance, we could begin 'We have decided on a thorough-going modernisation of the dockyards ...' We could end 'The main features of this bold and far-reaching plan are as follows'. We might even work in 'facelift' somewhere in the middle. It is only when we have carried out the duty of substituting order for chaos that we can indulge the pleasure of adding embellishment to order.

Specimens 5 and 6

Most White Papers are declarations of Government policy. They are normally drafted by officials; but when one reads the published version one does not know how many hands shared in the drafting or how much re-writing, for better or for worse, was done by Ministers. They often show inconsistencies of style which suggest that different writers contributed different passages, or that a good writer worked over the important bits but left other bits alone. Some of them read as if no good writer was ever allowed near them at all. The difficulty of 'drafting in committee' and finding compromise forms of words afflicts much official writing and fair allowance must be made for it. Moreover official writing often has to be rushed into print under almost unbearable stress of time.

Yet these handicaps can be overcome. Here are two extracts from White Papers, one by a Labour Government* and one by a Conservative Government †. Both deal with highly controversial matters and are addressed to a wide readership known to include many people who are unwilling to be convinced. Both therefore try hard to be persuasive and both rightly use good English for this purpose. Neither can be acclaimed as great literature, but neither can be condemned as incompetent.

* *In Place of Strife*, 1969, Cmnd. 3888.
† *The United Kingdom and the European Communities*, 1971, Cmnd. 4715.

This is the first (Specimen 5):

There are necessarily conflicts of interest in industry. The objective of our industrial relations system should be to direct the forces producing conflict towards constructive ends. This can be done by the right kind of action by management, unions and Government itself. This White Paper sets out what needs to be done.

Our present system of industrial relations has substantial achievements to its credit, but it also has serious defects. It has failed to prevent injustice, disruption of work and inefficient use of manpower. It perpetuates the existence of groups of employees who, as the result of the weakness of their bargaining position, fall behind in the struggle to obtain their full share of the benefits of an advanced industrial economy. In other cases management and employees are able unfairly to exploit the consumer and endanger economic prosperity. It has produced a growing number of lightning strikes and contributed little to increasing efficiency. There are still areas of industry without any machinery for collective bargaining at all. Radical changes are needed in our system of industrial relations to meet the needs of a period of rapid technical and industrial change.

Until action is taken to remedy these defects, conflict in British industry will often be damaging and anti-social. The Government places the following proposals before Parliament and the nation, convinced that they are justified on two main grounds . . .

This is the second (Specimen 6):

The strength and prosperity of the United Kingdom depend partly on the efforts of its peoples, and partly on the economic conditions prevailing in the world outside. We live, and have for long lived, by manufacturing for and trading with that world. The conditions under which we manufacture and trade are of vital national interest to us. We have to consider whether these conditions will be more favourable to us if we join the European Communities than if we do not . . .

As this White Paper shows, Her Majesty's Government are convinced that our country will be more secure, our ability to maintain peace and promote development in the world greater, our economy stronger, and our industries and people more prosperous, if we join the European Communities than if we remain outside them. The Government are also convinced – and this conviction is shared by

the Governments of the present six members of the Communities –
that British membership of the Communities will enhance the
security and prosperity of Western Europe. The Government are
satisfied that the arrangements for our entry agreed in the negotiations will enable us to adjust satisfactorily to our new position as
members of the Communities, and thus to reap the full benefits of
membership.

Both these passages are slightly rhetorical, being taken from
the introductory, or 'trumpet-sounding', sections of the two
White Papers. But they are not seriously out of tune with the
style of the rest. If you read these White Papers in full you will
be able to pick small holes here and there in both of them, but,
as I have suggested elsewhere, a writer with good habits can be
forgiven an occasional slip.

It would certainly be over-critical to find much fault with
either of these extracts. For my part, I instinctively fight shy
of *necessarily* because, like *inevitably*, it so often creeps in unwanted, particularly after *must*; so although *necessarily* is not
wrongly used at the beginning of Specimen 5 I would myself
probably have written *There will always be*. In the second paragraph I would substitute *great* for *substantial*, and *unfairly to
exploit* is not, I think, the best way of avoiding the split infinitive *to unfairly exploit*; I would either have put *unfairly* after
consumer or else have left it out altogether (since *exploit* already
connotes unfairness). And in the third paragraph I would have
preferred *Until these defects are remedied* (or *Until we remedy
these defects*) to *Until action is taken to remedy these defects*.
In Specimen 6 I think *are vital to us* would be better than *are of
vital national interest to us*, and I would write *and so are the
Governments* rather than *and this conviction is shared by the
Governments*.

But these are mere matters of taste, and though both passages
could doubtless be further improved by gifted writers most of
us would be delighted if our own writing were never thought
worse than this.

You will notice, incidentally, that *Government* is singular in
the Labour White Paper and plural in the Conservative (*the*

The Complete Plain Words

Government places, the Government are convinced). As has been said on pp. 179–80, either is right but the choice once made must be stuck to. Each of these White Papers sticks consistently to its choice, so both are right.

These writers may or may not have succeeded in 'affecting their readers precisely as they wish', but they have certainly tried. The arguments may fail to convince, but they have been given a fair chance.

Specimens 7 and 8

To cap these run-of-the-mill specimens, I append two very different ones. Neither can be described as 'plain words', and neither is offered as a model. The first is by a master of modern English prose*: the second is not †.

The first may not be the greatest passage Churchill ever wrote; for him it was perhaps run-of-the-mill writing. But his instinct for imagery and his genius for the choice and arrangement of words make it so vivid and appealing that we are at once more than half way to believing everything he says. The style is elevated, because he is excited by his subject, but the lurking humour saves it from bombast. Most good modern writers prefer a plainer style, but this is superb writing of its kind. There is not a single sentence that we lesser mortals could improve. In the second passage there is, quite literally, not a single sentence that we could not.

It would need a very long commentary to point out all the merits of the first passage or all the defects of the second. I have done no more than italicise a single word in each – *wave-lapped* and *otherwise*. Consider these two words in their contexts. It needed a genius to write one and a fool to write the other.

This is the first passage (Specimen 7):

*Sir Winston Churchill, *A History of the English-Speaking Peoples*, Vol. 1, pp. 49–50 (Cassell & Co. Ltd, 1956).

† It comes from a report by a council of worthies with a ministerial chairman.

A broader question is keenly disputed. Did the invaders exterminate the native population, or did they superimpose themselves upon them and become to some extent blended with them? . . . The evidence of place-names suggests that in Sussex extermination was the rule. Farther west there are grounds for thinking that a substantial British population survived. . . . Even where self-interest did not preserve the native villagers as labourers on Saxon farms we may cherish the hope that somewhere a maiden's cry for pity, the appeal of beauty in distress, the lustful needs of an invading force, would create some bond between victor and vanquished. Thus the blood would be preserved, thus the rigours of subjugation would fade as generations passed away. The complete obliteration of an entire race over large areas is repulsive to the human mind. There should at least have been, in default of pity, a hearing for practical advantage or the natural temptations of sex . . .

The invaders themselves were not without their yearnings for settled security. Their hard laws, the rigours they endured, were but the results of the immense pressures behind them as the hordes of avid humanity spread westward from Central Asia. The warriors returning from a six months' foray liked to sprawl in lazy repose. Evidently they were not insensible to progressive promptings; but where, asked the chiefs and elders, could safety be found? In the fifth century, as the pressure from the East grew harder and as the annual raiding parties returned from Britain with plunder and tales of wealth, there was created in the ruling minds a sense of the difficulty of getting to the Island, and consequently of the security which would attend its occupation by a hardy and valiant race. Here, perhaps, in this *wave-lapped** Island men might settle down and enjoy the good things of life without the haunting fear of subjugation by a stronger hand, and without the immense daily sacrifices inseparable from military and tribal discipline on the mainland. To these savage swords Britain seemed a refuge. In the wake of the raiders there grew steadily the plan and system of settlement. Thus, with despair behind and hope before, the migration to Britain and its occupation grew from year to year.

This is the second passage (Specimen 8):

In the sphere of physical activities, the best provision in a district is generally that of the local secondary school. In the context of out-

*Try, for instance, *sea-girt* instead. See what I mean?

door pursuits, although the secondary school may well provide the best base to working out plans etc., very often the pooling of resources to provide facilities for specific outdoor pursuits are most effective. Such pooling gives access to the PE advisory services of the LEA and to facilities at outdoor pursuits centres where such exist. The problems of trying to mount a wide range of physical activities by an individual youth club are considerable and most often not worth the effort – *otherwise* activities of other sorts which clubs can do more effectively tend to go by the board. Club activities of the table tennis and billiards/snooker variety, unless there is unlimited space on the premises, are prodigal of space which can be better used for other activities involving more members. Concentration on one or two physical activities only by the individual club may often be in its best interests . . .

The possibilities of following subjects and activities in school through to youth organisations and adult education are too numerous to be explored in detail. They may represent the only contact with non-commercial interests a young person will have. It is not our function to enumerate and develop an exhaustive list of curriculum subjects which have the potential for development in the after-school situation. The potential is best discovered by youth workers and adult educationists getting to know the curriculum approach in their local secondary schools and by teachers having an eye to the follow-on concern of these workers and developing some part of their work accordingly.

Look back, if you will, on these eight specimens. Very few of us are likely to rise as high as the seventh or sink as low as the eighth. But the others are all within our compass. If we never drop below the level of the fifth and sixth we can be well content; but not if we never rise above the level of the first four. The climb from the lower to the higher of these intermediate levels is neither long nor steep; but it makes an enormous difference to the freshness of the air and the beauty of the view.

13

A CONCLUDING MISCELLANY

> And even things without life giving sound, whether pipe or
> harp, except they give a distinction in the sounds, how shall it
> be known what is piped or harped? For if the trumpet give an
> uncertain sound, who shall prepare himself to the battle? So
> likewise ye, except ye utter by the tongue words easy to be
> understood, how shall it be known what is spoken?
>
> ST PAUL

WHEN preparing this revised edition I have collected much
material which I should have liked to use but which was difficult
to fit into the framework of Gowers' book without overstraining
it. Space forced me to discard a good deal of this material, and
I have adopted the lazy device of a concluding 'rag-bag' for
those odds and ends which seemed most worth keeping. This
chapter, like Chapters 11 and 12, is designed to be thrown away
when the work is next revised.

FOR AMUSEMENT ONLY

The boiled baby

The well-known example 'If the baby does not thrive on raw
milk, boil it' is quoted on p. 191. And we have all been familiar
from early youth with the sort of thing exemplified by the
advertisement 'wanted, a rabbit for a child with lop-ears'.
Some venerable examples are given on p. 163. Here are a few
more recent ones, which may be new to some readers:

I have discussed the question of stocking the proposed poultry
plant with my colleagues.
. . . county council employees can sit on district councils (and vice
versa).
Bulletin No. 160 on Housing of Pigs from Her Majesty's
Stationery Office.

He has given a number of lectures on methods of controlling the flow of gases and liquids to audiences of engineers.

Authority is given for you to proceed and gas, preferably yourself.

It was here that the Emperor liked to put on his grand alfresco spectacles.

There will be a meeting at desk level on bicycles in Conference Room A.

Nothing is less likely to appeal to a young woman than the opinions of old men on the pill.

People in the South East keep their teeth longer than people in the North.

Prices of different models vary and you should take the advice of an expert on the make.

Ladies who have kindly undertaken to act as school crossing wardens are reminded again that if they attempt to carry out their duties without their clothing on motorists are unlikely to take notice of them.

. . . there is more to California than the mask of the bizarre behind which the state hides.*

Let us not be too censorious about passages like these. They are careless, of course, but they add to the gaiety of life. Let him who is quite sure he has never committed one cast the first stone.

The roosting cow

'The sacred cows have come home to roost with a vengeance' is a stock example of the mixed metaphor. Here is a short selection of mixed or inappropriate metaphors to supplement the examples given on p. 110. The first has already been used on p. 114 to illustrate the liveliness of a *ceiling*.

Manpower ceilings are a very blunt macro-instrument and will be either ineffective or unduly restrictive if not based on the results of management reviews and other 'micro' activities . . . ceilings are biting, but this is what they were meant to do.

*Quoted by Walter Salant in the *Journal of Political Economy*. A journalist once referred to fence-sitting by politicians as 'bottomless futility'. A bizarre behind is perhaps what you develop if you do too much fence-sitting.

This pool [i.e. of staff] can also be used as a cushion.

Flexibility is one of the corner-stones of programme budgeting.

We now have 137½ pairs of surgical boots on our hands.

Instead of supersonic aircraft standing on their own feet by charging slightly increased fares, subsonic aircraft are required to cross-subsidise . . .

The road from X to Y has not yet got off the ground.

Thanks to a windfall of heavy tankers . . .

The recovery of the house-building programme will require action in a number of fields.

It has no real head of steam to which it can harness itself.

We are at the cross-roads and anyone making concrete forecasts is liable to come unstuck.

. . . a port apparatus that is cited as an example for qualified and fast turnover of ships.

Men and women want to know the future shape of their environment and expect candid guidelines to help them mould it.

No suitable framework for career streams was thrown up by the survey.

Architects have to undertake drastic cheeseparing to bring a project within sight of the yardstick.

'That's not what I meant!'

Several examples have been given in other chapters (e.g. on pp. 74, 135, 175–6, 203) of sentences where, through carelessness, turgidity or muddlement, the writer has ended by saying the opposite of what he meant. Here are a few more:

The New Ulster Movement may be non-sectarian: it is playing straight into the hands of those who are. (May not be sectarian.)

In selection procedures little weight was attached to good manners. Why on earth not? (Not much weight.)

Anyone with even a superficial knowledge of railways can hardly fail to be unaware of the constant negotiations between . . . (Aware, or omit *fail to*.)

It could well disclose some duplication of effort leading to a reduction of overall numbers. (The abolition of which would enable us to reduce staff. Note the futile *overall*.)

A very low proportion of people wish to be laden with full texts of a day or two-day seminar, and I suspect are unlikely to read them again. (Very few people want the full texts of a seminar lasting one or two days, or are likely to read them again if they get them. Note *a very low proportion of* instead of *very few*.)

The timing of each successive stage will depend upon progress with the last and upon the resources that can be made available for the next.

This mysterious sentence (also quoted on p. 128) has attained some notoriety in the Civil Service. (It comes from a progress report about certain changes being made in the Service.) It seems to say that the timing of any one stage will depend on the progress made with the one just before it and on the resources made available for the one just after it. Can so surprising a proposition be what is meant? More probably the writer meant to refer to the resources made available for the stage in question, not the next one after it: if that is so the sentence is so platitudinous that it would have been better to put it less pretentiously, or even to omit it altogether.

The buzz-phrase generator

I have pointed elsewhere to the baleful influence of American gobbledygook on certain sorts of writing, both academic and official. Defence is a subject which has suffered badly (owing, some say, to the Harvard influence imported by Mr McNamara into the United States Department of Defense.) But the phenomenon has not gone uncriticised, even on the other side of the Atlantic. The Canadian Defence Department is credited with the invention of the following 'buzz-phrase generator'.

Column 1	Column 2	Column 3
0. integrated	0. management	0. options
1. overall	1. organizational	1. flexibility
2. systematized	2. monitored	2. capability
3. parallel	3. reciprocal	3. mobility
4. functional	4. digital	4. programming
5. responsive	5. logistical	5. concept
6. optimal	6. transitional	6. time-phase
7. synchronized	7. incremental	7. projection
8. compatible	8. third-generation	8. hardware
9. balanced	9. policy	9. contingency

The procedure is simple. You think of a three-digit number at random and take the corresponding word from each column. Thus, 601 gives you the buzz-phrase 'optimal management flexibility', 095 gives 'integrated policy concept', 352 gives 'parallel logistical capability', and so on. The authors claim that the buzz-phrase generator gives its users 'instant expertise on matters pertaining to defence', enabling them to invest anything they write, not with any particular meaning, but with 'that proper ring of decisive, progressive, knowledgeable authority'.

I have seen a British development of this invention which has three columns of no fewer than sixty lines each and includes not only most of the vogue words mentioned elsewhere in this book but many others too. This may be over-elaborate for practical use, but its compilation speaks well for British civil servants. It is wonderful how slight the difference is between some of the serious writing produced nowadays on defence matters and some of the parodies produced with the aid of the Canadian or British buzz-phrase generator.

THE SATISFIED CUSTOMER

The following is a striking example of the effect of a well-written and sympathetic answer on an irate member of the public. Its references to the price of milk show that it is a few years old, but not many.

A.B. Esq., M.P.
Parliamentary Secretary,
Ministry of Agriculture.

Dear Sir,
Before the price of milk goes up again will you please tell me why I, and so many other people, have to put up with the dreadful stuff known as 'Homogenised' – it is horrible – does not keep and if boiled or used for sauces or puddings becomes 'stringy' and even more unwholesome looking.

If one buys a pint one has a choice, but for people such as I who live alone and only need half a pint, and countless OAPs who can only afford this quantity, this stuff is forced upon us willy-nilly as no other grade is put into half-pints.

My milkman tells me that all his customers complain but nothing is done. To add insult to injury, we already pay for this at the rate of 10d. per pint – 5d. per half-pint – instead of 4½d.

Yours faithfully,
(Miss C.D.)

Dear Miss D.,

The parliamentary Secretary, Mr B., M.P., has asked me to write and thank you for your letter of 10th September about half-pints of milk being supplied only in the homogenised grade in your district.

Mr B. has asked me to say that he has every sympathy with people, particularly elderly people, who require only a small quantity of milk each day. He does not like the taste of homogenised milk either; nor do I; but there are in fact some people who seem to prefer it. The difficulty is that the Government has no legal power to compel the dairyman to supply any given grade of milk, or to supply milk in half-pints at all. Some claim that half-pints are uneconomic, and so do not deliver them. Others compromise by selling only the dearer milk in half-pints. As for price, you probably know that this *is* controlled by Government. But homogenised milk may be sold at ½d. per pint above the price of ordinary pasteurised milk, and so at the moment works out at 9½d. per pint; and where half a pint of any milk could involve an odd farthing, the dairyman is allowed to round it up to the nearest ½d. So 5d. per half-pint of homogenised milk is quite legal.

Yours sincerely,
(E.F.)
Private Secretary

Dear Sir,

Many thanks for your Secretary's very courteous and human reply to my letter concerning homogenised milk – at least I have the satisfaction of knowing that I am in very excellent company in my dislike of this distasteful stuff!

Thank you for your explanation regarding the price.

Yours sincerely,
(Miss C.D.)

PHYSICIAN, HEAL THYSELF

Even the greatest writers occasionally write badly or incorrectly, just as great golfers or tennis-players occasionally play thoroughly bad shots; and their greatness matters more than their lapses. But anyone who writes about the proper use of English lays himself peculiarly open to derision if he fails to practise what he preaches. Here are a few examples.

The Report of a Committee on People and Planning (1969) uses these brave words:

> Whatever medium is used for the communication of ideas it is essential that the language or representation used should be readily understood ... The use of jargon between experts is understandable; between experts and the public it is unforgiveable. The recipient of the message must be able to understand it. Whatever is said must be said simply and clearly.

But elsewhere in the same report we find:

> The continuity of debate which is implicit in the participation process can itself be educative for both planner and public.
> The community forum can be the spring-board for involvement of the non-participators.
> The measure of the community development officer's success would largely be the extent to which he identifies and activates these points of contact.

What right, we may well ask, has this man (or this committee) to lecture us about saying things 'simply and clearly'?

An academic authority, commenting on the standard of writing among university candidates, wrote:

> ... it is very evident from much of the current work being produced that standards have undoubtedly slipped.

This, we must assume, was dictated by a man too busy to revise it by striking out *very*, *being produced* and *undoubtedly*. He went on to say that certain words

> come into usage, are gradually made meaningless by constant repetition and then suddenly drop out of usage altogether.

One of the words which will so drop out is, we must hope, the word *usage*, in contexts where *use* is meant. See p. 129.

Another academic writer starts an article about techniques of communication like this:

The efflorescence of a host of specialists in commerce and industry and the ever widening inroad that the Government is forging into our business lives are carcinogens of effective communication; for the jargon of, on the one hand, such people as computer programmers, systems analysts, cyberneticians, psychologists and, on the other hand, the complex prose of Whitehall constitute an invidious growth which is challenging our ability to express ourselves in clear simple terms.

How does one forge an inroad? How can an efflorescence of specialists and a forged inroad be carcinogens? The mixture of metaphors, and the muddled and illogical construction of the sentence after the semicolon, are so blatant that one begins to wonder whether the writer is doing it on purpose, with facetious intent. But the rest of the article expunges this charitable thought.

In a certain Government Department, a training leaflet dealing with 'the functional rather than the imaginative use of language' said:

The goal is optimal communication in terms of understanding and response rather than the stimulation of imaginative thought.

As suggested elsewhere in this book, *goal*, *optimal* and *in terms of* should always be treated with suspicion. All three should certainly not be condoned in a single line, least of all in a training leaflet on the use of language. If the writer had tried to practise what he preached he would have said something like:

The aim is to get the message over rather than to stir the imagination.

I do not think there was anything in the first edition of *The Complete Plain Words* to justify the taunt 'Physician, heal thyself'. If there is anything to justify it in this revised edition the taunt should be addressed to the reviser, not to the original author.

14

EPILOGUE

He that will write well in any tongue, must follow this counsel of Aristotle, to speak as the common people do, to think as wise men do; and so should every man understand him, and the judgment of wise men allow him.

ROGER ASCHAM

A BOOK designed as a guide to officials in the use of English runs the risk of giving a false impression. It cannot help being concerned mainly with faults to be corrected, and so may make the picture look blacker than it is. The true justification for such a book is not so much that official English is specially bad as that it is specially important for it to be good. The efficiency of government, central and local, depends to an ever-increasing extent on the ability of a large number of officials to express themselves clearly. At present there is a popular idea that most of them cannot – or will not – do so. The term *officialese* has been invented for what is supposed to be their ineffective way of trying. I do not know exactly what that word means, but that it is not ordinarily used as a term of praise is certain.

I should be sorry to be thought to support the popular notion that officials write a language of their own of a uniquely deplorable kind. Undoubtedly they have their peculiarities of style. So have journalists theirs. It is reasonable to attribute those of officialese in the main to the peculiar difficulties with which official writers have to contend. As we have seen, much of what they write has to be devoted to the almost impossible task of translating the language of the law, which is obscure in order that it may be unambiguous, into terms that are simple and yet free from ambiguity. And our system of government imposes on officials the need always of being cautious and often of avoiding a precision of statement that might be politically dangerous. Moreover, they do not easily shake off the idea that dignity of position demands dignity of diction. But it is certainly wrong to imagine that official writing, as an instrument for conveying thought, is generally inferior to the lamentably low standard now prevalent except among professional writers. It is not only the official who yields to the lure of the pompous or meretricious word, and overworks it; it is not he alone who sometimes fails to think clearly what meaning he wants to convey by what he is about to write, or to revise and prune what he has written so as to make sure that he has conveyed it. From some common faults he is comparatively free. Most officials write grammatically correct English. Their style is untainted by the silly jargon of commercialese, the catchpenny tricks of the worst sort of journalism, the more nebulous nebulosities of politicians, or the recondite abstractions of Greek or Latin origin in which men of science, philosophers and economists often wrap their thoughts. Sometimes it is very good, but then no one notices it. Occasionally it reaches a level of rare excellence.

The fact is not that officials do uniquely badly but that they are uniquely vulnerable. Making fun of them has always been one of the diversions of the British public. The fun sometimes has a touch of malice in it, but the habit springs from qualities in the British character that no one would like to see atrophied. The field for its exercise and the temptation to indulge in it are constantly growing. *De facto* executive power, which during the seventeenth and eighteenth centuries moved from the King to Ministers, is being diffused lower still by the growth of social legislation. The theory that every act of every official is the act of his Minister is wearing thin. The 'fierce light that beats upon a throne and blackens every blot' is no longer focused on the apex; it shines on the whole pyramid. So many people have to read so many official instructions. These offer a bigger target for possible criticism than any other class of writing except journalism, and they are more likely to get it than any other class, because a reader's critical faculty is sharpened by being told – as we all so often have to be nowadays – that he cannot do something he wants to, or must do something he does not want to, or that he can only do something he wants to by going through a lot of tiresome formalities.

Epilogue

So it is natural enough that official writing, with its undeniable tendency to certain idiosyncrasies of style, should have been worked up into a stock joke. The professional humorist, in print or on the stage or on the air, can always be sure of a laugh by quoting or inventing bits of it. It is a way of getting one's own back. It is pleasantly flattering to the critics' sense of superiority. Bagehot once pictured the public of his day as saying to themselves with unction:

Thank God *I* am not as that man; *I* did not send green coffee to the Crimea; *I* did not send patent cartridge to the common guns and common cartridge to the breech-loaders. *I* make money; that miserable public functionary only wastes it.

So we may imagine the critic of today saying: 'Thank God *I* am not as that man; when *I* write a letter I make my meaning plain; this miserable public functionary only obscures his, if indeed he ever had any'. He may be right about the functionary, but he is probably wrong about himself.

Though the spirit that still moves us to mock our officials may be healthy, the amusement can be overdone. One or two recent critics of so-called officialese have indulged in it to excess, deriding without discrimination, putting in their pillory good as well as bad, sometimes even mistaking the inventions of other scoffers for monstrosities actually committed. That is regrettable. It is a curious fact that attempts to teach 'good English' often meet with resistance. Probably the explanation is that an exaggerated importance was for so long given to things that do not greatly matter; the conviction still lingers that instruction in good English means having to learn highbrow rules of no practical usefulness. It will take a long time to put the truth across that 'good English' consists less in observance of grammatical pedantries than in a capacity to express oneself simply and neatly. Unfair criticism arouses reasonable resentment, and increases the difficulty of creating an atmosphere receptive of the new ideas. Even the notion that *officialese* in its derogatory sense is encouraged by authority has not wholly disappeared.

The truth is, on the contrary, that great pains are now taken to train staffs to write clear and straightforward English – greater pains, probably, than are taken by any employer outside the Civil Service.

It does not seem to me to be true to say that the language itself is in decay. Its grammatical and syntactical usages are carefully preserved, perhaps too carefully. It is constantly being invited to assimilate new words, and seems capable of digesting many of them without any great harm, some indeed with profit. Some of the changes that have taken place in the meaning of words have weakened the language, but others have strengthened it, and on the whole there is no great cause for disquiet here. The language remains as fine and flexible an instrument as it was when used by Shakespeare and Bacon; in some respects it has been enriched. There are some alive today, and some recently dead, whose exact and delicate English would bear comparison with the outstanding writers of any generation. What is wrong is not the instrument itself but the way we use it. That should encourage us to hope that we may do better. When we are tempted to say that we have fallen away from the high standard of our forefathers, we must not forget the vast increase in the part played by the written word in our affairs. With such an increase in quantity it would be surprising if there were not some deterioration in quality. The field in which these faults are most readily noticed – the writings of officials for the guidance of the public – is almost wholly new. We cannot say whether the crop that grows there is better or worse than it was a hundred years ago, for no crop then grew there.

However unfair it may be that official English should have been singled out for derision, the fact has a significance that the official must not forget. The reader is on the look-out for the tricks of style that he has been taught to expect from official writing. Shortcomings are magnified, and the difficulties that every writer has in affecting his reader precisely as he wishes are for the official wantonly increased. All the greater is his duty to try to convert *officialese* into a term of praise by cultivating unremittingly that clarity of thought and simplicity of expression which have always been preached by those who have studied the art of writing. Thus he may learn, in the words of the 400-year-old advice that heads this chapter, by thinking as wise men do, and speaking as the common people do, to make every man understand him.

BIBLIOGRAPHY

ALFORD, Henry. *The Queen's English.* George Bell & Co., 1889.

ALLBUTT, Sir T. Clifford. *Notes on the Composition of Scientific Papers.* Macmillan, 1925.

BALLARD, P. B. *Teaching and Testing English.* University of London Press, 1939.

Thought and Language. University of London Press, 1934.

BELL, Vicars. *On Learning the English Tongue.* Faber & Faber, 1953.

BERG, P. C. A. *A Dictionary of New Words in English.* Allen & Unwin, 1953.

BRADLEY, H. *The Making of English.* Macmillan, 1904.

BROWN, Ivor. *A Word in your Ear.* Cape, 1942 (and sequels to 1953).

CAREY, G. V. *Mind the Stop.* Cambridge University Press, 1939; Pelican Books, 1971. *American into English.* Heinemann, 1953.

Chambers' Twentieth Century Dictionary. Revised edition with supplement. Chambers, 1959.

CHASE, Stuart. *The Tyranny of Words.* Methuen, 7th edition, 1950.

COBBETT, William. *A Grammar of the English Language.* Oxford University Press, 1906.

COLLINS, V. H. *The Choice of Words.* Longmans, Green, 1952.

DAVIES, H. Sykes. *Grammar Without Tears.* J. Lane, 1951.

DUNSANY, Lord. *Donwellian Lectures,* 1943. Heinemann, 1945.

EDUCATION, MINISTRY OF. *Report of the Departmental Committee on the Teaching of English in England.* Her Majesty's Stationery Office, 1921.

EVANS, Sir Ifor. *The Use of English.* Staples Press, 1949.

FLESCH, R. F. *The Art of Plain Talk.* New York. Harper, 1946.

FOWLER, H. W. *Modern English Usage.* Oxford University Press. 2nd edition, revised by Sir Ernest Gowers, 1968.

FOWLER, H. W. and F. G. *The King's English.* Oxford University Press. 3rd edition, 1930.

GRAVES, R. and HODGE, A. *The Reader over your Shoulder.* Cape, 1943.

HARTOG, Sir P. *Words in Action.* University of London Press, 1947.

HERBERT, Sir A. P. *What a Word!* Methuen, 1949.

Bibliography

JESPERSEN, Otto. *Growth and Structures of the English Language.* Blackwell, 1946.

Essentials of English Grammar. Allen & Unwin, 1933.

JOHN O'LONDON. *Is it Good English?* Newnes, 1924.

KAPP, R. O. *The Presentation of Technical Information.* Constable, 1948.

LOUNSBURY, T. R. *The Standard of Usage in English.* New York. Harper, 1908.

MENCKEN, H. L. *The American Language.* 3 volumes. Routledge, 1948.

MONTAGUE, C. E. *A Writer's Notes on his Trade.* Penguin Books, 1949.

OGDEN, C. K. and RICHARDS, I. A. *The Meaning of Meaning.* Kegan Paul, 1946.

ONIONS, C. T. *Advanced English Syntax.* Kegan Paul, 1905.

ORWELL, George. *Shooting an Elephant and Other Essays.* Secker & Warburg, 1950.

Oxford English Dictionary. Clarendon Press. 2nd edition, 1953.

PARTRIDGE, E. *Dictionary of Clichés.* Routledge & Kegan Paul. 4th edition, 1950.

Usage and Abusage. Hamish Hamilton. 4th edition, 1948.

You Have a Point There. Hamish Hamilton, 1953.

PARTRIDGE, E. and CLARK, J. W. *British and American English Since 1900.* Andrew Dakers, 1951.

PEI, Mario. *Words in Sheep's Clothing.* George Allen & Unwin, 1970.

PERRIN, P. G. *Writer's Guide and Index to English.* New York. Scott, 1942.

QUILLER-COUCH, Sir A. *The Art of Writing.* Cambridge University Press, 1916.

ROSSITER, A. P. *Our Living Language.* Longmans, Green, 1953.

SMITH, Logan Pearsall. *The English Language.* Williams & Norgate, 1912.

Words and Idioms. Constable, 1949.

SOCIETY FOR PURE ENGLISH. *Tracts.* Oxford University Press, 1919–45.

TREBLE, H. A. and VALLINS, G. H. *An ABC of English Usage.* Oxford University Press, 1936.

VALLINS, G. H. *Good English: How to Write It.* Pan Books, 1951.

Better English. Pan Books, 1953.

WARNER, G. T. *On the Writing of English.* Blackie, 1940.

Webster's New International Dictionary. Bell & Son, 1928.

WEEKLY, E. *The Romance of Words*. British Publishers Guild, 1949.

Words and Names. Murray, 1932.

WESEEN, Maurice H. *Words Confused and Misused*. Pitman, 1952.

WESTWOOD, John. *Typing for Print*. Pitman, 1976.

WHITTEN, W. and WHITAKER, F. *Good and Bad English*. Newnes. 2nd edition, 1950.

WHYTE, A. Gowans. *An Anthology of Errors*. Chaterson, 1947.

WOOD, Frederick T. *Current English Usage*. Macmillan, 1962.

YOUNG, G. M. *Daylight and Champaign*. Hart-Davis, 1948.

Last Essays. Hart-Davis, 1950.

The extract on page 303 from Volume I of *A History of the English-Speaking Peoples* by Sir Winston Churchill is reproduced with the permission of the publisher, Cassell & Company Ltd. The permission of Dodd, Mead & Company and McClelland & Stewart Ltd, who control the United States and Canadian rights respectively, has also been given.

INDEX

NOTE. Words discussed are shown in roman type
and subjects in *italic*

Index

Index

Index

Index

Index

MORE ABOUT PENGUINS, PELICANS, PEREGRINES AND PUFFINS

For further information about books available from Penguins please write to Dept EP, Penguin Books Ltd, Harmondsworth, Middlesex UB7 0DA.

In the U.S.A.: For a complete list of books available from Penguins in the United States write to Dept DG, Penguin Books, 299 Murray Hill Parkway, East Rutherford, New Jersey 07073.

In Canada: For a complete list of books available from Penguins in Canada write to Penguin Books Canada Ltd, 2801 John Street, Markham, Ontario L3R 1B4.

In Australia: For a complete list of books available from Penguins in Australia write to the Marketing Department, Penguin Books Australia Ltd, P.O. Box 257, Ringwood, Victoria 3134.

In New Zealand: For a complete list of books available from Penguins in New Zealand write to the Marketing Department, Penguin Books (N.Z.) Ltd, Private Bag, Takapuna, Auckland 9.

In India: For a complete list of books available from Penguins in India write to Penguin Overseas Ltd, 706 Eros Apartments, 56 Nehru Place, New Delhi 110019.

THE PENGUIN ENGLISH DICTIONARY

G. N. Garmonsway with Jacqueline Simpson
Third Edition

MODERN
Unrivalled as a catalogue of English words as they are
now used in print and speech
Lists hundreds of post-war words and senses, including
new words of the last few years
Lists variant meanings in order of present-day
frequency

SIMPLE
Definitions given in the most direct form possible,
showing acquired overtones and the degree of
acceptance of words

NEW
Written and prepared by a team led by a distinguished
professor of English language, G. N. Garmonsway;
now thoroughly revised by Jacqueline Simpson

COMPREHENSIVE
Entries range from the most colloquial words to the
most formal

Reviews of the previous edition

'This is, above all else, a *modern* dictionary ... the
editors have performed an immensely difficult task
with tact and skill' – Eric Partridge in the *Guardian*

'The definitions are admirably simple and direct .... it
nowhere abandons a sound basis of scholarship in
order to be merely popular. Too much cannot be asked
of a work so exhaustively comprehensive, so
extraordinarily up-to-date, and withal so cheap' – *The
Times Educational Supplement*

ROGET'S THESAURUS
Edited and specially adapted for this edition
by Susan Lloyd

The first revision for twenty years – reflecting recent changes in spoken and written English.

Specially adapted for Penguins, this latest version is in direct line of descent from Roget's original. Now updated to include new concepts like data processing, hatchback, mole and sitcom, and still ranging from the literary to the colloquial, the scientific to the philosophical, *Roget's Thesaurus* is an invaluable work of reference – it is indeed a 'treasure house' of words!

'As normal a part of an intelligent household's library as the Bible, Shakespeare and a dictionary' – *Daily Telegraph*

'That hardy standby of authors, translators, advertising copywriters, crossword-solvers and indeed any of us with an interest in words' – *Sunday Times Magazine*

'Ms Lloyd has now improved it, with more new locutions and a touch of feminism' – *Sunday Telegraph*

'An established classic among works of reference' – *The Times Educational Supplement*